A COWARD IF I RETURN,
A HERO IF I FALL
STORIES OF IRISHMEN IN WWI

I wish the sea were not so wide
That parts me from my love;
I wish the things men do below
Were known to God above.

I wish that I were back again
In the glens of Donegal,
They'll call me coward if I return,
But a hero if I fall.

'Is it better to be a living coward,
Or thrice a hero dead?'
'It's better to go to sleep, my lad,'
The Colour Sergeant said.

'A Lament' by Private Patrick MacGill
Dec 1889–Nov 1963
From Glenties, County Donegal
1/18th London Regiment (London Irish Rifles)

D1342407

Neil Richardson studied Philosophy in University College Dublin and works as a creative writing teacher and editor. He is also a playwright and two of his plays, *Through the Dark Clouds Shining* and *From the Shannon to the Somme*, are inspired by stories from his book on the First World War. Neil is also a member of the Reserve Defence Forces and his family have a long military tradition stretching back over 150 years. His great-grandfather's experiences in the trenches inspired this collection of Irish veterans' stories.

Left: *A hand-sewn Connaught Rangers' crest, made no earlier than 1918. On the back there is a short message written: 'Remember the old flag. France, Mesopotamia, Palestine. Still to the good yet. The Gravel Crushers, are you looking.' The card was sent, and possibly made, by Private John Oliver to his friend Thomas Wall in Loughrea, County Galway. 'Are you looking' was a local Loughrea phrase.*

A COWARD IF I RETURN, A HERO IF I FALL

STORIES OF IRISHMEN IN WWI

NEIL RICHARDSON

THE O'BRIEN PRESS
DUBLIN

First published 2010 by The O'Brien Press Ltd., 12 Terenure Road East, Rathgar, Dublin 6, Ireland.
Tel: +353 1 4923333; Fax: +353 1 4922777; E-mail: books@obrien.ie; Website: www.obrien.ie
Reprinted 2010.

ISBN: 978-1-84717-131-3

Photograph credits:
The author and publisher would like to thank the families of the soldiers in this book who provided precious photographs and memorabilia for publication. Acknowledgement is also due to various archives and museums:
Front cover: Imperial War Museum (Q070168). Back cover: in background, Peter Doyle; top left, Cyril Wall and others, Neil Richardson.
Tim Aherne p301; Pádraig Broderick p314; Library and Archives Canada p181 (RG 150, Accession 1992-93/166, Box 3247–49) p205 (PA-149311); Jeremiah 'Jerry' Cregan Jnr pp193, 195; 'Darkest Dublin' Collection, The O'Brien Press p19; Mustafa Davran p62; Department of the Taoiseach pp14, 15, 32, 33, 42, 92, 98, 150, 164, 235, 281, 282; Imperial War Museum p6 (PST013626), p8 (PST02734), pp30-1 & 55 (Q013452), p35 (Q070451), p36 (Q070071), p52 (Q013818), pp68-9 & 93 (Q000052), p73 (Q000001), p76 (Q011586), p78 (Q003995), p94 (Q042261), p95 (Q002041), pp96-7 & 103 (Q005628), p99 (Q002636), p108 (Q012616), pp112-3 & 121 (Q47997), p123 (PST13657), p128 (FIR000046), pp126-7 & 130 (Q012063), p132 (Q060800), pp142-3 & 144 (Q023584), p148 (Q018593), p153 (Q055135), p155 (Q069876), pp162-3 &165 (Q066157), p176 (PST012424), p183 (Q030456), p189 (E_AUS_000672), pp198-199 & 212 (Q008099), p200 (Q008618), p208 (Q004256), p214 (Q003187), p217 (Q004922), p226 (Q018888), pp232-3 & 256 (Q005p35), p267 (Q010682), p269 (FIR009220), p270 (Q002628), p287 (HU0762548), p294 (W_AUS_001220), pp296-7 & 299 (Q00365), p307 (Q033693); Peter Doyle pp151, 157; Deborah and Marie-Louise Fitzpatrick pp27, 28, 298; Sean Hefarty p304; Mairéad Horkan pp324, 325, 328, 330; Irish Guards Archives p271; Eileen Kavanagh pp10, 311, 312, 313; Peter Langley p179, 185; McArevey family pp319, 320; Mark McLoughlin p332; Eddie Molloy p116; Terry Moran p263; National Library of Ireland p12 (IND_H_000311566), p100 (IND_H_000311566), p346 (IND_H_016611566); O'Keefe family pp273–275, p278; Mary O'Neill p264; Donal O'Sullivan p257; Public Records Office of Northern Ireland p248; Eugene Rooney pp82, 89, p222; Royal Inniskilling Fusiliers Museum pp49, 63, 64; Royal Irish Fusiliers Museum pp247, 248, 253; St Ignatius' College, Riverview, Sydney, Australia p17; Anne Sands pp53, 283, 284; Peter Sheen p215; Alison Schwalm pp63, 64, 67; Morrison Stewart p171; Trustees of the Royal Air Force Museum pp139, 140, 141; UK National Archives pp38, 288, 320; Cyril Wall pp24, 25, 41, 46, 105, 106, 110-111, 216, 295, 339, 341, 342, 343, 344, 347, 348; *The Westmeath Independent* pp236, 239.

The publisher acknowledges the support of the Taoiseach's Commemoration Initiatives Fund.

Every effort has been made to trace holders of copyright material used in this book, but if any infringement has inadvertently occurred, the publishers ask the copyright-holders to contact them.

Typesetting, editing, layout and design: The O'Brien Press Ltd
Printed and bound by Thomson Litho Ltd.
The paper in this book is produced using pulp from managed forests.

For Caroline – my inspiration

*This book is dedicated to
every Irish soldier in every army
– past, present and future*

Acknowledgements

I would like to thank my editor, Susan Houlden, for her hard work, meticulous eye for detail and her empathy with the subject.

With thanks to:

Richard Moles; Imperial War Museum; Sandra McDermott and the National Library of Ireland; Paul Johnson, Tim Padfield and the National Archives of the United Kingdom; Public Records Office of Northern Ireland; Cara Downes and the National Archives of Australia; Heidi Kuglin, Geordy Muir and the Archives New Zealand; Richard Lelièvre, Daniel Potvin and Library and Archives Canada; Mr DP Cleary MBE and RHQ Irish Guards; Amanda Moreno and the Royal Irish Fusiliers Museum; Major (ret'd) JM Dunlop, Catherine McGrath and the Royal Inniskilling Fusiliers Museum; Peter Devitt, Mary Jane Millare-Adolfo and the Royal Air Force Museum, London; Cathy Hobbs-Faulkner, James Rodgers and St Ignatius' College, Riverview, Sydney, Australia; Oliver Fallon and the Connaught Rangers Association; *Anglo Celt*; *Athlone Advertiser*; *Athlone Voice*; *Avondhu*; *Carlow Nationalist*; *Clare Champion*; *Connacht Telegraph*; *Connacht Tribune*; *Drogheda Independent*; *Family History* Magazine (UK); *Galway Advertiser*; *Ireland's Own*; *Kerry's Eye*, *Kildare Nationalist*, *Kilkenny Advertiser*, *Kilkenny People*, *Laois Nationalist*, *Leinster Express*, *Limerick Leader*, *Limerick Post*, *Mayo Advertiser*, *Mayo Echo*, *Mayo News*, *Meath Chronicle*, Midlands Radio 103FM, *Mullingar Advertiser*, *Munster Express*, *Nenagh Guardian*, *Offaly Express*, *Roscommon Champion*, *Roscommon Herald*, *Sligo Champion*, *Sligo Weekender*, *Southern Star*, *The Corkman*, *The Examiner*, *The Kerryman*; *The Kingdom*, *Tuam Herald*, *Tullamore Tribune*, *Western People*, *Westmeath Examiner*, Tadhg Carey and *The Westmeath Independent*, *Westmeath Topic*.

With thanks also to:

Tim Aherne, Michael Barry, Michael Black, Eilish Blacoe, Pádraig Broderick, Michael Brougham, Charlie Cavanagh, Angela Cleary, Bart Clifford, Tom Clonan, Pat Conlon, Geraldine Conway, Thomas Coote, James Cotter, Jerry Cregan, Matt Crowe, John Davis, Mustafa Davran, Patricia Dolan, Noreen Doolan, Joe Dowling, Peter Doyle, Michael Duffy, Jimmy Dunne, Edward Egan, Bridget Emerson, John English, Brian, Marian, and Fionnuala Fallon, John Finn, Deborah and Marie-Louise Fitzpatrick, Julie Fivey, Tony Gaffey, John Gorman, Tony Hadland, Sean Hefarty, Margaret Hendley, Tom Holian, Ger Holligan, Mairéad Horkan, Gordon Hudson, Cllr Ruth Illingworth, Mike Johnson, Andy Kavanagh, Eileen Kavanagh, Simon Kelly, Mary Kennedy, Arthur Kerr, Ken Kingston, Peter Langley, Brendan Lawrence, Pat Leavey, Peggy Lovell, John MacDonagh, Michael Maksymowicz, Sean Malone, Pat McCale, Patrick McDonnell, Tom McGrane, Catherine McHugh, Mark

McLoughlin, Steve McLoughlin, Eddie Molloy, Derek Molyneux, Mary Moore, Terry Moran, Assumpta Murphy, Geraldine Murphy, Kevin Myers, May Neary, Cllr Michael Newman, Stephen Nevin, Gearoid O'Brien, Kevin O'Byrne, Martin O'Dwyer, Mary O'Neill, William O'Reilly, Michael O'Rourke, David O'Sullivan, Donal O'Sullivan, Owen O'Sullivan, Kay Reilly, Michael Roach, Adrian Roache, Eugene Rooney, Peter Rooney, Margaret Royce, Billy Ryan, Sheila Ryan, Anne Sands, Alison Schwalm, Anne Shanks, Brian Spain, Morrison Stewart, Peter Toal, Cyril Wall, Peggy Whelan, Kieran White.

CONTENTS

INTRODUCTION

Opposite: Field Marshall Lord Kitchener depicted in his famous recruiting poster. Born and raised in County Kerry, he set up the New Army units filled with citizen volunteers that solved Britain's manpower shortages. Other famous historical figures, who were both Irishmen and British soldiers, include Daniel O'Connell – the Catholic emancipator; James Connolly – 1916 martyr; and Lord Wellington who defeated Napoleon at Waterloo.

When I decided to write this book, I was not sure how to go about it. How do you select a few men from 200,000 in order to tell the story of Irishmen in the First World War? There were some soldiers that I picked myself, men whose stories I wanted to tell, but for the majority I decided to submit articles to national newspapers, appealing for people whose ancestors had fought to contact me. Whoever contacted me, I would do my best to research and include the story of their ancestor.

The outcome was phenomenal. Not only was I contacted by hundreds of people from Ireland, I also received calls, post and emails from Irish in the UK, Australia, and America – people who had left these shores long ago but who still had the local papers sent to them, or who kept up on the latest news via the web. What I ended up gathering was a precious collection of first-hand oral accounts – stories that were told by the veterans themselves and then recounted to me by their children or grandchildren. These individual histories were perfect for giving a more personal edge to the famous battles and events of the war, and they allowed me to show what individual men went through – especially the ordinary private soldiers, those men who, for the most part, kept no diaries. When I cross-referenced these stories with surviving archival records, I was amazed by how accurately the veterans had imparted their experiences. These men's stories needed to be recorded and told.

Furthermore, I also never expected for the result of my newspaper appeal to be so representative of Irish First World War soldiers as a whole. There are men of all backgrounds and political opinions from nearly every county, including shopkeepers from Limerick, fishermen from Kerry, farmers from Waterford, labourers from Athlone, gentry from Cavan, Dublin men who worked for Guinness's, ardent republicans and diehard unionists. Many were killed, and although many came home, none really survived the war. The men who left Ireland's shores did not come back the same. There are officers and NCOs, privates and medal winners – those who were awarded the Victoria Cross, the highest award for bravery, and those who were executed for desertion.

I decided to write this book because of my great-grandfather, Martin Gaffey. I never met the man – he died years before I was born – but the story of him always held some intense interest for me. He had fought in the First World War, I was told. He had been shot through the neck, had survived and was sent home. There were a few medals in the house that the children used to play with. When Martin died he was buried in his hometown. He was remembered only by those who had met him, and the stories they would tell about him. I wanted to know more.

Martin Gaffey from Athlone, County Westmeath. Taken around the time he enlisted, it shows the hardened expression of an early twentieth-century Irish labourer.

What kind of man was he? Who was he before the war and what did it do to him? What did he go through when he was over there? Did he fight in any battles? Did he see the mud and shell craters and trenches of France and Flanders? Did he kill anyone?

The First World War suddenly turned into a sort of morbid fascination for me, perhaps because like so many other men who have only read about war on this scale, I wanted to know would I have measured up, would I have charged over the parapet, screaming at the top of my lungs, when the officer blew his whistle? Would I have been brave enough to go back out into no-man's-land to rescue a wounded friend, even when I had already managed to make it back to safety?

Then I realised something. Like so many other writers on the subject, I was starting to glorify the men who fought in the war and, by association, the war itself. Asking if I would have measured up suggested that there was some great masculine challenge involved, that the war really was a test that a soldier could simply pass or fail.

The truth is that the First World War was not a glorious struggle. A lot had changed since Carl von Clausewitz had written in his book, *On War* (1832), that 'War is nothing but a duel on an extensive scale ... Each [side] strives by physical force to compel the other to submit to his will.' Surviving a battle in this new style of industrialised, mechanised slaughter had very little to do with how strong, smart or well trained you were. It had very little to do with honour and nobility. Rather, it had everything to do with blind luck and pure chance. Survival often depended simply on where you were when a shell came screaming to earth, or when a blast of machine-gun fire raked across a patch of no-man's-land.

Even though Ireland has begun to acknowledge its First World War involvement, that acknowledgement often comes with qualifiers. On the one hand, there is the tendency to see the soldiers as heroes who went to fight for Belgium – for the freedom of small nations – or as proto-republicans who enlisted to secure Home Rule. This, of course, brings the Irishmen who fought in the trenches that little bit more into the nationalist fold – it makes them acceptable to a modern, republican Ireland. Another qualifier is that they had no choice, that they were poverty-stricken, ill-educated paupers who needed food in their stomachs and boots on their feet, while the older reason was that Irish First

John Redmond MP, leader of the Irish Home Rule Parliamentary Party, addressing a Home Rule rally from the Parnell monument, Dublin in 1912.

World War veterans were all foolish idiots that fought for the wrong side in the wrong war.

While the reasons why all these men went to war are certainly interesting, they should not form the basis of whether we remember them, acknowledge them, or mourn those who suffered tragic deaths. Why these Irishmen chose to go is worthy of mention, but when the artillery opened up, when the gas clouds rolled in across no-man's-land, and when the order was given to fix bayonets, those reasons melted away leaving each man – idealist, pauper, or idiot – exposed as a mere mortal. Therefore, the details that are really significant in any First World War story are who the men were, what they experienced, what they saw, and what it did to them afterwards.

In the past, in this country, there was a tendency to sideline veterans of the First World War in favour of remembering those of the 1916 Rising and the War of Independence. The men of the flying columns deserve their praise; they stood up for what they believed in, against the might of the British Empire. They lived in fear, moving constantly from place to place, giving up their homes and their loved ones to free their people from oppression. This book is not an attempt to deride the veterans of the War of Independence in favour of First World War soldiers; it is merely seeking to acknowledge the experiences of the latter.

The Irish State awarded 2,411 medals to commemorate participation in the 1916 Rising, and 62,868 for service during the War of Independence (with only 15,224 of these being issued to fighting men of the flying columns). These figures can be taken to represent the number of soldiers who took part in these two pivotal events in Irish history, but when we compare this with the fact that 200,000 men from the island of Ireland (and a further 300,000 Irish emigrants or sons born to Irish parents elsewhere) served in the First World War, and between 35,000–50,000 of them (as much as eighty percent of which may have been from the south), perhaps more, never returned home, we really cannot afford to ignore the significance of the First World War in Ireland. The 1911 census recorded 2,192,048 males living in Ireland. Approximately 700,000 were in the seventeen to thirty-five age bracket and this means that twenty-five to thirty percent of Irishmen eligible for recruitment fought in the war. Of course, this figure still does not include men and women who worked in industries that supplied the war effort or Irish people who emigrated to Britain to work in munitions factories, and so, in the early days of republican rebellion, it is easy to see why there was fierce opposition to such aggressive nationalism – because so many Irish families had sons, husbands, and brothers fighting overseas, while thousands of Irish women played their part in war-related industries. But for whatever reasons, the memory of all this has been deleted from our national psyche.

What the Irishmen (and indeed every other man) in the First World War went through has no parallel in all of history. The Second World War may have been bloodier and far costlier in terms of human life, but the First World War had its own unique psychology. The Second World War was the war of movement that the First World War was meant to be but never was. Men sat in their trenches and waited for death to rain down on them, or they died in their thousands, as wave after wave were sent walking towards a wall of machine-gun

bullets. The First World War was also, as the name implies, the first of its kind, and the scale of the destruction and the killing produced a cultural aftershock that resonates down to the present day. The horror of the Second World War was, on many levels, a continuation of the madness of the First, and while the concentration camps and the atomic bomb shocked the world in a way that the First World War never did, the 1914–1918 conflict introduced the globe to industrialised slaughter and mindless devastation.

We are used to ten or twenty people being killed by insurgents in the Middle East – or the deaths of two or three soldiers in a roadside bombing. These are terrible events, and any loss of life like this is tragic. But in the First World War, deaths were not measured by the dozens, or even the hundreds, but in the thousands. The worst and most famous example is the first day of the Battle of the Somme. Twenty thousand were killed and a further 40,000 wounded on the British side alone. Can you imagine if Croke Park, packed to capacity, was blown up, with one quarter killed outright and the rest severely injured? Now imagine it happening perhaps two or three times a year, over and over and over. That was the First World War – men died in their thousands, men were blown apart in their thousands and, in Ireland, men were forgotten in their thousands.

The Irish Times security analyst and former Irish Defence Forces officer Tom Clonan refers to this as Irish 'collective amnesia', and in an RTÉ radio interview he once said that 'to put this in context, and I don't mean to trivialise casualties, but of twenty years' involvement in the Lebanon we lost maybe fifty people,

Above: *London Irish Rifles' cap badge: Irishmen at home were not the only ones to enlist. Others, Irish emigrants or the sons of Irish parents, served in regiments that recruited amongst the Irish communities in Britain, such as this one, the London Irish Rifles. Originally raised in 1859 as the 28th Middlesex (London Irish) Rifle Volunteer Corps, the London Irish Rifles became part of the reserve Territorial Army in 1908 and was re-designated the 18th (County of London) Battalion London Irish Rifles. During the First World War, they raised three battalions, and in common with many regular Irish regiments, their Latin unit motto was Quis Separabit – 'who shall separate us'.*

there or thereabouts. In the opening hours of the Battle of the Somme you had 60,000 troops were killed. ... in the whole of Vietnam there were 66,000 troops killed and the American involvement in Vietnam stretched over nearly fifteen years. In one morning, 60,000 troops. And that's the extraordinary thing about the Irish casualties. I mean ... approximately 50,000 Irish soldiers died in the First World War. Now that is approximate to the number of Americans that were killed in Vietnam. Vietnam is a big scar on the American psyche; its commemorated, we're all aware of it. But that's out of a population of nearly 200 million people. We had 50,000 people killed out of a population of what, two and a half million ... America commemorates Vietnam ... and for us, as such a small nation, we've swept them under the carpet. We do not remember them. All those boys ...'

The answer as to why the Irish people have this 'collective amnesia,' as Tom Clonan calls it, is simple. The independent, republican Ireland of the post-War of Independence years had no place and no tolerance for those who had formerly served the crown, not unless they were willing to put their years of imperial service to good use by joining the IRA or the National (Free State) Army. But why the bitterness? Why the hatred? It could be a reflection of just how bad the Irish considered life under British rule, or of the path that the fledgling Irish State took as it tried to carve out its own identity in the world, but either way, the effect was the same. First World War veterans, as perceived symbols and reminders of the old colonial power, were shunned, ignored and made to feel ashamed. It was one thing to reject all things English, but when that included

Above: *8th (Irish) Battalion King's Regiment Liverpool cap badge: Another regiment which recruited amongst the Irish in Britain was the Liverpool Irish regiment. In 1860, the Irish emigrants living in Liverpool filled the ranks of the 64th Lancashire Rifle Volunteer Corps, many of whom were Irish nationalists in search of military training. Known as the 'Liverpool Irish', they later fought in the Boer War and were then transferred into the reserve Territorial Army in 1908 and renamed before serving in the First World War. Their unit motto was the Irish phrase* Erin go Bragh, *meaning 'Ireland Forever'.*

Irishmen who had worn the British uniform, that had a terrible effect on so many thousands of lives.

This shunning of Irish First World War veterans had other effects. On the one hand, men were completely erased from family histories, while, on the other, the stories of trench veterans were altered and warped to 'justify' their actions. In many cases, while I was interviewing surviving family of veterans, I found that the details of stories had been changed over the years, to include facts that were not true or simply could not be true. In some instances, I was told that 'Paddy died, only seventeen years old, the poor young lad' when military, census, birth and baptism records prove that 'Paddy' was really in his twenties when he was killed. While many Irish soldiers were underage – many of whom were killed in action – some families curiously made their veterans younger when the story was passed on. In other instances, I heard that 'the reason why Paddy went was because he was conscripted. They forced him into the trenches.' Conscription was never introduced in Ireland, and in all of these conscription and false-youth stories, I have always found that the soldier's family at the time turn out to be ardently republican. The conscription and false-youth stories then turn out to be merely an attempt to remove 'blame' from the soldier for having signed up to the British Army – if he was young, then he was not old enough to know any better, and if he was conscripted, then it was not his fault that he served the crown (Curiously, on more than one occasion, I was also told that 'Paddy fought in the First World War alright, but not in the British Army. He would never have taken the king's shilling. No, he served with the Irish Army in the trenches'. In each instance, it was the fact that the relative served in a regiment with the word 'Irish' in the title that led to the misunderstanding. But each time when I tried to delicately explain that their relatives had served in Irish regiments of the British Army, and that the Irish Army did not yet exist at the time of the First World War, the mood of the conversation quickly changed).

Also, I have heard 'Paddy died dragging two wounded friends through the muck. They were all killed by a shell.' Now this might be accurate, but I have found in several cases that deaths were often glorified, sometimes by surviving friends from the trenches and, on occasion, by the families themselves, in order to give some purpose to what was invariably a senseless and horrible end to the

Capt. Joseph Clonan,

O.R. '93-95.
Accidentally killed in France on the 10th Nov., 1917.

Irish-Australian Lieutenant Joseph Clonan. This is a picture of him from the 1917 Alma Mater of his old school in Sydney. His tragic end was covered up to disguise the senseless horror of his death.

life of a loved one. This was certainly true in the case of Lieutenant Joseph Clonan – an Irish-Australian. When Clonan died on 10 November 1917, one day before the end of the Third Battle of Ypres, an account of his death soon appeared in the Alma Mater of Clonan's old school in Sydney, Australia, stating that he rode out 'at the head of a transport column going up to the lines when a shell burst five yards away, and struck both rider and horse. His men ran to his assistance and propped him up. He opened his eyes for a moment, and smiled at those who were helping him. He died almost immediately, and was buried in a village about ten miles from Armentières.' The truth was that Joseph Clonan did not die cheerily while urging his men on to glorious victory. A transport officer, Clonan had been ordered to join an infantry company in the front-line trenches – a role he knew nothing about – and so, while in his billet on the morning of 10 November, he put a gun to his head and shot himself. However, witnesses state that he did not die instantly. Clonan lingered on for as long as thirty minutes before finally dying, drenched in his own blood. His family never learned the truth.

What these examples all show is that Irish people have always felt the need to qualify our involvement in the war. The truth is that service in the British Army has been an element of Irish life for centuries. No matter which side you pick, we all fought for English kings at the Boyne; Irish rebels fought Irish regiments in 1798; thousands of us wore the redcoat, and thousands more the khaki uniform of the First World War. It is part of our history, and, until recently, part of our national identity. There are Irish war graves on every continent, and names such as Rita and Ursula are used today in Ireland because Irish soldiers in the British Army brought them back from India in the nineteenth century.

But while the politics of all these various wars, battles and centuries interest me, what really matters are the lives of the Irishmen who fought, survived, or died in them. So who were they? The answer to that question must include the Ireland they grew up in, the situations that they faced in life, and invariably, the reasons why they enlisted. Their lives were very different from the lives led by Irish people today – many of the men who fought in the First World War came from large families; not finding work often meant that you and perhaps the rest of your family might starve, and they knew poverty and deprivation, the like of which is difficult for us to comprehend.

Two views of tenements in Dublin, 1913. Single rooms in poor states of repair would often house entire families. Disease, extreme poverty and premature death were commonplace.

Dublin is the best example of what Irish urban life was like nearly one hundred years ago. On the one hand, there was the up-and-coming Catholic middle class who, along with the well-established, wealthy Protestants, had been flocking in their thousands out of the inner-city for years to the clean and prosperous suburbs. The Georgian homes that they left behind had become the slums for thousands of destitute Dubliners. These tenements housed 26,000 families, 20,000 of which lived in just one-room accommodation. Henrietta Street was the most infamous street in the capital – in just fifteen houses, there were 835 people struggling to survive. Several generations of several families lived together and the possibility of death was never far away. Even if you were lucky enough to survive infancy, you might die from disease caused by the non-existent sanitation. Tuberculosis, or 'consumption' as it was called, was a common killer – doctors would often prescribe milk, eggs and butter to build you up, assuming you could afford these luxuries. Or perhaps, as happened in many cases, your house might literally collapse on top of you from lack of repair.

Old Dublin, then, was a dying city. Unlike the industrialised northern city of Belfast, Dublin had yet to enter the modern mechanised age. Belfast had the same problem with tenements and slums, but Dublin was more of a hub than a producer, a place where the paperwork was done and a place where things passed through on their way to somewhere else. The cattle boat sailed to Britain seven times a day, eighty times a week from Dublin ports, often carrying as many Irish emigrants as livestock.

Outside the capital, in the various towns in the various counties, life was no better. Most of the population of the big rural towns survived as unskilled labourers. They started work young, most before they reached their teens, to earn much-needed, but meagre, extra income to supplement the family. The local workhouse was also a common feature throughout the land, and served as hospital, poorhouse, home for the elderly, and mental asylum. Children, when not born at home, were often born in a workhouse ward. Many might then find themselves, years later, forced to enter the workhouse because they had no money, no hopes of finding work, and therefore no chances of surviving outside its walls. Others ended up in the workhouse because they were too old to care for themselves, too sick, or perhaps even dying. Even those with mental illnesses were often committed into a workhouse. They truly were horrific places, where men were separated from their wives, and parents from their children.

Several families I interviewed swore that the huge numbers of Irish priests at the time could be ascribed to the condition of the country in the early 1900s. It was not faith but desperation that drove them to the Church. After all, the priesthood was a great career move – it offered financial security, a fine house, and local respect.

Meanwhile, in the outlying rural villages, dotted along the periphery of the west coast of Ireland, life was perhaps at its hardest. While the city-dwellers of Belfast toiled in their factories, and the labourers and tradesmen of Dublin and the other southern towns struggled to get by, the farmers of the west of Ireland lived life from year to year, crop to crop. Alcoholism was rife among a population that were never far away from famine and starvation. Emigration was the only option for thousands of Irish people – in Kerry, the population had nearly halved since the end of the Great Famine.

Life was so desperate in these rural areas and land so vitally important, that it was not unusual for violent and bloody family disputes to erupt over who owned a tiny field, or an even tinier garden where some extra precious crops could be grown. Sometimes, these arguments ended with fathers and sons, or brothers, never speaking to each other ever again. Sometimes, they even ended in murder.

Of course, this old world *was* beginning to change. 1914 was a world of empires and monarchs clinging to power and their colonies, and flexing their muscles in the form of massive armies. But it was also a world of revolution. Workers' Labour parties, women's suffragettes, and nationalist movements demanded change. Ireland had already seen the Home Rule movement, workers' strikes and the 1913 Lockout, so there was a sense in the air that a new way of life might be on the way – one where small nations could decide their own destiny, and where ordinary workers would finally have a voice in society. Unfortunately though, for Ireland, not everyone welcomed the change.

On 11 April 1912, the Third Home Rule Bill had been introduced to the House of Commons. Unlike the previous two bills, the House of Lords could now only postpone it for two years and not veto the bill out of existence. So in

1914, Home Rule would be a reality – it was only a matter of time before Ireland had its own parliament. However, not everyone on the island had been happy at this prospect.

Ulster unionists believed that if they were subjected to the rule of a southern Irish parliament, they would be facing policies geared towards the more agrarian south. The industrialised north feared economic ruin. Furthermore, southern Ireland was predominantly Catholic, and Ulster Protestants were determined to resist Home Rule, which they often referred to as 'Rome Rule'. They wanted to avoid becoming a religious minority, and avoid the risk of discrimination. The unionists demanded to remain a part of Britain.

To ensure that this happened, the Ulster Volunteers were set up to defend unionist ideals and reject Home Rule, by force if necessary. Tens of thousands of men flocked to the organisation and they marched, drilled, and trained all across Ulster. In September 1912, just under a quarter of a million male unionists signed the Ulster Covenant in protest against a southern parliament. Some took the signing of the covenant so seriously that they signed in their own blood.

The following year, it was southern nationalists' turn to reply. 1913 had seen the setting up of the Irish Volunteers to defend Home Rule at all costs. However, secretly involved in the organisation was the Irish Republican Brotherhood (IRB), with a motive to create an Irish republic, completely separate from Britain. Like their northern opponents, the Irish Volunteers began training and drilling. However, initial weapon shortages saw columns of men marching with hurls instead of rifles. And while the Ulster Volunteers (or Ulster Volunteer Force – UVF – as they soon became) had no trouble importing arms and ammunition – ironically from Germany – the Irish Volunteers were constantly plagued by supply shortages. Still, they prepared and readied themselves. So by 1914, it looked as though the moment that Home Rule became a reality, civil war would break out in Ireland.

This then, was the world that the Irishmen who would soon become trench veterans were born into. It was a world of inequality, danger, and suffering – but a world that seemed on the verge of change. Given the aggressive tension that was building up in Europe, the catalyst for this change was only ever going to come in the form of violence. With the European empires having been at each other's throats for decades, war was the only outcome. Each country had been building up its army and its stockpiles of weapons for years. Then, on 28 June 1914, Archduke Franz Ferdinand – heir to the Austro-Hungarian throne – was shot dead in the streets of Sarajevo by a Serbian nationalist named Gavrilo Princip. The Serbian situation was probably one that many Irish of the time could relate to – it was the story of a small country ruled over by an imperial superpower. All of a sudden, alliances between various countries were activated and, soon enough, Britain, France and Russia were at war with Germany and Austria-Hungary. In Ireland, the regular career soldiers were shipped to the battlefields, while, to meet the requirements for this new type of total war, recruitment campaigns were launched throughout the country. Fresh Irishmen were needed to fill the ranks of the expanding British Army. Here, now, it is time to turn to the reasons why these Irishmen enlisted, or, indeed in some cases, re-enlisted.

Irishmen had always served in the British Army. In the sixteenth century, the Tudor monarchy had acknowledged their Irish soldiers as a hardy and fierce fighting force. During the Peninsular War against Napoleon, thirty percent of Wellington's army had been Irish. This figure rose steadily over the following decades. By 1831, forty percent of the British Army were Irish. By the 1860s, the number peaked at sixty percent claiming to be either Irish-born or of Irish descent. The number then gradually reduced until by the Boer War, twenty percent of Britain's fighting men were Irish. By 1914, the British Army numbered 247,000 troops, of whom 20,000 were Irish, with a further 145,000 ex-regular reserves that could be called upon, 30,000 of which were Irish (meaning that in 1914, Irishmen made up twelve percent of the total British Army). Over the centuries, Irish soldiers had developed a reputation for being dependable fighting troops. The Connaught Rangers were nicknamed the 'Devil's Own' because of their hard-fighting spirit. Similarly, the Royal Irish Fusiliers had the motto 'Faugh-a-Ballagh'. It means 'clear the way', and was earned because of their skills as first-strike shock troops.

The picture of Ireland as it was in 1914 would suggest that the majority of men enlisted to escape the poverty and the general hopelessness of life at home. There are many cases such as that of my great-grandfather Martin Gaffey, who was orphaned young and – according to his daughter Eileen Kavanagh – raised

Soldiers of 1ˢᵗ Connaught Rangers, who were members of the League of the Cross, at their station in Daghshai, India, 1908. Founded in 1873, the League was a Catholic organisation whose members took oaths of total abstinence.

by a tyrannical aunt who sent him to work in the fields while still only a boy and took every penny he earned. He enlisted in October 1915 to escape the harsh life of an unskilled labourer in his hometown of Athlone.

Then there were those like Fred Kelly and Thomas Byrne, who signed up to escape the law. Byrne was from the village of Timahoe in County Laois, and for some misdemeanour that has been lost to time, he was wanted by the law when war broke out. Byrne, seeing the army as his only escape from capture and a prison sentence, enlisted under his mother's maiden name of Dowling, only to be killed in action in 1915. As for Fred Kelly from Athlone – according to his granddaughter who now resides in New Zealand – he grew up with a terribly abusive father and, when only fifteen years old, during one of his father's more violent moments, Fred produced an axe and nearly killed his father on the spot. He then turned and walked out of the family home, never to return. A few years later, Fred found himself in an English jail for killing a man. He then went on to enlist upon the outbreak of war, and ultimately survive the conflict. Unable to return home to Ireland, and not exactly wanted in England either, Fred chose to emigrate to America, where he married a local girl. But, breaking with marriage tradition, Fred Kelly took his wife's maiden name in order to leave his past behind.

However, there were numerous reasons why Irishmen joined up for the khaki uniform. For some, although this only really applies to those who enlisted pre-war, the army offered some attractive perks. A single man might travel to India. He would be expected to remain there for several years at a time, but while there, even a private soldier might have an Indian manservant. Besides this, a married man could bring his wife and children out to India and start a new life in an exotic land, far away from the drudgery of Ireland.

There was also the wage and job security, and the army pension. Some men, faced with learning a trade or joining the army, simply weighed up their options and made the decision based on what was the best career move. For others, especially in the garrison towns such as Athlone, Birr, Castlebar, Cork, Drogheda, Mullingar, Naas, Newbridge, Templemore, Tipperary, and Dublin (to name but a few), family tradition played a large role in a young man's decision. If his father or grandfather had been a soldier, he might be expected, or indeed might want to continue the custom. The outbreak of war against Germany simply gave many men like this the extra nudge they needed to walk in the barrack gate.

Some, of course, joined for purely political reasons. There were those who were disgusted by Germany's invasion of small, Catholic Belgium – men who felt it was their duty to stand up and teach Fritz a lesson. Others, Catholic and Protestant, felt that they simply had to play their part for King and Country, and that being a British citizen meant answering the call when it was asked of them. But most of the Irishmen who went to war for political reasons were members of either the Ulster Volunteer Force or the Irish Volunteers. The UVF wanted to show its rock-solid determination to stay a part of the union, and knew that fighting for Britain would certainly strengthen their case. As for the Irish Volunteers, who numbered around 190,000 at the start of the war, they suffered a great disappointment on 18 September 1914 when, after Home Rule was granted to Ireland by royal assent, its implementation was

immediately postponed until the end of the war (or for one year if the war turned out to be short). Therefore, the Irish Volunteers still had Home Rule to protect. They felt that to prove their worthiness of Home Rule, they had to fight alongside Britain in the war – to basically show critics in England that if Ireland was granted Home Rule, it was not going to turn into a fiercely anti-British country. It would still come to Britain's aid if need be (Surprisingly, the south ended up surpassing the north in terms of initial recruitment figures. As noted by Philip Orr in his book *The Road to the Somme*, the historian Alice Stopford Green discovered from a Viceroy's report of 14 January 1916 that, as of that date, '1.36 percent of the population had volunteered in counties Antrim and Down ... whereas 1.7 percent had done so in Kilkenny, Tipperary, Waterford and Wexford.').

However, not every man in the Irish Volunteers agreed with fighting this new war. The organisation split, and while 180,000 renamed themselves the Irish National Volunteers with many marching off to the recruiting stations, the

Above: A studio photograph of Private John 'Jack' Fallon of the Connaught Rangers from Loughrea, County Galway, taken pre-war in Ahmednagar, India. It shows the uniform and fashion style of pre-war soldiers.

remaining 10,000 refused to fight for the British flag. They kept their old name, the Irish Volunteers, and being heavily influenced by the Irish Republican Brotherhood, this breakaway movement started to plan a war of their own. Ultimately, this would become the Easter Rising of 1916.

Then there were the down-right ordinary reasons why some Irishmen enlisted. Some naively saw war as just a great adventure, or were simply bored with their monotonous life in Ireland. Working day in day out, perhaps as clerks in dreary offices, and raised on stories

of glorious battles of past conflicts, they had no idea of the horrors that awaited them in the trenches. Some were swayed by contemporary propaganda, depicting the Germans as stupid gorilla-like brutes who did not know which way to point a rifle. It was also widely believed that the war could not possibly last beyond Christmas 1914, and that any man who did not sign up and fight in time would be looked down upon when the glorious heroes returned.

Lastly, there were those who were forced to go by peer pressure. Patrick Hickson was one such man. He lived on Adelaide Terrace, just off the South Circular Road in Dublin, and worked as a compositor for Lecky, Brown and Nolan printing firm. The only son out of eleven children, he was a good-humoured,

Above: *Gunner Patrick Hickson from South Circular Road, Dublin (first on right), posing with two comrades for a postcard photo. All the soldiers were allowed to say was that they were 'somewhere in France'. The back of the original contains the message 'To Mother. From Paddy. With best love.'*

outgoing man who could always be found whistling or singing cheerily. The family were firm British supporters, but when the war broke out, Patrick did not see it as his duty to go. However, his twin sister thought otherwise, and hounded him, insulting him with lines such as, 'If I was a man, I'd go. If you were a real man, you'd go,' until Patrick finally enlisted into the Royal Field Artillery. He was wounded at Ypres, survived the war, but ultimately suffered from shellshock for the rest of his life, which was, unfortunately, filled with hardships. He retreated into himself after the war – his former cheeriness gone – and married an aggressive schoolteacher in the 1920s who was always 'giving out' with a 'loud, fattish voice', according to Patrick's niece. Later, Patrick Hickson also had to suffer the death of his only son when aged six.

This then, was the world and the reasons which brought Irishmen to the trenches. What they endured and suffered there was beyond anything they could have imagined. Even Irish veterans of previous wars – such as the Boer War – could not possibly have known what the First World War would bring. Britain's previous wars had been colonial ones, where small expeditionary armies manoeuvred across wide tracts of land. This war was a sit-tight, stay-alive, mass-slaughter war on a gigantic scale. The men of Ireland who entered the trenches were to experience a living nightmare.

This book is not an attempt to tell the geo-political story of the First World War with a sprinkling of the individual anecdotal stories of Irishmen thrown in. The main focus of this book *is* the stories of forgotten Irish soldiers, and as such, this book is not a traditional military history text – the movements of corps and divisions and the tactics and strategy of generals are not my prime concern, and so the wider history of the war, where mentioned, is included only to give necessary background information.

These Irish soldiers were not traitors; they were not fools. It does not matter if they were nationalist or unionist, pauper or career soldier. They were all human beings and deserve to be remembered. What they went through can be difficult to understand – but it should **never** be forgotten. This is their story.

May God **have mercy on their souls.**

Above: *Soldiers and nurses sharing a dance. Gunner Patrick Hickson is part of the second pair from the left (dancing with the nurse with eyes closed).*
Below: *Gunner Patrick Hickson and soldiers of the Royal Field Artillery, posing for a group photograph in France.*

CHAPTER 1

BAPTISM OF FIRE

'Even to Jimmie's inexperienced eyes the battalion had changed since he had left it. The men were weary, but the raw soldiers had been tested in battle and seemed to him to have gained the self-confidence of veterans.'

Captain Edward King, 6th Royal Inniskilling Fusiliers, in his memoir *Haphazard*

From the initial phase of the First World War onwards Irishmen played a significant role; one of the first New Army divisions of citizen volunteers to go into action was Irish; on the Somme, it was Irishmen that made the most remarkable achievements on the first day of battle; and as the war dragged on, the Irish divisions often suffered most at the hands of the enemy. Time and time again, the Irish were at the forefront of the war and earned their place in the history books. Irishmen were even some of the first to die in the war. On 6 August 1914 – barely two days after the start of the conflict – twenty-five year old Signalman Joseph Pierce Murphy of Thorncastle Place, Ringsend, Dublin and thirty-nine year old Petty Officer Second Class Joseph Lynch from Ringaskiddy, County Cork were killed when their ship, HMS *Amphion*, hit a mine in the North Sea. Today, both men are commemorated on the Plymouth Naval Memorial.

Above left: *North Irish Horse cap badge: The North Irish Horse was not a regular unit of the British Army but rather a Special Reserve Yeomanry unit comprised of part-time soldiers. However, unlike other non-regular units, elements of the North Irish Horse actually departed with the original BEF for France upon the outbreak of the war. Formed in 1903, the unit had squadrons based in Belfast, Derry/Ballymena, Enniskillen and Dundalk, and in March 1918, the unit was turned into a Cyclist Battalion due to the lack of need for cavalry in modern warfare.*

Above middle: *6th Inniskilling Dragoons' cap badge: Raised in 1689 as Sir Albert Cunningham's Dragoons, this unit was ultimately one of the most famous dragoon regiments in history. After fighting at the Boyne – where they were personally led by King William of Orange on his final assault against the Hilltop of Donore – they went on to fight at Waterloo, and then at the Battle of Balaclava in the Crimean War where they charged, as part of the Heavy Brigade under Lord Lucan, in support of the famous Light Brigade. Like their fellow Inniskilling infantry regiment, they were also known as 'The Skins', and their unit motto was 'Inniskilling'.*

Above right: *8th King's Royal Irish Hussars: Originally raised in Derry in 1693 as Henry Conyngham's Regiment of Dragoons, the unit is most famous for having participated in the ill-fated Charge of the Light Brigade during the Battle of Balaclava in the Crimean War. Nicknamed 'The Crossbelts', the unit motto was Pristinae Virtutis Memores – 'mindful of former valour'.*

THE FIRST SHOT

EDWARD THOMAS

When Britain declared war on Germany on 4 August 1914, it began to mobilise an expeditionary army to send to the Continent, to aid France and Belgium. Initially, the British Expeditionary Force (BEF) was comprised of approximately 86,000 officers and men and, within days of war being declared, the first waves began landing in France. Among them were Irish units such as 1st (Battalion) Irish Guards, 2nd Royal Munster Fusiliers, 2nd Connaught Rangers, 2nd Royal Irish Regiment, and 2nd Royal Irish Rifles. There were also Irish cavalry units, such as elements of the North Irish Horse, South Irish Horse and the 4th Royal Irish Dragoon Guards. The BEF immediately began marching towards the German Army in Belgium.

By 22 August, the BEF was entrenched in the little Belgian town of Mons, and at 7am that morning to the north of Mons, C Squadron of the 4th Royal Irish Dragoon Guards was on patrol. It was dawn, and the two armies of the British and German empires had yet to encounter one another. The Germans had steamrolled through most of Belgium already on their way towards France, and the British knew that the Germans were heading straight towards them. Therefore, they had decided to make a stand at Mons, and had sent out patrols such as C Squadron, to give them advance warning of the German approach.

As the patrol neared the village of Casteau, they spotted four enemy cavalrymen belonging to the German 2nd Kuirassiers. Realising that they had encountered the enemy, the Germans turned and fled. Major Thomas Bridges quickly ordered the men of C Squadron to open fire, and when the first bullet whizzed through the air, it came from the rifle of Private Edward Thomas of 4th Troop. Thomas was from Nenagh, County Tipperary, and had originally enlisted as a drummer into the Royal Horse Artillery. Now, however, he had just gone down in history as the first British soldier of the First World War to fire at the enemy. It is uncertain whether or not he killed or just wounded the German, but Captain Charles Beck Hornby of 1st Troop then led a charge after the enemy. Hornby killed several German soldiers, using his officer's sword and

Above right: 4th *(Royal Irish) Dragoon Guards' cap badge: Originally raised as the Earl of Arran's Regiment of Cuirassiers in 1685 by King James II, in order to defend his throne during the Monmouth Rebellion, the regiment later fought under the command of King William III of Orange at the Battle of the Boyne in 1690. It later served in the Peninsular War, but a series of unfortunate circumstances saw the regiment unhorsed and sent home after just under two years in the field.*

returned later in the day, the blade red with German blood. Edward Thomas would go on to win the Military Medal for bravery and reach the rank of sergeant, before transferring into the Machine Gun Corps in 1916. He ultimately survived the war, served a few more years with his old regiment – the 4th Royal Irish Dragoon Guards – and was then discharged in 1923.

And so, the two enemies had encountered one another. It would only be a matter of time before they came face to face in battle.

THE FIRST VICTORIA CROSS

MAURICE DEASE

Entrenched in Mons that same day was Lieutenant Maurice Dease. Dease was an Irishman from Gaulstown – situated about halfway between Coole and Castlepollard – in County Westmeath. He was twenty-four years old, and his father, Edmund Fitzlaurence Dease, was a land agent and former justice of the peace. Serving with the 4th Royal Fusiliers, Dease, like Private Edward Thomas, was another of the veteran Irishmen who constituted the original BEF – the men who had been sent to the continent immediately after the outbreak of war.

On 22 August, the 4th Royal Fusiliers were positioned at Nimy, just north of Mons, where they were tasked with guarding two crossings on the Mons canal – a railway bridge and a road-swing bridge. The German Army needed these crossings and others like them to press on into France and so the BEF knew that they must be defended at all costs. According to the battalion war diary, orders were simple: 'Had orders to hold on to this position as long as possible.' So the men dug hasty trenches and rifle pits for protection, and Lieutenant Dease set up his machine-gun detachment of two guns to cover the crossing. According to Max Arthur in *Symbols of Courage*, 'Dease got flour sacks from the local mill and filled them with shingle to protect his guns on either side of the bridge, and they worked into the night, all the time hearing the sounds of the Germans moving in the woods to the north of the canal.'

The next morning, an enemy aircraft flew overhead, followed by a German cavalry patrol which tried to approach the bridge but was fired upon. Then, at

Lieutenant Maurice Dease from County Westmeath. Educated in Stoneyhurst College in England – a Catholic institution – and later Wimbledon College, Dease was commissioned out of Sandhurst as a second-lieutenant into the Royal Fusiliers in May 1910. Two years later, he was promoted to lieutenant.

A Company of the 4th Royal Fusiliers – Lieutenant Maurice Dease's battalion – resting in the Grand Place, Mons, 22 August 1914.

around 9am, all along the British line, the Germans descended on the canal crossings. Dease ordered his gunners to open fire while British riflemen let loose with rapid fire – the 'mad minute' of at least fifteen aimed rounds in sixty seconds. The fire was so murderous that the more inexperienced German units actually believed that they were solely on the receiving end of machine guns. The enemy were held back, but then German shells started falling amongst the British, and with very few artillery guns with which to return fire, the British soldiers were forced to suffer the enemy bombardment and simply wait it out. When it finally ended, around 11am, the enemy infantry advanced again.

Defending Nimy railway bridge, C Company of the 4th Royal Fusiliers – which included Lieutenant Maurice Dease – was suddenly faced with, as the war diary records: 'at least four battalions of [enemy] infantry, also cavalry and artillery. We suffered severely on the bridges over the canal by rifle and artillery fire.' Dease's left-side machine gun was soon knocked out by the enemy and, as Max Arthur states, 'the machine-gunners, under constant fire, were killed and wounded in such numbers that bodies had to be moved aside so that

replacement gunners could take their place.'

Dease had been fifty yards to the rear of the bridge up to this point, directing fire, but when he saw a break in the enemy fire, he dashed forward. Reaching the silenced left-side machine gun, he was hit in the leg by the enemy. A superior officer insisted that Dease withdraw to have the wound tended to, but the young officer refused and began crawling across the line of fire to his second gun. On the way, he was shot in the side but still refused to withdraw. He made his way back to his only working gun on the right-side of the bridge, and was shot for a third time.

Dease was soon personally manning this machine gun, as all the rest of its crew had either been killed or wounded, but he was in a terribly exposed position. The right-side gun was positioned on top of an embankment, and the Germans pounded him with rifle, machine-gun and artillery fire. He was shot a fourth time, and then a fifth – around 3.30pm – after which he finally collapsed, unable to continue. It was now obvious that the Mons canal could not be defended, and the BEF command sent orders to begin a withdrawal. Private Sidney Godley volunteered to rush out under enemy fire, to get the gun working again, in order to cover the retreat of 4th Royal Fusiliers, but he was ultimately wounded and taken prisoner by the Germans.

One month later, a telegram, dated 22 September 1914, arrived to Lieutenant

Above: Short Magazine Lee-Enfield (SMLE) No 1 Mk 3 rifle: The standard British infantryman's rifle of the First World War, the Lee-Enfield was a reliable weapon and simple to use. When fully loaded the rifle held ten rounds of .303 calibre ammunition (compared to the German's Gewehr 98 which held five rounds). A bolt-action weapon, its maximum range was 550 yards. The soldiers were trained to perform the 'mad minute' of at least fifteen rounds in sixty seconds – a rate of firepower that the soldiers of other armies could not match. The rifle is still in service today in Indian, Pakistani and Bangladeshi reserve military and police units.

Dease's father at his home in Drumree, just outside Dunshaughlin in County Meath, informing him that 'Lieut. M.J. Dease Royal Fusiliers has been dangerously wounded.' This telegram was followed by another, four days later, which stated that 'Lieut. M.J. Dease Royal Fusiliers is now reported killed in action. Lord Kitchener expresses his sympathy.' However, on 30 September 1914, a third telegram arrived, its contents casting doubt on the previous one. 'Lieut. M.J. Dease Royal Fusiliers reported killed Sept 5th is now (Sept 12) reported to be wounded and missing. Both reports from O.C. Battalion.' It must have been a difficult time for Dease's family, not knowing whether Maurice was alive or dead.

The truth was that Maurice Dease from Westmeath had died not long after being relieved by Private Godley. Obviously having tried to

Top: First telegram received by Maurice Dease's father, 22 September 1914.
Middle: Second telegram received by Dease's father, 26 September 1914.
Bottom: Third telegram received by Dease's father, 30 September 1914.

crawl away from the machine gun in a final search for medical assistance, he was found draped across the nearby railway lines and taken to a dressing station where he died soon after arriving. He was twenty-four years old and was soon awarded the first Victoria Cross of the First World War. His citation, which later appeared in the *London Gazette* (16 November 1914), read 'Though two or three times badly wounded he continued to control the fire of his machine guns at Mons on 23 August until all his men were shot. He died of his wounds.' Private Sidney Godley, the man who relieved him, was awarded the second VC for his bravery.

Today, Dease's body lies in St Symphorien Military Cemetery, close to where he died.

THE WESTERN FRONT

Four days before the Battle of Mons, the German Kaiser, Wilhelm II, had issued an 'Order of the Day', stating that 'It is my Royal and Imperial Command that you concentrate your energies for the immediate present upon one single purpose, and that is that you address all your skill and all the valour of my soldiers to exterminate first the treacherous English [and] walk over General [Sir John] French's contemptible little army.' He had actually referred to the BEF as a 'contemptibly' little army – insulting their size – but the word had been wrongly reported as 'contemptible'. Now, as far as the British were concerned, their 'contemptible' army had shown what it could do, and they adopted the name as a badge of honour. From then on, the British soldiers who had fought in the first battles of the First World War would be forever known as the 'Old Contemptibles.'

At Mons, the British were ultimately forced back in the face of superior German firepower. They had suffered 1,600 killed or wounded, and had inflicted an estimated 5,000 casualties on the Germans. This was due to the high level of skill and experience in the BEF – most of its soldiers had learned their trade over many years in places such as India, Burma, or Malta, and some were even veterans of the Boer War. They were the furthest thing from raw recruits.

However, there was simply not enough of them to repel the massive German

Army, and in France and Belgium along the Western Front, the next few weeks saw the Germans fight to within a few miles of Paris. Then, when the war seemed all but lost, a gap in the German line was exploited and a renewed Allied offensive miraculously pushed the Germans all the way back to a defensive line on the Chemin des Dames Ridge along the River Aisne. Here, the Germans dug in, and no matter how hard they tried, the British could not breach the enemy defences. So they too dug in, and before long, parallel lines of Allied and German trenches stretched from the Belgian coast to the borders with Switzerland. Trench warfare had begun.

The British soon found themselves centred on the crumbling Belgian town of Ypres. They launched a renewed offensive against the Germans, hoping to break through before the enemy became too firmly entrenched in this latest position. But the offensive failed, only ending when the winter snows arrived in late 1914, costing the British 58,000 casualties, the French 50,000, while the Germans suffered 130,000 killed and wounded. So, with a state of deadlock existing on the Western Front, the Allies turned their attention to new battlefields.

GALLIPOLI

Turkey, Germany's ally, was considered a good target. If the Allies could force their way through the Dardanelles – a narrow strip of water separating European Turkey from Asiatic Turkey – they would have a route from the Aegean into the Black Sea, and this would allow the western Allies to link up with Russia and surround Germany on all sides. But after forts along the Dardanelles coastline prevented the British Navy from reaching the Turkish capital of Constantinople, it was decided to send in the infantry to capture the forts by land. That way, once the forts were neutralised, the navy could sail up the Dardanelles unopposed.

The place selected for the infantry attack was a peninsula of chalk and sandstone hills separated by steep ravines; a place of rock, dust, heat and scrub. Its name would soon become synonymous with the struggling and sacrifice of Irishmen.

A group of Connaught Rangers pose for a photograph in tropical uniform.

THE INITIAL LANDINGS

JAMES CLIFFORD

On 25 April 1915, the infantry attack was launched. Five beaches on the Turkish peninsula of Gallipoli would be assaulted simultaneously, in order to gain footholds for further advances inland. On four of the five beaches, the attacks would follow the standard plan for amphibious landings – men would row ashore in small boats and leap into action – but on the fifth beach, a new plan would be tried out. In had been inspired by the fact that the ruins of Troy were not far away – where the Greeks had used their famous Trojan horse to trick their way inside the city walls. At V Beach, the British generals of the First World War had decided to use a modern Trojan horse against their Turkish enemies. And the soldiers selected for this bold plan were the Irishmen of the 29th Division.

At 6am, the preliminary naval bombardment of V Beach ceased, and towards the shore sailed the SS *River Clyde*, an old collier ship converted into an armoured landing craft. The idea was to literally beach the ship, open its doors, and have infantry flood out to capture the beachhead, beside which was the ancient Turkish fort of Sedd-el-Bahr. In the *River Clyde* that day was Private James Clifford of the 1ˢᵗ Royal Munster Fusiliers. A regular soldier, Clifford was from Killarney, County Kerry, and had joined the army in 1910 having lied about his age – he was only seventeen at the time. He was now twenty-two and currently serving as a batman to an officer.

On board the *River Clyde* and fast approaching the Turkish peninsula, Clifford got ready to disembark. It was clear that the ship was too large to make it all the way to dry land. When it beached itself, it would still be surrounded by deep water. For this

Above: *Royal Munster Fusiliers' cap badge: Formed in 1881 by the amalgamation of two former East India Company regiments – the 101ˢᵗ and 104ᵗʰ Foot (Bengal Fusiliers) – the Royal Munster Fusiliers could trace its lineage back to 1652. It had the nickname 'The Dirty Shirts' and the Latin motto* Spectamur Agendo *– 'let us be judged by our acts'. Its recruiting grounds were counties Cork, Kerry, Limerick and Clare, with the regimental depot in Tralee barracks.*

Below: *A view of V Beach and Sedd-el-Bahr fort, taken after the disastrous* River Clyde *landings, 25 April 1915. This is the gauntlet that Private James Clifford from Tralee, County Kerry, had to run to reach the shore. Bodies of dead Royal Munster Fusiliers can be seen on the lighter in the foreground, and a mixture of Royal Munster Fusiliers and Royal Dublin Fusiliers survivors can be seen huddling under cover on the beach.*

reason, a smaller steamship – the *Argyll* – was to beach itself in front of the *River Clyde,* to make a bridge to shore. To cover this manoeuvre, Irishmen of the 1st Royal Dublin Fusiliers were to row ashore in lighters ahead of the *River Clyde* landing. Clifford waited anxiously as the ship neared the land.

As the Dublin men landed in their boats, Turkish machine guns at either end of the beach and in Sedd-el-Bahr fort opened up, raking the beach with enfilading fire. The Irishmen were caught out in the open and were gunned down. Survivors scrambled to a low sandbank which gave them just enough cover from the enemy, but within a few minutes, over fifty percent of the 700 men who had just landed were dead.

Inside the *River Clyde*, bullets started pinging and ricocheting off the hull. V Beach was defended by only a handful of Turks, but they were determined to keep the British from gaining a foothold on Gallipoli. The *River Clyde* shuddered and ground to a halt as its keel got stuck in the sand. However, the *Argyll* failed to finish the bridge to land, and so the captain of the *River Clyde* was forced to gather some sailors and try and build a bridge out of lighters. Machine-gun bullets raked the water as the navy men tried desperately to lash the boats together.

The ship's doors opened and the infantry assault was launched. Two companies of Royal Munster Fusiliers ran out on deck, heading for the gangways down to the lighters. But since the doorways out of the hold were tiny and few, the enemy gunners had easy targets. Munster men were cut down as they poured out of the doorways. Bodies had to be pushed and kicked aside as men continued in their frantic efforts to reach the lighters and the bridge to shore.

James Clifford took his turn to run the gauntlet. He sped out of the bowels of the ship and raced down the gangway, leaping over his fallen comrades. Clifford was a good swimmer and as bullets were splashing into the sea all around him, he dived into the water to get to shore. Along the way, he passed a lighter with two navy men sitting in it. One man had his kneecap torn open by enemy fire, and the two begged Clifford for help. 'For Christ's sake,' they pleaded. 'Help us.' As Bart Clifford – James Clifford's son – would later recount, all that James Clifford could do was to push the lighter out to sea and away from the gunfire.

Clifford managed to make it to shore but was shot in the leg in the process. He joined his Dublin comrades and together they huddled behind the sandbank. Then, two and half hours later, at 8.30am, the order was given to try again. Men of the 2nd Royal Hampshire Regiment, who had also been in the *River Clyde*, tried desperately to get to shore but were slaughtered in the process.

After this final attempt to storm ashore, out of the 2,000 men who had taken part in the attack, only 200 were on the beach, and these men were effectively trapped behind the sandbank. Seventy percent of the two companies of Royal Munster Fusiliers who had charged out of the *River Clyde* had fallen. From where he lay, James Clifford looked out to sea and could not believe his eyes. The water around the *River Clyde* was literally red – red with blood.

V Beach was finally secured the following day after bitter fighting. For Private James Clifford, the same day he entered the war was the same day he was wounded. He was evacuated to a hospital ship, and when he was fit to serve again, Clifford was posted to the Western Front. Then, while serving in the Loos sector in 1916, a lump of shrapnel sliced his arm nearly clean off, and with the limb dangling from a sinew and while completely in shock, Clifford stumbled to a dressing station. His son, Bart Clifford, remembers the story. 'Along the way, my dad came across a man who he thought was a priest. "Father," he asked, "Could you spare me a cigarette?" The man looked round and turned out to be a Protestant minister. He said, "I'm not of your flock, but you can certainly have a cigarette."' After receiving medical treatment, Clifford's arm was ultimately amputated.

This was enough to get Clifford sent back to his native Killarney, and, seeing as he was friendly with a colonel who was one of the Earls of Kenmare, he managed to get work caddying on the Kerry golf courses. In fact, James Clifford had once been a very good golfer.

However, years later, when the family home was inherited by Clifford's elder brother, and when this brother married a fiercely nationalistic woman, Clifford was no longer allowed to speak of his First World War experiences. Worse still, his new sister-in-law binned his war medals, along with all keepsakes that the former soldier had to remind him of his days in uniform.

Back in Gallipoli in 1915, after the lukewarm successes of the initial landings, the fighting on the Turkish peninsula quickly started to mirror the Western Front. Soon enough, Gallipoli was a mess of trenches, barbed-wire defences and machine-gun emplacements. As in France and Belgium, there was no movement or swift advances – only stalemate and stagnation.

The Turks turned out to be a dogged and determined enemy who were passionate in the defence of their homeland. Initially, they became infamous for launching suicidal bayonet charges towards Allied lines, screaming 'Allah! Allah!' as they rushed forward in their droves only to be mown down by British or Australian/New Zealand Army Corps (ANZAC) fire. Later, however, as the campaign dragged on – after Allied soldiers started meeting face to face with Turkish soldiers through the odd regional truce or through the latter being taken prisoner – soldiers realised that the Turks were the same as they were. They were men with families, who would rather be with their loved ones than

Trenches, stalemate and stagnation. Gallipoli soon became just another Western Front. Here, a Royal Irish Fusilier teases a Turkish sniper by holding his helmet on his rifle above the parapet.

fighting and killing. They were, towards the end of the campaign, fondly referred to as 'Johnny Turk', but in the opening days of Gallipoli, they were seen as a fanatical enemy to be feared and defeated.

THE FIRST VOLUNTEERS

The regimental drums and pipes of the Connaught Rangers. Regimental bands led the way during marches, and would have instilled great pride in soldiers.

EDWARD KING

After the initial landings at sites such as V Beach, it was decided that new troops and new divisions were needed if there was to be any hope of pressing inland. The regular soldiers of pre-August 1914 were mostly dead or wounded. These were the veteran men of many years' experience, but Britain needed new troops to continue the fight. It was time to call on the men of the New Army units, Kitchener's volunteers who had signed up for service at the outbreak of war. It is true that some units had been formed out of men from the same background, such as the 'Dublin Pals' – volunteers who formed D Company, 7th Royal Dublin Fusiliers, and who were mostly professional graduates who had refused officer's commissions, many of whom were talented rugby players and IRFU members – but in many of these volunteer formations, men of all classes, professions, religions and political opinions from up and down the social hierarchy served together.

By summer 1915, they had been training for several months, drilling, marching, parading, shooting, learning to dig trenches and prepare defensive positions, but they had never seen combat. They were eager and enthusiastic – full of patriotism, the spirit of adventure, or the desire to get away from their home for whatever reason – but they had a severe lack of experience. For most of these men, war was a concept, an ideal, far removed from the blood-and-filth reality of the trenches. Furthermore, there was criticism that these New Army units had not been adequately trained, so while these volunteers had no idea of what they would face at the front, they had also not been fully provided with the skills to survive.

The first New Army division, the 9th (Scottish) Division, was detailed for the Western Front, but the next one, the 10th (Irish) Division, was ordered to make ready for Gallipoli. This unit was an historic first as never before had a British division contained the name 'Irish', and never before had such a mass of Irish troops been gathered into a single fighting formation. Made up of 'Service' battalions that had been created for the duration of the war, the 10th (Irish) Division was comprised of men from all across the island of Ireland. They were one of the first batches of First World War volunteers to go into action anywhere.

One such citizen-turned-soldier in the 10th (Irish) Division was Edward King. He ultimately survived the war, and in later life wrote a memoir entitled *Haphazard*, detailing the significant events in his life. Regarding his beginnings, King wrote that 'Munterconnaught Rectory, where I was born in August 1894, was a small white house on a knoll overlooking Lough Ramor near the southern border of County Cavan.' King's father was the Church of Ireland Reverend Albert Edward King, later the Dean of Kilmore, and the family had come to Ireland in the 1600s, but Edward's father hated being referred to as Anglo-Irish. 'Nothing annoyed him more than to hear Protestant families like ours referred to as West Britons or Anglo-Irish. "Ireland has been our homeland for hundreds of years," he would declare. "Creed and politics do not affect nationality. Does anyone suggest that Dean Swift, WB Yeats or George Bernard Shaw were not as Irish as James Joyce?"' As far as Edward's father was concerned, Ireland was his home, as it had been the home of his father and his father before him. The family were Irish, and that was that.

Edward had two younger siblings, Marjory and Richard, and not far from his childhood house was the old home of the Sheridan family. It was in this building that Dean Swift was reputed to have written part of *Gulliver's Travels*. Literary influences seemed to have surrounded the young Edward, and when his family moved to Kildallon near Killeshandra in 1899 – the only town around for miles, which had the 'nearest doctor, railway station and public houses (only nineteen of them – all too few on a thirsty market day)' – King was not far from Ardlougher, where Edgar Allan Poe's ancestors were said to have lived before moving to the New World. Pat McLoughlin, a local man, was known throughout the land as a powerful story-teller and used to entertain Edward for hours with his yarns, but, 'unlike a retired naval petty-officer who lived nearby, [Pat] never interrupted a yarn to teach me arms-drill with a broom handle until my back ached.'

King also grew up with military stories from a young age. He always remembered that one of the Sheridans – Philip, born in 1830 – had emigrated to America and rose to become Commander-in-Chief of the United States Army,

Above: Royal Inniskilling Fusiliers' cap badge: 'The Skins', as they were known, were originally raised in Enniskillen in 1689 as Colonel Zachariah Tiffin's Regiment of Foot. The following year, they fought at the Battle of the Boyne on the side of King William, and in 1746, the regiment took part in the Battle of Culloden. The Skins later fought in the American War of Independence and were the only Irish regiment of infantry on the field at Waterloo. In 1881, the old East India Company regiment – the 108th Foot (Madras Infantry) – was absorbed into the unit. The Skins recruited from Donegal, Derry, Tyrone and Fermanagh, with the regimental depot at Omagh. Their Latin motto was Nec Aspera Terrant – *'by difficulties undaunted'.*

Lieutenant Edward King from County Cavan, 1914.

Citizen volunteers joining D Company, 7ᵗʰ Royal Dublin Fusiliers (the 'Dubin Pals')
at Lansdowne Road rugby ground.

and he also once met an old army pensioner with an interesting past. 'It was not given to every boy to hear the story of the charge of the Heavy Brigade at Balaclava from the lips of one who, as a young trooper in the Dragoon Guards, had ridden against the Russian guns, in 1855, to save the remnants of the Light Brigade immortalised by Tennyson.'

Years after, Edward King entered a new phase of his life, later remembering that 'In winter, cold, chapped hands, chilblains and, at all times, hunger and claustrophobia were part of our daily existence. The infirmary was seldom empty.' This had nothing to do with the war however; this was King's experience of school. He was educated in King's Hospital School in Dublin, a place that he hated, feeling that school only 'stifled imagination and bred mediocrity ... There was a grimness about the School as I knew it to match the grey walls that shut us in.' However, he was very close to Royal Barracks (now Collins Barracks Museum), where he would later serve.

According to King, 'One of my most vivid memories [from school] is of gazing from the window of No. 1 Dormitory across the football ground and in the Officers' Mess of the Royal Barracks, glimpsing the blue and scarlet and gold of the uniforms and listening to the strains of waltz tunes played by the band. To the callow lad it seemed another world. It never crossed my mind that the day would soon come when as a newly-fledged subaltern I would join my regiment in those self-same barracks, though wearing the khaki of war-time and in surroundings totally divested of the colour and glamour of pre-war years.'

In 1913, Edward left King's Hospital and entered Trinity College, where he studied classics and history, perhaps inspired by the literary surroundings of his youth. Then in 1914, the war came.

Because King had been a university student, he was considered a prime candidate for a commission. He applied to become an officer in the army and was successful. Soon enough, twenty-year-old Edward King found himself serving with the 6th Royal Inniskilling Fusiliers, which had been formed at Omagh in August 1914. He was soon promoted from second-lieutenant to lieutenant and in April 1915, along with his battalion, he departed the Curragh for Basingstoke to join the rest of 10th (Irish) Division in preparation for deployment. On 8 July, the division sailed for war, with the bulk of the division assembling on the Greek island of Lemnos in advance of landing on Gallipoli. However, in the case of Edward King, his battalion – the 6th Royal Inniskilling Fusiliers – went into bivouac on the island of Mitylene. King was left alone in command of a small detachment on Lemnos.

In reference to the period starting with July 1915, while 'stranded' on Lemnos away from the rest of his battalion, until the end of the Gallipoli campaign, King strangely changed the way he wrote *Haphazard*. Instead of writing in the first person, as he had done up to this point, and to which he would return afterwards, Edward wrote the Gallipoli sections of his memoir in the third person and referred to himself as 'Jimmie Todd', as though he was a character in a novel. It is unusual, but perhaps this was an unconscious move by King to distance himself from the war?

King's classical education certainly enhanced his appreciation for Lemnos, and he recalled, 'with some amusement, the story of the mythical Argonauts who landed at Lemnos during their search for the Golden Fleece. The women of the island had murdered all the men in revenge for some ill-treatment. They were delighted by the arrival of Jason and his crew and received them with open arms. When the Argonauts resumed their voyage a year later, Lemnos was well on its way to being re-populated ...'

The harbour of Mudros on the island of Lemnos, where the Allied armada had assembled prior to the invasion of Gallipoli. As Lieutenant Edward King recalled in his memoir, 'Agamemnon is said to have assembled his fleet in this great natural harbour [Mudros] on the island of Lemnos before he sailed for Troy to recapture the beautiful Helen'.

Unfortunately for Edward King and his fellow Royal Inniskilling Fusiliers, however, the local villages were off-limits to soldiers. As King was aware, 'there must have been young women on the island, but they were kept at a safe distance from the soldiery, leaving only aged crones, well protected by voluminous garments, to sell water-melons, tomatoes and tiny eggs to soldiers tired of rice, bully beef, and army biscuits.'

However, King's classical appreciation did nothing to help him cope with the difficulties of life on Lemnos. 'On the shore was a vast encampment of tents and bivouacs, swarming with troops and resembling a gigantic colony of ants. Working-parties were the order of the day. There were no pioneer corps or gangs of stevedores equipped with proper tackle for the shifting of munitions and stores from ship to shore or onto lighters. At Mudros all this had to be done by the manual labour of unskilled soldiers, working under a blazing sun and on a meagre ration of tepid water brought from Egypt because, in summer, Lemnos was parched and almost waterless.' Edward recalled 'Homer's description of the succulent flesh of Lemnos' tall-horned cattle. In July 1915 Mudros was unable to provide a canteen or even a Greek shop where a bottle of beer, much less a beef-steak, might be found.'

Dust and flies were everywhere, and most soldiers looked forward to having enough time to dive into the crystal blue sea, but then, 'even a bathe had its drawbacks for the shore was infested by some marine creature which left a legacy of festering sores where its sharp spines had pierced the bather's feet.'

By this point, the war was nearly a year old, and the men knew that the earlier landings on Gallipoli by battalions of regular soldiers had met with stiff Turkish resistance. Gallipoli was the Western Front all over again, though it had the added difficulties of unbearable heat, dysentery, raging thirst, bush fires, grit and sand that got into everything, swarms and swarms of flies like men had never seen before, and an enemy that would not be easily beaten.

A soldier of the South Irish Horse in front of a bivouac. This photo is a good example of what accommodation was like in the field.

On the lighter side, Edward King was responsible for censoring his men's mail, and although he did not enjoy invading the privacy of his troops, he found it could be a humorous task. 'Fusilier McHugh wrote vivid accounts of the battles in which he had claimed to have played a hero's part; his wife must have been impressed when she read them, for she could not know that his only battles hitherto had been with the Military Police! But it was Corporal Coles who gave the reluctant censor most of his smiles: a fireman on the railway in civil life, Coles was something of a Casanova, judging by the passionate letters with which he stoked the fires of love in half a dozen girls at home; he had no favourites – each letter was a copy of the others – but there was no chance of comparing notes because the addresses were as far apart as Glasgow, London and Crewe.'

Then, on 7 August 1915, the bulk of 10th (Irish) Division sailed to Gallipoli, landing at Suvla Bay in the north of the peninsula. But Lieutenant Edward King did not join them straight away. Finally, though, the orders came, and King and his detachment packed up their kit on Lemnos and 'climbed aboard a former Thames pleasure-steamer for their voyage of sixty miles.'

On the journey, Edward King noticed that his canvas valise, along with everything inside – everything he owned except what he had on his person – had disappeared, another victim of the army scroungers.

The ship steamed on and 'soon there appeared on the horizon a long line of hills, like a dark purple smudge beneath the azure sky from which the sun blazed down almost perpendicularly ... eyes began to distinguish sandy beaches and little knolls, with a background of ridges cleft by gullies and sparsely covered with trees and scrub. It was rugged, inhospitable country. It was the Peninsula at last.'

Edward King landed at Suvla on 12 August 1915 with shrapnel shells bursting in the distance over the inland ridges. His men 'scrambled ashore, hastened on their way by taciturn naval ratings, under the command of a midshipman who looked about fourteen and had the wealth of language of the admiral that he doubtless became if he survived the war.'

The beach was a hive of activity. 'Working-parties, stripped to the waist, sweated under the hot sun; stores, ammunition and guns were being manhandled ashore from landing-craft of various shapes and sizes; scores of men were bathing; an officer was supervising the roofing of a dug-out by a squad of

Suvla Bay. This is where the 10th (Irish) Division landed in August 1915. Note the large number of horses. In the background, the Kiretch Tepe Sirt Ridge can be seen. The Karakol Dagh, where Lieutenant Edward King was reunited with 6th Royal Inniskilling Fusiliers, is on the left.

sappers; long lines of men, draped with strings of water-bottles or carrying camp kettles, patiently waited their turn at the hoses which stretched like the tentacles of an octopus from a floating water tank.

'The only discordant notes in a peaceful scene, the only indications that this was not part of a training exercise, were the occasional whine of an approaching shell, momentarily halting every activity, and the processions of stretcher-bearers carrying wounded men down to the beach on their way to the hospital ship lying out in the Bay.'

In the few days since the Irishmen of the 10th (Irish) Division had landed at Suvla Bay, they had already seen some tough, bitter fighting. Many had been killed in the initial struggles to press inland, and for the wounded, even reaching the hospital ship did not guarantee survival. Hospital ships were often grossly understaffed, with too few doctors to treat far too many casualties, and in such confined, humid conditions, if the wound did not kill you, a subsequent infection might.

On 13 August, Lieutenant Edward King's detachment was guided towards the front. To the east of Suvla Bay was a dried-up salt lake, but to the north was a crescent of hills that made up the Kiretch Tepe Sirt Ridge – now the front line. The westernmost region of this ridgeline was the Karakol Dagh, and it was up the Karakol Dagh that Edward King was led along with his men. 'On the way Jimmie [Edward King] smelled for the first time the sickly stench of corruption that pervades a battle-field. It was seldom out of his nostrils for many days to come. "Smell of dead Boer," muttered an old soldier, pausing for a moment to ease his shoulders from his heavy pack. "Smell of some mother's son," was Sergeant Moran's dry retort.' Then, 'in a hollow among the rock,' the detachment was reunited with the rest of 6th Royal Inniskilling Fusiliers.

The battalion had already been involved in the assaults on Chocolate Hill and Green Hill, and, suffering from exhaustion, caused by a tiring march through sandy expanses, intense thirst, and hindered by constant enemy shrapnel shelling, they had also managed to help secure a part of the Keretch Tepe Sirt Ridge east of the Karakol Dagh. They were already becoming painfully familiar with land mines and vigilant enemy snipers, and in just five days since landing, the battalion had lost a third of its men. Scimitar Hill had been stormed on 11 August, but in the organisational nightmare that was Gallipoli – the troops were ordered to withdraw back to Suvla after securing their objective.

Edward King frequently heard older soldiers – the few veterans that had been attached to the New Army divisions – grumbling about what should have been done but had not, the positions that should have been reached, the initial inland push that should have been made, the supplies that should have been provided. These veterans of the South African campaigns knew that smaller strike parties, like the flying columns employed by the Boers, could have captured the high ground and driven the Turks back. They lamented the fact that the enemy still overlooked their positions, dominating the ridges, while their generals poured more and more inadequately supplied men onto a desolate beachhead, which only created more problems and a demand for ammunition and water. At this rate, the British would be too busy trying to sort themselves out to organise an attack, and when the Turks inevitably counter-attacked in order to drive them into the sea, there were fears that they might even succeed.

Men were soon being picked off by snipers. On the subject, King once heard a major from another Irish regiment remark to a Royal Inniskilling Fusiliers captain: 'The Turk is a damned good fighter. His snipers are everywhere, even behind our lines. This morning two of my best sergeants were killed while at the latrine. We got the chap that did it – hidden up a tree. He looked so young that we thought it was a girl, but our Doctor says he was a male, and he ought to know the difference, even if the rest of us have forgotten.' With snipers, you had to be extremely cautious just walking about. If your head appeared for even an instant in the wrong place, or you looked around the corner at a given mound, it might be the last thing you ever did.

Edward King's account of Gallipoli makes it clear that the Turks knew where the Irishmen were weak. They knew exactly how to beat the invader, and it did not involve bombs, bullets, or shells – it involved water. More often than not, 'the wells which the Staff had expected to find were either non-existent or had been destroyed [ie poisoned] by the Turks as they retreated back on to the hills. On that sun-scorched terrain the scanty supplies of water that could be landed from tankers were utterly inadequate for the needs of such a large force of thirst-racked men.'

Men were driven out of their minds with the thirst, and, although the Turks did render many wells unusable, others were soon made foul by the Irishmen themselves, although not on purpose. With an initial lack of designated latrines, men relieved themselves all along the ridges and up and down the slopes. As men wiped their arses with their shirts and sleeves and came down with dysentery in their hundreds, vital wells turned putrid. Water was still being shipped from Egypt, in dangerously low quantities, and all orders to ration it were ignored by this army of citizen volunteers. 'The troops were unacclimatised. They lacked the hard and life-saving skills of regular soldiers. Orders were unavailing. Full water-bottles in all too many cases were emptied within an hour or two.'

The other massive problem was the flies. As soon as a soldier lifted a piece of food to his mouth, or worst of all, opened a jam tin, it would literally be crawling with flies. Men had to cope by eating with one hand while waving the pests away with the other. The flies, like the rats of the Western Front, had no respect for privacy – they flew into your mouth, up your nose, and buzzed in swarms around your face. And, like the rats, they had no respect for the dead. Out in no-man's-land, 'they bloated and gorged on the flesh of corpses,' covering the swollen, rotting bodies of Irishman and Turk alike.

Over the days that followed, attack after attack went in, but Edward King managed to stay out of the fighting. His battalion was never in the thick of battle, or as King himself put it, they did not 'add to its butcher's bill'. Their sister battalion, the 5th Royal Inniskilling Fusiliers, however, had not been so lucky. After advancing just 1,000 yards across no-man's-land, with barely any artillery support and no diversionary attacks to draw away Turkish attention, they only managed to fight their way to a position just in front of the enemy trenches, before being withdrawn at night. When they returned to British positions, the 5th Royal Inniskilling Fusiliers – a battalion with a normal compliment of roughly 1,000 men – had been reduced to three officers and 200 other ranks.

At the end of the Battle of Keretch Tepe Sirt, Edward King had lost many friends. He recorded that the 6th Royal Irish Fusiliers had only one officer left, and had lost three-quarters of its men in the fighting. 'Lads, full of the zest of life; staid, older men, with wives and families waiting and praying for their safe return – most of them were gone. Some – the lucky ones – were on a hospital-ship; the rest had been cut off suddenly and uselessly on this barren, sun-baked "corner of a foreign field" … Among the Division's dead were, no doubt, many other men of equal ability and promise – potential leaders of their generation in various walks of life, now thrown away on the scrap-heap of war.'

No gains, insane losses, and a well-prepared enemy – stalemate now characterised the Gallipoli campaign. Edward King remembered the books that he had read as a youth. Books like *Deeds that won the Empire* and *Fights for the Flag*. Years ago, he had read them with wide-eyed enthusiasm, fascinated by the tales of heroism and valour. Now, faced with all of Gallipoli's plagues, along with the shelling and the accompanying feeling of helplessness, Edward was quickly realising that the glory of war that he had read about did not exist. He now knew 'that there never had been any, save in the imagination of authors or in the arm-chair anecdotes of retired warriors.' All that was to be seen was 'the courage and endurance of ordinary men in the face of hardship, danger, and death.'

After being relieved for three days and after bathing and receiving mail from home, Lieutenant Edward King and the men of 6th Royal Inniskilling Fusiliers were ordered back to the front on 21 August, initially stopping in an area between Lala Baba and Chocolate Hill. Here, they were ordered to wait behind friendly artillery, which was currently in the process of laying down support fire for an attack on Scimitar Hill by the 29th Division – pre-war regulars, some of which were the Irish survivors of the *River Clyde* landing back in April. 'Up among the hills in front there was an incessant crackle of musketry, interspersed with staccato bursts of machine-gun fire. Every few minutes the ground seemed to quiver as warships out in the Bay fired broadsides from their heavy guns towards unseen, distant targets.'

Scimitar Hill had been secured back on 11 August, but in a baffling display of mismanagement, the British soldiers had been ordered to withdraw as soon as they had captured it. Now, the generals were sending thousands of men to re-take Scimitar Hill, having decided that they needed it, but now, of course, the Turks had dug in on the high ground and were not going to give it up without a fight.

Even though this battle was a good distance away, the 6th Royal Inniskilling Fusiliers were not out of harm's way. Positioned where they were, behind friendly artillery, they were being hit with 'a flippin' double ration,' the 'overs', as they were called – enemy shrapnel and shells that were meant for the British guns, but which were overshooting the target and falling on the infantry behind. The second attempt to take Scimitar Hill raged on all day and before long, Edward King was looking into the distance towards the battlefield where 'soon there appeared the flicker of bush-fires on the scrub-covered ridges where the 29th Division was endeavouring to break through the Turkish defences. Such was the reputation of those regular soldiers that it seemed they could not fail.'

But they did fail. Scimitar Hill was not re-taken, and by evening, the scrubland of the hill was littered with British corpses, men who had been killed by shrapnel before they had even got near the enemy.

With the fighting having died down, Edward King and his battalion received orders to move forward. There were fears that the enemy would counter-attack, and the exhausted 29th Division and their supporting units were in no state to mount a strong resistance. The 6th Royal Inniskilling Fusiliers entered the trenches on Chocolate Hill in preparation. 'There was no rest for anyone that night: trenches had to be allocated to companies; machine-guns sited and ranged; supplies, above all of water, had to be brought up; wounded to be rescued from no-man's-land and the dead brought in for burial. The stretcher-bearers reached all they could; the slightest movement brought a hail of fire from the Turks. Much further out, and beyond reach of help, there were still more wounded. For them, the scrub, set alight by shell-fire, was an inferno. For the dead, it was a funeral pyre.'

On 24 August, Edward King celebrated his twenty-first birthday. He met up with his best friend, Second-Lieutenant Irvine Smyth – the son of a Methodist minister – who he had known since childhood, and the two sat down in a slit-trench to catch up. Edward joked that this was not exactly where he would have pictured himself being on his twenty-first birthday, and together they shared a tot of rum. In a nearby Turkish trench, however, a mortar shell was fired at the British lines. Unbeknownst to the enemy gunners, the shell was a dud – it was never going to explode. The shell arced up into the air and then sped down towards the slit-trench where Edward and Irvine were sitting. As the pair celebrated Edward's birthday, the dud mortar plunged into Irvine Smyth's body, killing him instantly. Edward King was left sitting there, staring at his best friend's corpse – a mortar shell lodged in his chest. If the dud had fallen only two feet away, the pair would have been startled but completely unharmed. It was a one-in-a-million shot, but it ended the life of Irvine Smyth. He was only twenty-three years old, from Green Road, Knock, in Belfast, and today his body lies in Green Hill Cemetery on the Gallipoli Peninsula.

Within days, Edward King was promoted to captain and given command of a company, 'replacing Captain R.H. Scott who, like so many others, had been invalided by the prevailing dysentery.' The Turkish counter-attack never came, the enemy 'seemingly content to hold the Suvla sector in a vice and to allow dysentery and their own artillery to fight their battle for them. Nor did the British mount any more attacks; they had "shot their bolt."' For the Irishmen on Gallipoli, life settled down into a routine of monotony, blight, and death.

Then in the last week of September, Edward King remembered that a rumour had begun to circulate, 'one of the countless rumours that buzzed like flies from man to man achieved the miracle of being true: the Division was to leave the Peninsula.' Having finally realised that the campaign was futile, British Command in Gallipoli ordered the evacuation to begin. Edward King's turn came on 29 September 1915. 'That anyone should sail away, except on a hospital-ship, was incredible! It was not until the battalion had handed over their sector of trenches to an English unit, had filed down to the beach and were on board a transport heading out to sea, that the sceptic was prepared to believe that an episode in his life was over and that he had "lived to fight another day."' The 6th Royal Inniskilling Fusiliers sailed back to Mudros Harbour on Lemnos Island, but as they went, Edward King 'leaned over the ship's rail, [and] thought of those whom they had left behind. Nearly fifty years later [I] still see them – the irrepressible McHugh; dour, imperturbable Sergeant Moran; good companions like Irvine Smyth, and many other.'

At Gallipoli, the Allies had suffered 140,000 casualties – approximately 4,000 of which were Irishmen – for very little gain in the face of stiff and dedicated opposition from the Turks. However, there were other battles to be fought, and the battered divisions were soon redirected elsewhere. After evacuating Gallipoli, the 10th (Irish) Division was sent to nearby Salonika and the fight against the Bulgarians. Men like Edward King were soon back in the war.

These men were the first Irish volunteers to go to war and one of the first New Army divisions to enter the fight, only to be slaughtered on the shores of a distant Turkish peninsula. To this day, the bleached-white bones of First World War soldiers are still being discovered by Turkish farmers – hidden under scrub or buried beneath a thin layer of dirt. How many of these skeletons belong to Irishmen who should have been allowed to grow old and be buried in their hometowns? How many of these piles of bones belong to Dubliners in the Royal Dublin Fusiliers, Galwaymen in the Connaught Rangers, men from Kerry and Cork in the Royal Munster Fusiliers, or Royal Inniskilling Fusiliers soldiers from Northern Ireland? They were the ordinary citizens of Ireland – the clerks, labourers, students, idealists, paupers, loyalists, nationalists and youth of our country.

Today, Gallipoli is still the isolated peninsula it was in 1915, only now, graveyards and memorials dot the landscape, such as the one near Sedd-el-Bahr fort on V Beach where Dublin and Munster Fusiliers lie in graves close to the water's edge where they died in battle. On one of the monuments commemorating the sacrifices of Turkish soldiers, the words of Mustapha Kemal are engraved in stone. Kemal was a thirty-four-year-old lieutenant-colonel in the Turkish Army during the Gallipoli campaign. A brilliant strategist, he was instrumental in organising the successful defence of the peninsula after the initial Allied landings, and later went on to become the Republic of Turkey's first president – changing his name to Kemal Ataturk ('Ataturk' meaning 'Father of Turks') when he took office. The following is what he had to say about both sides in the conflict:

'To those heroes who shed their blood and lost their lives, you are now lying in the soil of a friendly country. Therefore, rest in peace. There is no difference to us between the Johnnies and the Mehmets [referring to both Allied and Turkish soldiers], where they lie side by side, here in this country of ours. You, the mothers who sent their sons from far-away countries, wipe away your tears. Your sons are now lying in our bosom and are in peace. Having lost their lives on this land, they have become our sons as well.'

As for Captain Edward King, he went on to serve in the Salonika campaign,

Above: *Gallipoli, 2008: Looking south towards V Beach where the Royal Dublin Fusiliers and Royal Munster Fusiliers landed in the* River Clyde. *The ancient Turkish fort of Sedd-el-Bahr still stands in the background.*

The taking of Kareina peak

where he developed severe vertigo from leading his frostbitten company around icy ravines – ravines where mules often vanished over the edge if they lost their footing – while the wind tried to pick men up and throw them to their deaths. During the atrocious Balkan winter of 1915, King tried to enliven things by paying his men to give him any ancient coins that they found while digging trenches, in an effort to boost morale and combat the effects of cold, misery and hardship.

Above: *In later life, Captain Edward King acquired a watercolour entitled 'The taking of Kareina Peak', recording the day, 27 December 1917, when he won his Military Cross. Under the painting is written the following: 'At this point the troops are seen successfully surmounting the hill top. The Turks are retiring northwards by the low ridge toward Ain Arik. The R.E.s [Royal Engineers] and pioneers have just passed along, making a road for the guns as the infantry advance, and by evening on the same day the guns were again facing the enemy. The following day a special order was issued by Lieut. Gen. Sir Philip W. Chetwode, commanding the 20th Corps. "I have again to thank the 20th Corps and to express to them my admiration of their bravery and endurance during the three days' fighting on Dec. 27th, 28th & 29th. The enemy made a desperate attempt with five corps to retake Jerusalem, and whilst their finest assault troops melted away before the staunch defences of the 53rd and 60th Divisions, the 10th [Irish] and 74th were pressing forward over the most precipitous country brushing aside all opposition, in order to relieve the pressure on the right. Their efforts were quickly successful and by the 27th we had definitely regained the initiative and I was able to order a general advance".' The caption concludes with a short remark: 'A splendid three days' work.'*

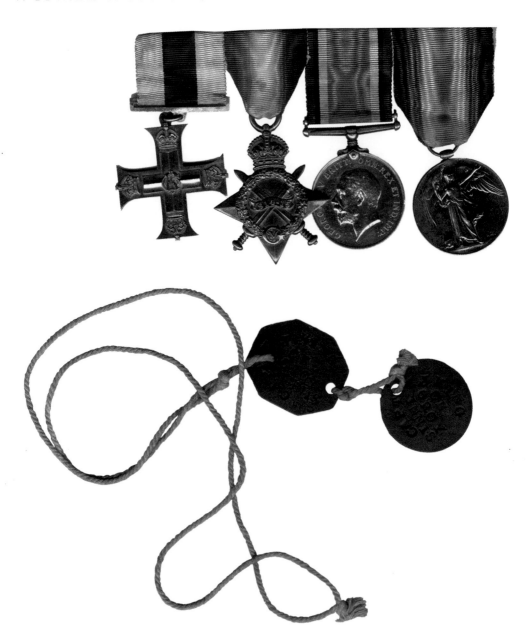

Captain Edward King's medals and identity disc (the medals are, from left to right, the Military Cross, 1914–15 Star, War Medal, and Victory Medal). The Military Cross was the officers' equivalent of the other ranks' Military Medal, and was established on 28 December 1914.

Later, while on leave, King was torpedoed aboard a vessel in the Mediterranean. He survived, and was rescued by an Italian fishing boat and taken to a convent in Naples where the nuns looked after him. They taught him some Italian and, coming from a classical background, Edward King spoke to them first in Latin. In late 1916, he was informed that his canvas valise, which he had noticed was missing while on his way to Gallipoli back in August 1915, had turned up in Alexandria with a note inside – 'Thanks for the nice kit', and signed, 'A Base-rat'.

In autumn 1917, after nearly two years in Salonika, the 10th (Irish) Division was shipped to Egypt and from there they marched into Palestine. Edward King and the 6th Royal Inniskilling Fusiliers returned to the fight against the Turks. They aided in the capture of Jerusalem in December 1917, and then, on 27 December, Edward King was involved in the capture of Kareina Peak. The bravery and leadership that he displayed during this battle earned him the Military Cross, which he was to receive several months later.

With the Turks soon defeated in the Holy Land, Captain Edward King and the 6th Royal Inniskilling Fusiliers were redeployed to the Western Front, finally coming into contact with the Germany Army in 1918. They were in the vicinity of Mons towards the very end of the war, where King narrowly missing being killed when his battalion was accidentally shelled by friendly artillery. King was on the staff at HQ behind the lines, and so was out of the trenches when the bombs started falling. Several of his Royal Inniskilling Fusiliers comrades were not so lucky.

As for the rest of his life, Edward King was appointed to the Egyptian Ministry of Finance in Cairo as an inspector in 1919. Egypt was a fascinating place to Edward, full of many interesting characters, and he recalls in *Haphazard* that, 'One of the greatest racing coups that I heard of was pulled off by a Greek in Alexandria. He had an accumulator on five horses. When his first four selections won at good prices he stood to win several hundreds of pounds, but with the risk of losing all if his fifth selection failed to win the last race of the day. Having tried unsuccessfully to lay off the bet, he wasted no time in prayer or wishful thinking, as any ordinary man might have done. Instead, he found the owner of the fifth horse – another Greek – and bought the animal. He promptly withdrew it from the race, paid the fine of fifty pounds for scratching it on the post and collected his winnings on what he had now converted into a successful four-horse accumulator. The story goes that he re-sold the horse to its original owner the next day for almost as much as he had paid for it, and one can well believe it. The whole episode was in character. The Levantine Greek has many qualities but slowness of wit and innocence in money matters are not among them.' Not long after, King took up a new post – as personal assistant to Sir Fabian Ware, vice-chairman of the Imperial War Graves Commission.

Edward King later went on a climbing expedition to British Columbia – ironic for a man who panicked on cliff walks – before journeying to Jamaica and Haiti where he encountered the influence of voodoo among some of the people on these tropical isles. He never returned to live in Ireland, and was living in England when the Second World War broke out. His two sons were evacuated to Clovelly in North Devon in 1941, but the eldest died of diabetes aged only three and a half. In 1942, Edward was coming home from work at the Ministry of Trade – he was on a bus on his way to Waterloo Station – when a German 'Doodlebug' bomb crashed into the upper deck, killing everyone upstairs. Edward King normally sat upstairs on the bus and smoked, but today he was on the lower deck and survived. He was slightly wounded in the shoulder but carried on home to Surrey, although the injury meant that in later years, he was unable to do continuous work.

For Edward, loud noises used to make him nearly hit the floor. The shellfire and explosions, the constant detonations of Gallipoli never left him. He visited Ireland regularly enough, holidaying in Courtown in the late 1940s and early 1950s, and he also enjoyed going to the Dublin Horse Show and the National Stud. In 1958 he went on a trip to Kerry with his daughter, Alison, and she remembers that 'he just loved being back in the country where he felt at home.'

Edward King, a former captain in the 6th Royal Inniskilling Fusiliers and Military Cross recipient, died on 13 November 1971, aged seventy-seven. Today, his ashes are interred in Clovelly, North Devon.

Captain Edward King, c1918. Note the four overseas stripes (one for each year of service) on his sleeve.

CHAPTER 2

THE SOMME AND 1916

'The Brigade moved off as if on parade, nothing finer in the way of an advance has ever been seen but alas no sooner were they clear of our own wire, when the slow tat tat of the Hun machine guns from Thiepval Village and Beaumont-Hamel caught the advance under a deadly cross fire, but nothing could stop this advance and so on they went.'

Battalion War Diary, 14th Royal Irish Rifles, 1 July 1916

While Gallipoli was turning into a disaster, the situation on the Western Front in 1915 was just as challenging. The shortcomings of British industry – totally unequipped to provide for a war on this scale – meant that attack after attack was launched with little or no artillery support. The gunners lacked sufficient quantities of shells to adequately 'soften up' the enemy positions, and so, 1915 brought only more stagnation and misery.

Towards the end of 1915, however, supply levels finally began to improve and a grand plan was devised for 1916. Having previously failed to defeat Germany with independent attacks, the Allies agreed to coordinate their efforts in 1916 and attack Germany on all fronts at the same time, the idea being to put the German Army under such strain that it would be forced into defeat.

The name of the place where France and Britain decided to mount their joint assault now resonates through history. This scene of one of the bloodiest battlefields of the First World War is full of landmarks like 'Usna Hill', 'Tara Hill', and 'Munster Alley', landmarks that got their nicknames from the tens of thousands of Irish soldiers who fought at this place. Irishmen were also praised for making the greatest successes in the opening phase of this battle. That place is the Somme.

THE BIG PUSH

From December 1915, tens of thousands of New Army men began disembarking in France, in preparation for the British element of the 'Big Push', as it was called. With them were two new Irish divisions, neither of which had yet seen action. They were the 16th (Irish) Division and the 36th (Ulster) Division. Unlike their 10th (Irish) Division comrades, the men of these two new formations were more distinct from each other in terms of political opinion. Many of the men of the 16th (Irish) Division came predominantly from the ranks of the Irish National Volunteers and had answered Irish Parliamentary Party leader and Home Rule MP John Redmond's call to defend Home Rule, while the bulk of the 36th (Ulster) Division were made up of former unionist UVF soldiers. The two divisions also differed in that, while the men of the 16th (Irish) Division – like those of the 10th (Irish) Division before them – had been required to serve under mostly English officers, the men of the 36th (Ulster) Division served under their old UVF commanders. The 36th (Ulster) Division was also far more prepared for active service, since its troops had been undergoing military training for years before the war. But, like all New Army units, the soldiers of both of these new Irish divisions were enthusiastic, but utterly green and inexperienced when it came to real warfare. The generals knew that these units, as they now stood, did not constitute the future of the army – the future lay in the men who lived beyond their first day of fighting, the lucky ones who survived long enough to gain that elusive experience.

ENGLAND'S DIFFICULTY, IRELAND'S OPPORTUNITY

1916 looked to be a promising year as such a concerted effort by all of the Allies had not yet been attempted. If it worked, the war might be ended before economies and populations were destroyed by endless fighting. Little did they know it, but for the Irishmen marching down the gangways of ships docked in Le Havre, Boulogne, Marseilles or St Nazaire, 1916 would prove to be an eventful year back home. This year, gunfire, explosions and death would not be limited to the fronts of the First World War; the people back in Ireland would become intimately familiar with them as well. And as the Irish soldiers in the British Army sailed away to enter the trenches, plans were set in motion by another army of Irishmen to rebel against foreign rule. Operating on the principle that 'England's difficulty is Ireland's opportunity', and that 'the enemy of my enemy is my friend', the IRB and the Irish Volunteers had been in contact with the German government, with a view to securing arms in order to mount an insurrection against the British in Ireland. They had been successful – the Germans hoping that at the very least, a rebellion in Ireland might divert British troops away from the Western Front – and the weapons were on their way.

It is interesting to note here that, as well as weapons, leading Irish Volunteer Sir Roger Casement also tried to secure the release of Irish prisoners of war from the Limberg internment camp. These were Irishmen of the British Army who had been captured during the battles of 1914 and 1915. Casement's hope was to form an Irish Brigade, which would then return to Ireland to fight for Irish independence. The Germans gave Casement the go ahead to begin recruiting, but he was met with difficulties from the start. Due to the lack of enthusiasm for the plan from Irish POWs, incentives were offered (such as money or extra rations), but still very few took Casement up on his offer. After attempting to recruit volunteers from 2,500 Irish prisoners, Casement only managed to secure fifty-three men for his Irish Brigade. The rest simply refused to betray their comrades still fighting and dying in the war. They jeered Casement when he held meetings with them, refused to go to Mass, said by a fiercely nationalistic priest who was present at the camp, and they ripped up recruiting forms given to them by Casement. A prisoner delegation is on record as having proclaimed: 'In addition to being Irish Catholics, we have the honour to be British soldiers.' The Germans, less than satisfied with the outcome of Casement's recruitment drive, abandoned the idea of an Irish Brigade altogether.

THE SOMME

Back on the Western Front, the British were making sure that the Big Push of 1916 would be the greatest offensive the war had yet seen. The shell shortages were finally coming to an end and British industry was catching up at last with the demand for explosives and artillery. The area around the River Somme – the site selected for the offensive – was far to the south of the old battlefields of Ypres and Loos. It was an area of gently sloping hills dotted with forests. Here, over the following months, thousands of guns were towed to the front by trucks or teams of horses, while battalion after battalion of men entered the trenches. The artillery pieces were hidden under camouflaged nets and three million shells were stockpiled in massive depots. Training grounds and rest areas were designated, and huge army kitchens were set up to feed the enormous influx of troops. It was only now that protective headwear was issued to the men – Brodie helmets, known as 'shrapnel helmets' or 'Tommy helmets', that looked like upturned bowls. For the previous two years, men had still been wearing just their caps to save them from chunks of razor sharp, searing hot metal.

However, the opposing German trenches were well placed up the slopes from the British positions, providing the Germans with a perfect view of enemy activity. The Germans were quickly made very aware that an attack was planned, and so they dug deep to fortify their positions. They dug twelve-foot deep trenches, forty-foot deep dugouts made of concrete that could withstand anything an artillery gun could throw at it, and erected fifty-yards-thick rows of barbed wire out in no-man's-land; concertina wire, spool barbed wire and strand barbed wire wrapped around immovable iron stakes. Meanwhile, the British generals, ever-determined to foster the spirit of advance and attack, did not permit their troops to construct trenches nearly as advanced as those that the Germans were building – anything so permanent might get men into the mindset of the defensive. And so, as the British poured men and resources into the area behind the Somme front, across no-man's-land, their enemy knew that they were coming, and they had prepared accordingly. The element of surprise was lost.

Then, to upset the Allied plans even more, the Germans attacked first. Out of

A party of Royal Irish Rifles resting in a communication trench during the early phase of the Battle of the Somme, possibly on 1 July. Some men smile for the camera, others stare on anxiously, knowing that it will not be long before they have to go over the top.

the blue, on 21 February 1916, the Germans launched a massive offensive against the southern French citadel of Verdun. Verdun was a symbolic city within French society – a fortress town which was famous for standing defiant against invading armies – so the French redirected thousands of men and vital resources from the Somme front to keep Verdun in French hands. It could not be allowed to fall and the fighting there was some of the most desperate and brutal in the war where the flamethrower – a new German invention – made its first appearance on the battlefield. Verdun became nicknamed 'The Mincer', and the French soon started begging the British to move forward the launch date of the Somme offensive. They desperately needed to distract German reinforcements that would otherwise be sent to Verdun. And so, with the French Army under severe pressure, the British were forced to select 1 July 1916 as the day to launch the Big Push. Then, as the pace of preparations began to pick up, the Easter Rising broke out on the streets of Dublin.

THE EASTER RISING

The Easter Rising began on 24 April after Pádraig Pearse occupied the GPO and read the Proclamation of the Irish Republic from its steps. At the time, both the Irish Volunteers and the British Army in Dublin numbered roughly 1,200 soldiers each. Five days later, when bitter, desperate fighting and shellfire had reduced whole streets to crumbling ruin, Pearse was forced to surrender to Major-General John Maxwell. Marshal Law had been declared; Dublin was now garrisoned by 12,000 British soldiers; many of the Irish Volunteers were dead or wounded, and there was no hope of a rebel victory. Angered by the destruction of their city, and cursing the rebels for having brought hunger and further deprivations on an already poor populace, Dubliners were outraged at Pearse and his followers. Many families were disgusted at this betrayal of their sons, fathers, and brothers in the trenches. The *Irish Independent* and the *Irish Times*, mirroring the opinion of thousands of Irish citizens, even demanded the executions of Pearse and his fellow leaders.

But public sentiment began to change when the executions started on 3 May,

The aftermath of the Easter Rising. This view of the Daniel O'Connell Monument shows the scale of the destruction.

only four days after the rebels had surrendered. The Irish public might have been baying for blood at the end of the Rising, but the swiftness and harshness of the British response to the rebellion was shocking. Soon enough, public opinion started to shift in sympathy for the rebels, and when word was released that James Connolly, who had been badly wounded during the Rising but who had subsequently received medical treatment, had been strapped to a chair and executed while barely strong enough to hold his head up, elements of Irish society were outraged. Irish opinion was to change to support the ideals of a free, independent Ireland – a republic – and the fate of 200,000 Irishmen in the British Army would be sealed. They would soon be viewed as traitors and fools, while the ideals of the leaders of the Rising gained more and more widespread support. When the Irish prisoners of the Easter Rising were released on 25 December 1916, many were welcomed home as heroes. By the time the Irish soldiers of the First World War started coming home two years later, they would be yesterday's heroes and today's traitors.

In all, the Rising had taken the lives of about 450 people: eighty rebels, 200 Irish civilians and 150 British soldiers. In terms of wounded, the rebels had suffered over 1,600 wounded, 600 Irish civilians had been wounded, and a little over 300 British soldiers.

THE HULLUCH GAS ATTACK

In the same week however, the 16th (Irish) Division was gassed in the trenches at Hulluch, north of Loos. Germany had first used chlorine gas as a weapon back in 1915. The British had been initially outraged, fuming that this weapon was cowardly and barbaric. But all that changed very quickly. Gas was effective; it killed the enemy in large numbers, and in this total war, winning had nothing to do with playing fair – it was simply about how many of the enemy you could slaughter. The British had soon started using gas themselves.

Twenty-eight-year-old Private William Lawrence – a farmer's son from Slieverue, Ballinglen, County Wicklow – was serving with the 8th Royal Dublin Fusiliers during this time. He was one of two brothers in the war, and his younger brother – Private Matthew Lawrence, a former gardener who served

British troops, blinded by tear gas, wait outside an Advance Dressing Station, near Bethune, during the Battle of Estaires, 10 April 1918. The Irishmen gassed during Easter Week 1916 were poisoned by chlorine gas. It blinded them and suffocated and burned their lungs.

variously with the Royal Dublin Fusiliers, Royal Irish Regiment, and Royal Inniskilling Fusiliers during the war – had previously had a lucky escape that sounded like something out of a work of fiction. He was shot by the enemy, only for the bullet to lodge in his pocket watch, thereby saving his life. Also at Hulluch during this time, and also in 8th Royal Dublin Fusiliers, was nineteen-year-old Joseph Spain. He had been born in a tenement block on Lower Dorset Street in Dublin, but had been living on Sullivan's Quay in Cork and working as a draper's porter when he had enlisted.

At night on 27 April 1916, the Germans opposite the Irishmen at Hulluch waited for the wind to blow towards the Irish trenches and then released clouds of smoke. The Royal Inniskilling Fusiliers were directly in the path of the smoke and when they saw it coming they raised the alarm. Grabbing their phenate-hexamine goggle helmets (gas masks) they quickly put them on. The smoke rolled in across the dark uneven surface of no-man's-land and the Irish soldiers held their breath, literally. But no German attack materialised. Nobody got sick from gas poisoning. And when one soldier realised that the smoke was just smoke, the confused men took off their gas masks.

An hour and a half later, a different cloud came blowing across the battlefield – chlorine gas. Thinking it was again just regular smoke, the Irishmen did nothing. The German trick worked and Irish losses were devastating. The gas initially blinded men, then, as their faces blackened and burned, a dark foamy liquid started to form in their lungs. Soldiers started dying, writhing in agony at the bottom of their trenches, clutching at their throats as the foamy liquid spewed up and out of their mouths. Also, the gas was heavier than air; it actually 'flowed' down and into the trenches. Anyone who attempted to escape by scrambling over the top would be caught by enemy machine-gun fire.

Then the Germans launched their attack. Other battalions of the 16th (Irish) Division which had escaped the gas attack were ordered to the front to push the Germans back. The fighting that followed was nightmarish, in amongst the dead and the writhing, dying wounded.

The two battalions of the Royal Dublin Fusiliers (8th and 9th) in the 16th (Irish) Division suffered roughly 800 casualties, mostly from the gas. Two of those casualties were twenty-eight-year-old William Lawrence and nineteen-year-old Joseph Spain. They both died an agonising death as the gas slowly killed them, and today, with no known graves, both men are commemorated on the Loos Memorial. Also commemorated on the Loos Memorial is seventeen-year-old Private Joseph Pender from Brookfield Place, Blackrock, Dublin of the 9th Royal Dublin Fusiliers, and fellow seventeen-year-old Private Patrick Byrne from Summerhill, Dublin of the 8th Royal Dublin Fusiliers – both underage soldiers, both victims of the gas.

The Battle of Hulluch continued for a further two days. All German attacks were eventually repulsed but at a cost of 538 killed and 1,590 wounded, many of whom were members of the Irish National Volunteers and who had previously served alongside the men of the Irish Volunteers – many of whom had carried out the Rising – back when they had all been one organisation. Over those three days, the 16th (Irish) Division incurred as many wounded as the rebels had suffered in all of Easter Week, and they had more dead than all the rebel, British, and civilian fatalities of the Rising put together.

A British Vickers machine-gun team, wearing anti-gas helmets (phenate-hexamine goggle type) in 1916 – these were the type of gas helmets that the Irishmen at Hulluch failed to put on when the real German gas attack was launched.

We remember the martyred leaders of the Rising – sixteen men who were executed by the British. But there were 538 other Irishmen who died that week who are not remembered – 538 who were erased from our history because of politics.

BOMBARDMENT

Back at the Somme, the preparations continued right up to 24 June – one week before the launch date. Then, along an eighteen-mile front, 2,000 artillery guns opened fire at the German lines. The idea was to pulverise the German trenches with a 24/7 unending bombardment. It was believed that nothing could live through such a fire storm, and that at the end of the shelling, the rows of barbed wire which blocked the way forward would be reduced to nothing.

However, the Germans were far from being ground into dust. They were hunkered, albeit extremely uncomfortably, in their forty-foot-deep dugouts where even the heaviest shells could not touch them. And even though the constant pounding of shellfire – or 'drumfire' as they called it – drove men out of their minds, filled their heads with incessant noise that would not let them sleep, would not let them rest or finally made them completely deaf, the Germans were far from exterminated by the British barrage. Worse still, out of the 2,000 guns that the British were using to lay waste to enemy positions, 1,800 of them were eighteen-pounders that were firing mere shrapnel. Shrapnel shells are essentially hollow shells filled with metal 'shrapnel balls' and an explosive charge. When the shell detonates in mid-air, the shrapnel balls pepper the ground beneath. While shrapnel is lethal to human flesh it will do nothing to destroy barbed wire or collapse enemy trenches and bunkers. Shrapnel is an infantry killer, and with all the German soldiers securely underground, the British might as well have not being firing it at all. That left only 200 heavy guns to cover the eighteen-mile front, which was an average of one heavy gun to roughly every 160 yards. Furthermore, thanks to the bonuses offered to munitions workers – an incentive designed to help end shell shortages – shells had been made rapidly and badly, which resulted in thirty percent of all shells fired in the Somme bombardment being duds.

As the barrage continued and the clock ticked down towards zero hour, the enemy barbed wire remained intact. Although flung about by shellfire, this only made the spools of wire form massive twisted sculptures of razor-sharp interlocking steel – totally impassable.

OVER THE TOP

THE ROONEY BROTHERS

Two Irishmen surveying the heavy rain of shells during this period were brothers Private Thomas Rooney and Private Peter Rooney, both serving with the 14th Royal Irish Rifles – the Young Citizen Volunteers Battalion – part of the 36th (Ulster) Division. Unlike the majority of their comrades in the 36th (Ulster) Division, the Rooneys were Catholics in a predominantly Protestant and unionist division. When the brothers were born, the family had been living in the gate lodge of the Kilmorey Estate near Kilkeel, County Down – the boys' father, Laurence Rooney, was head keeper to Lord Kilmorey. As one of Thomas Rooney's grandsons – Peter Rooney – recalls, one of the Rooney sisters, Mary, was 'as a very young girl adept at sewing together the lips of ferrets before they were sent down warrens for rabbits and she sat on the King's lap when he visited Kilmorey and demonstrated this for him, much to his amusement.' However, since Laurence Rooney and his wife Sarah went on to have a large family, Laurence was 'let go' from the Kilmorey Estate when the gentry became annoyed at so many children playing around the gate lodge. However, Lord Kilmorey gave Laurence Rooney a parting gift – a swordstick (a walking stick with a concealed rapier inside).

The family ended up living at 43 Kilmood Street in Belfast, having been, as the Rooney family recall, 'transported from the splendour of the hills of Carlingford to a two-bed, mean, cramped, damp, poverty-ridden slum in a Catholic ghetto at the bottom of the Newtownards Road in Belfast.' Here, the Rooney brothers grew into men, and in January 1915 they enlisted – according to another of Thomas Rooney's grandsons, Eugene Rooney – after the local parish priest told them that it was their duty to fight against the 'German menace'.

14th Royal Irish Rifles' (Young Citizen Volunteers battalion) cap badge: This battalion wore a different cap badge to the rest of the Royal Irish Rifles due to the fact that, when it was formed in September 1914, its ranks were filled with Belfast UVF men who had been former Young Citizen Volunteers. The YCV had been formed in 1912 as a 'non-sectarian and non-political' organisation with the aim to 'assist ... the civil power in the maintenance of peace' – some Catholics even volunteered to join – but due to grievances with the British government, the YCV soon changed to become a Belfast battalion of the UVF.

At this time, anti-German propaganda was rife. It was said that the Germans hacked the hands off small children, raped nuns, tortured priests, and burned down cathedrals. They had also trampled across small Catholic Belgium, and that was enough in the eyes of many priests to demand that the Germans be stopped.

The Rooney brothers entered the war in October 1915, in preparation for the Big Push, and on 30 June 1916, the night before the attack was due to commence, they found themselves marching under a starry sky through viscous mud towards the front – the incessant thundering of shell detonations growing louder and louder as they neared the trenches. The Big Push they were here for was about to begin.

Both Thomas and Peter Rooney were each carrying 66lbs of equipment, which included rifle, bayonet, gas mask, canteen, 220 rounds of ammunition, helmet, rations, field dressing, entrenching tool, grenades and sandbags, while some of their comrades were carrying a lot more, with various men also weighed down by machine guns and ammunition, ladders, barbed wire spools, satchels of bombs (hand grenades), wirecutters, wooden trench supports and sledgehammers. When you take into account that the average man of 1916 weighed about 140lbs, the soldier with the lightest burden was still lugging half his own bodyweight. It was lucky then, perhaps, that the men had been ordered to advance at a walking pace during the coming assault. It was believed that there would be no point in rushing, seeing as the Germans were sure to be dead or shellshocked to hell, and since the troops were carrying such great weights and were inexperienced in rapidly manoeuvring from cover to cover, and therefore sure to split up if they ran across no-man's-land, the decision seemed to make practical and tactical sense.

The 14th Royal Irish Rifles were in position in Elgin Avenue and Paisley Avenue (both front-line trenches) facing Thiepval by 12.15am on 1 July. At 1.10am, the battalion war diarist – the adjutant – recorded:

> As I passed the assembly trenches I gave zero time to all officers, watches were set and final instructions given. At this time a lull seemed to settle over all the earth, as if it were a mutual tightening up for the great struggle shortly to commence. A water hen called to its mate midst the reedy swamp, and a courageous nightingale made bold to treat us with a song.

Private Peter Rooney from Kilmood Street, Belfast. Unlike most of their Ulster comrades, Peter Rooney and his brother Thomas were Catholics in a predominantly Protestant and unionist division. They were the sons of Laurence Rooney – a sailor. Thomas, at twenty-two, was the eldest. Peter was two years younger.

Two hours later at 3am, the enemy started shelling the Ulster lines, and 'the shells were falling all around and the candles in the Battalion Hd. Qrs. kept going out.'

Zero hour was designated – at 7.30am, 1 July 1916, the Battle of the Somme would begin. 14th Royal Irish Rifles were due to support 9th and 10th Royal Inniskilling Fusiliers and follow them over the top alongside 11th Royal Inniskilling Fusiliers. The Rooney brothers must surely have been nervous and terribly anxious. Then the dawn broke and at 6.15am the British artillery bombardment intensified (which was so loud it could be heard in London). The war diary continues:

> Our intense bombardment has opened and shells of all sizes, including the big trench mortars are raining upon the Hun lines which are covered with smoke and dust. It is marvellous how anything can live under such a hail of shells.
>
> But through the swirling clouds of earth kicked up by heavy trench mortars and heavy howitzers, officers observing no-man's-land through their periscopes started to spot untouched coils of deadly barbed wire in their path.

Irishmen in 14th Royal Irish Rifles started dying even before the battle was launched. On the morning of 1 July, Private William 'Billy' McFadzean from Rubicon, Cregagh, Belfast – a soldier in C Company – was 'in a concentration trench and opening a box of bombs for distribution prior to an attack, [when] the box slipped down into the trench, which was crowded with men, and two of the safety pins fell out. Private McFadzean, instantly realising the danger to his comrades, with heroic courage threw himself on the top of the bombs. The bombs exploded blowing him to pieces, but only one other man was injured. 'He well knew the danger, being himself a bomber, but without a moment's hesitation he gave his life for his comrades.' This is the citation from Billy McFadzean's Victoria Cross (*London Gazette*, 8 September 1916), which he would receive posthumously for this selfless act of bravery. He died aged twenty, and has no known grave. Today his name is commemorated on the Thiepval Memorial on the Somme.

But although the Germans had been very aware of the British build-up on the

Somme, they knew nothing about the seventeen massive mines that had been laid under their positions and out under no-man's-land. In June, Scottish and Yorkshire miners had finished tunnelling passages, shafts and chambers down to a depth of fifty feet under enemy strong points and these man-made caverns had been packed with high explosives. They were due to be detonated at 7.28am, two minutes before zero hour, to vaporise key enemy emplacements. For some inexplicable reason, however, the mine at Hawthorne Ridge in front of Beaumont Hamel was blown at 7.20am, a full eight minutes too early. The idea behind the mines had been not only to destroy German defences, but also to create cover for advancing infantry. British machine gunners could man the rim of each mine crater and have a clear field of fire. Eight minutes later and the remaining sixteen mines were set off. The largest one contained 60,000lbs of explosive and created Loughnagar Crater, 450 feet wide and ninety-five feet deep – it is still there today. Earth and rock shot thousands of feet into the air and the ground erupted upwards. Whole German trench networks and dug-outs were blasted apart. British soldiers could physically feel the shockwaves from the explosions kicking them in the chest. The Rooney brothers had two minutes to go.

Suddenly, the British barrage ceased and men were called on to summon every ounce of courage that they could gather. These men were not veteran pro-fessionals, and although most of them had been in France for months at this point, they had never left the relative safety of the trenches and gone 'over the top'. They had never gone into battle. At 7.30am, whistles and bugles were blown (the latter being the custom in Irish units) to signal for the attack to commence.

In the 36th (Ulster) Division, the first waves did not have to scramble over the parapet to advance towards the enemy, nor did they slowly walk shoulder to shoulder into the German machine guns. Some time before zero hour, the lead units had crawled out into no-man's-land and so were much closer to the enemy lines than their comrades elsewhere when the attack was launched. And when the Ulster bugles were blown, they jumped to their feet and charged – not walked – at their German enemies. However, for the Rooney brothers and 14th Royal Irish Rifles, they did have to go over the top and climb over the parapet in order to enter the fight, since, as second wave troops, they would have remained in the trenches until the battle had begun. When their time finally came, the war diarist noted that:

> The Brigade [109th, containing 14th Royal Irish Rifles] moved off as if on parade, nothing finer in the way of an advance has ever been seen, but alas no sooner were they clear of our own wire, than the slow tat tat of the Hun machine guns from Thiepval Village and Beaumont-Hamel caught the advance under a deadly cross fire, but nothing could stop this advance and so on they went ... as the 14th [Battalion] moved off, I received a written message from Capt. Slacke, O.C. 'A' Coy, stating that they were moving, this was the last I ever heard from him.

Private Peter Rooney was in A Company.

Some men barely made it a few yards before they were cut to ribbons. Although the Germans had been driven to the brink of madness by the week-long bombardment, they were still in one piece and able to rush out of their dugouts and get into position once the barrage had stopped. At Hawthorne Ridge, they had even managed to set up machine guns on the rim of the mine crater – eight minutes being more than enough time to set up defences before the British infantry advanced.

All along the British line, the first waves of each attacking division were fired upon while crossing no-man's-land. But, with the exception of the Ulstermen, they did not run; they just kept walking, exactly as they had been ordered to, and the Germans shot them down in their droves. When they encountered the massive tangles of barbed wire, completely undamaged by seven days of shell-fire, they were shot on the spot or got snagged on the wire and died draped across the razor-sharp barbs.

The battlefield was soon filled with the screams of the wounded, the sound of flying bullets and the pounding German artillery fire. Within minutes, hundreds of soldiers were lying shot out in no-man's-land. Some tried to drag themselves into craters; others cried out for water; others shook terribly as they tried to wrap bandages around their gaping, bloody wounds. Some lay there, unable to move as they bled to death from a severed arm or leg, while others, superficially wounded, were forced to gather themselves before pressing on.

In the 36th (Ulster) Division's sector, however, this was not immediately the case. Due to the division's first waves having charged enemy positions at zero hour from a starting point deep inside no-man's-land, within twenty minutes they had entered the enemy front lines and were fighting and bayoneting their way up trenches stacked with dead towards the Schwaben Redoubt – a fortress of German bunkers and machine-gun posts that guarded the northern approach to Thiepval. Fire from Schwaben, Thiepval and Beaumont Hamel was relentless but still the Ulstermen advanced into the teeth of the enemy guns. German prisoners were soon flowing back towards British lines as the Irishmen attacked, consolidated and moved on yard by yard.

Then the Germans started pounding the attackers with heavy artillery – 5.9-inch shells. Out on the battlefield, the Ulster troops were cut down and, due to the fact that (as the war diarist recorded) 'the 32nd Division [were] badly held up in front of that heap of brick dust, Thiepval Village,' the enemy machine guns there were able to fire on the Ulstermen unopposed. Still, the men of the 36th (Ulster) Division fought on bitterly and succeeded in capturing the impregnable Schwaben Redoubt. They had suffered appalling casualties in the process and three hours into the battle, reinforcements were desperately called upon. But they did not come.

The Ulstermen had achieved the impossible and, if they were supported by fresh units, they stood a very real chance of breaking through the German lines. Schwaben was to the north of Thiepval, and if British troops stormed down towards the town from this direction, they would not encounter the same fierce defences that guarded the western approaches. The Germans realised the severity of the situation and planned a counter-attack for as soon as assaulting units could get into place – 4pm – and then pummelled the Schwaben Redoubt with every gun they had at their disposal, along with no-man's-land in front of Schwaben and the trenches that led up to it. Their objective was to kill every last Ulsterman in the redoubt and prevent any reinforcements from reaching them. These Irishmen suddenly understood what the German infantry had gone through over the last week.

Ulstermen in Schwaben were screaming for help. The battalion war diarist makes several entries recording such desperate requests. But Lieutenant-General Thomas Morland, in command of this sector of front, refused to put the divisional reserves at their disposal. The original battle-plan had outlined the capture of Thiepval from the west. Thiepval had not yet been taken by a western, frontal assault and so instead of redirecting men to attack Thiepval from the north via Schwaben, he just ordered more waves of men to march straight into Thiepval's western defences.

Back in Schwaben, the situation worsened. The men were being killed by shrapnel and heavy shelling: 'trees knocked down, stones & splinters flying ... I could hear the 5.9s walloping down on them ... the wood is stiff with shrapnel,' are some of the comments made by the war diarist. Assistance was called for over and over by frantic commanders in the field. Finally, at 4pm, HQ replied that reinforcements were on their way, but by then it was too late.

The Germans were not plagued by the same lack of flexibility and, even though only one of the three German assault groups due to counter-attack at Schwaben was in place by 4pm, the attack went in anyway. The German field commanders realised that it was better to attack now with a weak force rather than give the Ulstermen time to dig in and consolidate. The Germans poured into Schwaben like a tidal wave and the 14th Royal Irish Rifles' adjutant soon received a report that 'the whole line had given way'. Even though reinforcements had been promised for 4pm, they did not arrive until 6pm. Even then, HQ only sent a single battalion of confused Territorial soldiers that had no idea where they were going – one battalion, to strengthen what was left of four battalions clinging to a corner of the Schwaben Redoubt. The story was the same in other units of the 36th (Ulster) Division – little or no reinforcements provided when thousands more troops were needed.

By 7.30pm, exactly twelve hours after the attack had been launched, the 36th (Ulster) Division were steadily losing ground in the Schwaben Redoubt in the face of overwhelming firepower. They were forced to fall back to a new line of defence. But as they retreated and their comrades elsewhere withdrew, men were slaughtered thanks to little tin triangles pinned to the back of their packs. These triangles had been devised in order to give British artillery observers an idea of where the advancing infantry were at any given time – they would glint in the sun and therefore be easy to range. What no one had considered was that when the infantry were heading the other way, these shining triangles would give excellent range to German gunners and would make British troops incredibly visible to enemy snipers. The remnants of the Ulstermen were picked off as they retreated. At 10.30pm, the Schwaben Redoubt was back in German hands.

By nightfall, the following was the situation: the 36th (Ulster) Division had made the greatest advance along the whole of the British line. Other divisions had had other successes elsewhere, but the Ulstermen had achieved the impossible – only for their sacrifices to end in defeat. The failure was attributed to poor and inflexible leadership. Now, all along the eighteen-mile front, frontline trenches were clogged with debris, wounded, corpses and wide-eyed survivors, milling around in a desperate attempt to reinforce forward positions against counter-attack. Officers were trying to reach rear headquarters, trying to get a telephone connection, ordering runners to take notes to higher command; they were frantic to learn what was going on. There were no orders reaching anyone; no one knew what had happened, and no one knew what to do.

Out in no-man's-land, there were literally thousands of screaming, moaning soldiers begging for water in the darkness. Hordes of rats were descending on the fresh corpses and they even started nibbling on the living wounded. Lying in shallow craters, some injured officers pulled out their revolvers and opened fire, anything to keep the rats away. The trenches were overflowing with wounded and so were the casualty clearing and dressing stations. The doctors simply could not believe the numbers of wounded that were pouring in, and to add to the millions of expended shell cases lying behind British lines, ever-growing piles of amputated arms and legs were soon building up as doctors – hurriedly working in cold sweats – did what they could to save men's lives.

In total, the British had managed to gain seven desolate miles of land at a cost of some 57,470 casualties. The following morning, the adjutant of 14th Royal Irish Rifles looked out across the battlefield and saw:

> ... a few bare poles of trees ... that were once a wood, [which] bore eloquent testimony to the severity of the fire ... Trench full of debris, fallen trees & men lying in all positions of death.

1 July 1916 was the bloodiest day in the history of the British Army, and out

Private Thomas Rooney from Kilmood Street, Belfast and 2nd Platoon, D Company, 14th (YCV) Royal Irish Rifles in Randalstown Camp during training, 1915.

of those 57,470 casualties, 19,240 had been killed. The 36th (Ulster) Division had suffered an unbelievable 5,104 casualties, 2,069 of which had been killed. Among the wounded was Private Thomas Rooney of 14th Royal Irish Rifles. He had received a bad gunshot wound to his left thigh – the bullet had also fractured his tibia – but he had managed to take off his belt and wrap it around the wound to slow the bleeding until help had arrived (most likely a stretcher-bearer party) and he was carried back to the British lines. His younger brother, however, had not been so lucky. While Private Thomas Rooney was tended to in a dressing station, Private Peter Rooney's remains lay scattered out in no-man's-land or in the Schwaben Redoubt. Thomas Rooney had actually seen his brother die – he had seen a shell slam into Peter Rooney's position on the battlefield. Peter had been only twenty years old, and in the madness that followed the first day of the Battle of the Somme, his body was never recovered. Today, along with the names of 73,334 other British soldiers who have no known graves, he is commemorated on the Thiepval Memorial on the Somme. Strangely, the Rooney family also have a story of how, back home in Belfast on 1 July 1916, Sarah Rooney – the brothers' mother – turned to walk up the stairs at home when she was confronted with a vision of Peter standing at the top of the stairs in his uniform and smiling at her. Concerning the story of this ghostly apparition, Eugene Rooney said, 'These people [the Rooney family] were extremely religious and I suspect they were not telling an untruth.'

Other Irish brothers suffered similarly that day. Both Private Ezekiel Smyth (aged twenty-three) and his older brother Private Andrew Smyth (aged twenty-five) were killed, while serving in 11th Royal Inniskilling Fusiliers. They were from Convoy, County Donegal, and with no known graves they are commemorated on the Thiepval Memorial. Private John Burke (aged twenty) and Private Joseph Burke (age unknown) lie in separate cemeteries; John in the AIF Burial Ground, Flers, and Joseph in Puchevillers British Cemetery. They were from Guardhill, Newbliss, County Monaghan, and they served in the Royal Irish Fusiliers. Finally, Private James McGowan (aged nineteen) and Private John McGowan (aged eighteen) of 12th Royal Irish Rifles from King Street, Ballymena, County Antrim are both commemorated on the Thiepval Memorial. Neither of them has known graves. All of these men died on 1 July 1916.

And so, it was the Irish, once again, who ended up suffering terribly, but also succeeding against desperate odds. However, the Irish involvement on day one of the Battle of the Somme is not as forgotten as other Irish aspects of the war – in fact, the 36th (Ulster) Division's struggle to enter the Schwaben Redoubt is part of modern unionist identity. That said, there is no reason why all Irishmen cannot acknowledge the sacrifices made on 1 July 1916. After all, fighting just north from the 36th (Ulster) Division – across the River Ancre – was the 1st Royal Dublin Fusiliers in the 29th Division, the veterans of the *River Clyde* landing at Gallipoli. They were in the first wave of the attack and suffered 147

Royal Irish Rifles' cap badge: The unit's history began in 1793 when two regiments of infantry – the 83rd (County of Dublin) Foot and 86th (Royal County Down) Foot – were raised as part of Britain's response to the war with the new French First Republic. In 1881, these two regiments were amalgamated to form the Royal Irish Rifles. By the First World War, the unit recruited from Antrim, Down and Louth, with the regimental depot at Belfast. The Latin motto was Quis Separabit – 'who shall separate us'.

casualties and sixty-four missing. Some of the Dublin dead included seventeen-year-old Private Timothy O'Connor from Lower Gloucester Street, Dublin, who enlisted at Howth and is today buried in Auchonvillers Military Cemetery; eighteen-year-old Private James Mahon from Mary's Abbey, Dublin, who died of wounds and is buried in Couin British Cemetery; nineteen-year-old Private William Feely from Pender's Court, Dorset Street, Dublin, who with no known grave is commemorated on the Thiepval Memorial; and nineteen-year-old Private Patrick McLean from Martin Street, South Circular Road, who is buried in Hawthorn Ridge Cemetery No.2, Auchonvillers. Meanwhile, the 2nd Royal Dublin Fusiliers in 4th Division were in the second wave. Fourteen out of their twenty-three officers became casualties along with 331 other ranks out of 480 total; three of the dead were twenty-year-old Private William Carroll who was originally from Dalkey but residing at Killiney View Cottages, Kingstown, County Dublin (buried Sucrerie Military Cemtery, Colincamps); twenty-year-old Private John Geraghty from Prebend Street, Broadstone, Dublin; and twenty-five-year-old Dubliner Lance-Corporal Matthew Reardon (who served under the alias surname O'Rearden) who came all the way back to Europe from his new home in Montreal, Canada, to enlist. With no known graves, both Geraghty and Reardon are commemorated on the Thiepval Memorial.

As for Private Thomas Rooney, although evacuated back to England after 1 July 1916, he was ultimately sent back to the war after his leg injury had healed. He was back with 14th Royal Irish Rifles in time for the Battle of Cambrai in 1917, but when the winter cold started biting at his old wound, Thomas Rooney had to be evacuated again on 19 December 1917, although he did not leave France. On 3 January 1918 he transferred into the Labour Corps as he was now unfit for front-line service. On 20 September 1918, he was still in the field as on this date he was fined five days' pay for disobeying an order and for going absent without leave for twenty-four hours, though his service file does not say why he did it. Thomas Rooney was probably still in France when the armistice was declared, and was only finally discharged on 19 March 1919. He returned home to Belfast, having enlisted as a healthy man with his brother. Now, he was returning alone, suffering from a terrible leg wound that would flare up badly from time to time.

Thomas Rooney married Isobel Dempster – a local beauty – and had two sons. She used to pose for a local photographer and his shop window was full of her portraits. Then one day, as Thomas Rooney's grandson – Peter Rooney – recalls: 'There is then a dark absence of information but Isobel was found in a pool of blood on the living-room floor. Suicide was mentioned, as was falling off a chair while mending curtains.' Either way, Thomas Rooney walked away from his two sons and left them to be cared for by his sister, Sarah. So as the boys grew up, not only had they to suffer the lack of a father – who went on to have other children with another woman – but they also had to deal with constantly seeing portraits of their mother in the photographer's shop window.

When Thomas Rooney was dying in the 1970s, one of the sons that had been brought up by his sister went to visit Thomas on his deathbed. This son, John, claimed that as the end came near, his father started ranting about being in the trenches.

THE END OF THE BATTLE OF THE SOMME

The rest of 1916 saw the Allies make slow but steady gains on the Somme. The strain was finally relieved from Verdun, and when September 1916 arrived and the tank made its debut on the battlefield, the Germans realised that the Somme was draining them of men and resources and that British pressure was literally slaughtering their armies. They knew that they could not continue paying the cost in lives required by the Somme, and so, miles behind the front lines, they began construction of a fortified wall of elaborate trench networks, concrete pillboxes, rows of barbed wire and machine-gun emplacements. The Germans called it the Siegfried Line, but to

Tyneside Irish shoulder title: The four Tyneside Irish 'Pals' battalions were battalions 24–27 of the Northumberland Fusiliers. Together they comprised the 103rd (Tyneside Irish) Brigade, and included men of Irish birth or extraction living in Newcastle-upon-Tyne. It is possible that the Tyneside Irish badge was only ever worn as a shoulder title, and that the men still wore the Northumberland Fusiliers' badge on their caps.

Unlike most images of men going 'over the top', this one was not staged for the camera. It shows the Tyneside Irish (103rd Brigade, 34th Division) advancing from the Tara-Usna line to attack La Boisselle on 1 July. They incurred heavy casualties, with the 34th Division suffering higher losses than any other division that day.

the British it was known as the Hindenburg Line – after the famous German general, Paul von Hindenburg – and it was designed to allow fewer men to defend a wider area.

The Battle of the Somme officially came to an end on 18 November 1916. Again, the fighting was halted by the arrival of a bitter winter. In just under five months, 420,000 British soldiers had been killed, wounded or had gone missing, along with 205,000 Frenchmen and 435,000 Germans. Added up, this totalled 1,060,000 dead and wounded on all sides – just over 310,000 of these had been killed – and while it is impossible to obtain an accurate number, out of this massive amount of casualties, at least 3,500 Irishmen are believed to have been killed on the Somme and at least twice that figure wounded. If you take into account that each one of these Irishmen had a mother and father, siblings, aunts, uncles, cousins, friends, girlfriends, wives or even children, then the amount of grieving Irish people could spiral into the hundreds of thousands for this number of dead alone. Statistically speaking, for every foot of ground gained by the British on the Somme, thirty of their men were killed or wounded in the process.

By February 1917, even though the fortifications were still not fully

The body of a dead British soldier on the Somme.

complete, the Germans began withdrawing units from the Somme to the Hindenburg Line. When it was fully manned, the Hindenburg Line was designed to be impenetrable. By mid-March, the German withdrawal was well underway – they covered their retreating units with excellently placed rearguard snipers or machine-gun crews – and the British soldiers never caught up with the bulk of the German Army. After months of fighting and thousands of deaths, the Germans simply surrendered the whole Somme battlefield and fell back to the Hindenburg Line. The Allies were back to square one.

The British fought the Battle of Arras (just north of the Somme) in April and May 1917 to try and break through the Hindenburg Line in support of a major French offensive, but even after incurring 160,000 casualties, they still failed. Then, on 6 April, they received a serious morale boost with news that America had just declared war on Germany. However, it would be a long time before America entered the war proper, and so the Allies would simply have to wait.

A NEW IRELAND

Meanwhile, back home in Ireland, the Irish people were also seeing their fair share of political changes. On 10 May 1917, Sinn Féin candidate Joseph McGuinness won a by-election in south-Longford against the local Irish Parliamentary Party representative. For John Redmond, leader of the Irish

Parliamentary Party, losses like this were crippling. Politically, his party was quickly becoming an impotent force in a rapidly changing Ireland. For the previous several decades, aside from the Land Acts, Home Rule had been *the* dominating issue of Irish politics. Now with the rise of ardent republicanism and support for Sinn Féin, Home Rule had been tossed aside. British Prime Minister David Lloyd George tried to stem the tide when, six days after the south-Longford by-election, he called for the southern twenty-six counties to be granted immediate Home Rule. But Home Rule was now yesterday's concern. On 20 July, Eamonn de Valera defeated Home Rule's Patrick Lynch in east-Clare, proving that the country was steadily shifting towards support for total independence. The days of the Home Rule supporter were numbered. The reason behind so many Irishmen going to war was being made redundant.

A dead German soldier at Beaumont Hamel on the Somme, November 1916. Three hundred and ten thousand men died on the Somme – French, British and German – one out of every three casualties incurred on that battlefield.

CHAPTER 3

MESSINES RIDGE AND THE HOLY LAND

'It [the war] would be a fine memorial to the men who have died so splendidly if we could, over their graves, build up a bridge between North and South [of Ireland]. I have been thinking a lot about this lately in France – no one could help doing so when one finds that the two sections from Ireland are actually side by side holding the trenches!'

Major William Redmond MP, 6th Royal Irish Regiment, in a letter to his friend Arthur Conan Doyle – December 1916

Along the Western Front in late-spring of 1917, the British had a decision to make. America had not yet entered the war, so they had to press on alone for now. The area around Arras and the Somme had not yielded any successes, but with the French Army having recently mutinied – an event which left it incapable of taking the field against the enemy – the British had to open up a new battlefront in order to divert German attention away from the ailing French. So they set their sights on returning to an old battlefield. The orders were written and on 30 May the men were informed. The British Army was heading back to Belgium – they were returning to Ypres.

Ypres was the nemesis of the British – they had fought the Germans here in 1914 and 1915, and while their focus had turned to the Somme during 1916, they had never forgotten about the 'Immortal Salient' as they called it. Ypres had never fallen to the Germans, the salient had never been pinched out, and like Verdun to the French, Ypres was a symbol to the British – a symbol of determination, resistance and sacrifice. 'Wipers' was a point of honour to the British, a national struggle. So they prepared to launch the Third Battle of Ypres.

RETURN TO BELGIUM

MICHAEL FITZGERALD

One of the opening battles of the renewed offensive at Ypres would also go down in history as one of the most poignant battles of the war in terms of Irish involvement. The British plan in the lead up to launching the Third Battle of Ypres was to firstly capture the Messines Ridge to the southeast of Ypres and use this as a platform to advance further. Attempts to storm the high ground on any battlefield in the past had nearly always resulted in massive losses, such as the assaults made on the Chemin des Dames Ridge in 1914, or the endless fighting on Gallipoli hillsides in 1915, so the British devised a way of levelling the playing field – literally. For over a year, British miners had been tunnelling towards German positions at Ypres. The plan was to lay mines under the enemy trenches and strong points, exactly as they had done on the Somme, although at Ypres, the mines would be far larger. Shafts had been dug, and wearing felt slippers, using rubber-wheeled trolleys and speaking in whispers, with air pumps needed to supply oxygen to the men as they got deeper, sappers of the Royal Engineers had laid over 1 million lbs of explosive in various locations. The job had been successfully completed, and a time and date for the assault on the Messines Ridge was set – 3.10am, 7 June 1917.

In the lead up to the attack, Second-Lieutenant Michael Fitzgerald of the 6th

Above: *Royal Irish Regiment cap badge: The oldest of the Irish infantry regiments, the Royal Irish Regiment was originally formed in 1684 by the Earl of Granard. Elements of the regiment later fought at the battles of Lexington, Concord and Bunker Hill during the Seven Years' War in America (1756–63). Its recruiting grounds were Tipperary, Waterford, Wexford and Kilkenny, with the regimental depot at Clonmel. It gained a 7th Battalion in 1917 when the South Irish Horse was dismounted and turned into infantry.*

The old world meets the new: a trio of 2ⁿᵈ Irish Guards wearing German plate and body armour which they have picked up off the battlefield, July 1917. They are examining a German 1908 pattern machine gun. Armed with the weapons of the modern age, they are wearing body armour that would not have been out of place on medieval battlefields.

Royal Irish Regiment found himself in the trenches below Messines Ridge. However, he had not started out in the war as an officer. Born in Templederry, County Tipperary, but raised in Thurles, twenty-three year old Michael Fitzgerald was educated in the Hughes Academy, Belfast. The son of a Royal Irish Constabulary sergeant, he joined the RIC himself in 1911 and served as a constable until deciding to join the army in November 1915 when he enlisted as a private in the Irish Guards. However, after displaying good organisational and leadership ability – which saw him quickly-promoted to lance-corporal – Fitzgerald was recommended by his commanding officer for a commission in September 1916. His application was successful, and by 1917 he was serving as a second-lieutenant with the 6th Royal Irish Regiment, itself a part of 16th (Irish) Division.

Second-Lieutenant Fitzgerald joined his battalion in the field on 1 May 1917. Training was intensified as the date for the upcoming attack drew near. Then on 25 May, Fitzgerald heard a story that was making its way around the battalion. Someone in the 6th Royal Irish Regiment had shot a local civilian – in an act of deliberate violence. The following day, the battalion war diary recorded that 'the civilian shot by the man of the battalion (Pte Kenny) died on Whit Sunday,' and on 27 May that 'Pte Kenny identified as the culprit, by daughter and wife of the murdered man, on parade. Scenes of emotion on the part of the French people followed.' It is not recorded what punishment, if any, he received.

The preliminary bombardment of Messines Ridge began on 31 May. Then, on the night of 6 June, Michael Fitzgerald's twenty-fourth birthday, the 6th

John Redmond (centre) and William Redmond (far right), 1912. Upon the outbreak of war, Willie Redmond had been one of the Home Rule figureheads who had advocated enlistment, in order to secure an Irish parliament. Even though he was aged fifty-three at the time, he declared in a recruitment speech at the window of the Imperial Hotel, Cork: 'I do not say to you Go – but grey haired and old as I am, I say Come, come with me to the war.'

Royal Irish Regiment moved into battle positions for the attack.

That night, Major William Redmond – MP for Wexford since 1884 and brother of Home Rule MP John Redmond – joined the battalion. When war broke out in 1914, Willie Redmond had re-joined the army, putting back on a British uniform for the first time in thirty-three years, and was made captain in his old regiment – the Royal Irish Regiment. With his promotion to major in 1916, Redmond was taken away from a combat role, but the day before the assault on Messines Ridge was due to be launched, he managed to secure permission to return to A Company and take part in the fight, although he was under orders to return to the trenches after the first enemy line had been taken. According to Major Charles Taylor, Major Willie Redmond spoke to every man in the 6th Royal Irish Regiment on the eve of the battle.

The British preliminary barrage was now a week old and it continued into the early hours of 7 June. High explosives and shrapnel shells screamed overhead and officers like Second-Lieutenant Michael Fitzgerald would have checked their watches over and over. Zero hour was 3.10am, but the infantry had been promised some assistance. The bombardment ceased a few minutes before zero hour and, as on the Somme the year before, German troops poured out of their dugouts to man their defences. The men of 16th (Irish) Division glanced up at the Messines Ridge.

IRISHMEN UNITED

Suddenly, the earth shook. Messines Ridge seemed to rumble and burst upwards as though a huge fist was punching its way up from underground. Percussion waves shot across the battlefield and men were literally thrown off their feet as nineteen massive mines detonated under the earth. One million lbs of explosive erupted and rock and dirt were thrown 5,000 feet into the air. Whole companies of Germans were destroyed. The town of Messines, on top of the ridge, was virtually flattened. Miles away, French citizens far behind the front were woken up in their beds. The blast registered on the Richter scale in England, felt like an earthquake in London, and could even be heard in Dublin. Soldiers nowhere near Messines Ridge were showered with soil. It was the loudest man-made sound in history and the greatest man-made explosion that the world had ever seen. It would be another twenty-eight years before the record was broken, and that was when the first atomic bomb was dropped on Hiroshima.

The deafened British officers blew their whistles and the assaulting infantry raced out of the trenches behind a creeping barrage. However, even though the mines had been set off at one of the best possible times, when the German units on the ridges were being relieved, so that troops completing their tour of the front and troops beginning a fresh tour had both been caught in the blast, many remaining Germans still put up a fight. Some enemy survivors simply dropped their weapons and put their hands on top of their spinning heads, but others – even though they were deafened and disorientated – decided to mount a resistance. And if they could still aim and fire a rifle, or load an artillery gun, then they were still a threat.

Second-Lieutenant Michael Fitzgerald began to lead his men across the battlefield. As the 16th (Irish) Division moved towards its objective – the village of Wytschaete (which the troops called 'Whitesheets'), south of Messines – they were advancing side by side with the 36th (Ulster) Division. Both Irish divisions had been ordered to fight alongside one another and secure the same target, and what an unusual sight it must have been. Here were two Irish divisions, one recruited from mostly northern Irish unionists, the other from predominantly southern Irish nationalists, fighting as comrades-in-arms. There was no animosity between them – just a common goal and soldierly professionalism – while back home in Ireland, tensions between unionists and nationalists were at an all-time high. However, on the Messines battlefield, both sides worked together, fought together, and died together.

In fact, after Major William Redmond of A Company, 6th Royal Irish Regiment led his men over the top and was shot in the wrist and leg, it was stretcher-bearers of the 36th (Ulster) Division – die-hard unionists who would have cursed his name in civilian life – who carried him from the field. And when Willie Redmond subsequently died in hospital, the Ulstermen agreed to a £100 donation to his memorial fund. They also formed the Guard of Honour at his grave. Back in the 'real' world, they were his political enemies, but not here – here, they were brothers.

Large group shot of 16th (Irish) Division after the Battle of Messines Ridge, 7 June 1917. It was during this battle that the predominantly nationalist 16th (Irish) Division advanced alongside the unionist 36th (Ulster) Division. Second-Lieutenant Michael Fitzgerald, from County Tipperary, never got to take part in these celebrations. He was wounded during the battle and evacuated.

William Redmond was fifty-six years old when he died, and today his body lies in Locre Hospice Cemetery. Redmond died on the very battlefield that would become this memorial – a place symbolic of Irish unity.

Meanwhile, as Second-Lieutenant Michael Fitzgerald continued his advance up Messines Ridge, a shell burst exploded near him, sending shrapnel slicing into his left arm and right thigh. The wounds were not life threatening, but they necessitated that the Tipperary officer be evacuated back to England. As Michael Fitzgerald was carried away to the rear thousands of Germans had already surrendered and, at this rate, the high ground would soon be in British hands. So along with an impending victory, he could celebrate having survived the Battle of Messines Ridge, having seen the two Irish divisions fight side by side, and having lived beyond his twenty-fourth birthday.

At the end of the Battle of Messines Ridge, the British had captured 7,000 enemy prisoners and inflicted 25,000 casualties on the Germans, although they suffered about the same number of killed and wounded themselves. The mines had set the scene for a fantastic victory – shock tactics and rapid movement had been put to good use – but there was pressure to follow up with another equally successful battle. What happened was the Third Battle of Ypres, otherwise known as the Battle of Passchendaele. Like every major battle before it, it failed to bring about a decisive victory for either side. The subsequent Battle of Cambrai equally came to nothing.

As for Michael Fitzgerald, his involvement with famous Irish moments of the war did not end with Messines Ridge. Second-Lieutenant Fitzgerald soon found himself posted to a place that was dear to the hearts of most Irish men and women of his time. In November 1917, having recovered from his wounds, Michael Fitzgerald set sail to re-join the war, having just returned from three weeks leave to visit home in Thurles. His journey started with a ship from Southampton to Le Havre, then an overland trip across France to Marseilles, where he boarded another boat to Alexandria in Egypt. From Egypt, he set out across burning desert to join the 1st Royal Irish Regiment. This battalion was now a part of 10th (Irish) Division, the division that had fought in Gallipoli, been redirected to Salonika, and had recently been redirected to Palestine. Michael Fitzgerald was going to the Holy Land.

THE CRUSADE

The fact that an Irish division fought in Gallipoli is starting to become common knowledge in Ireland, but the fact that this division went on to fight in Palestine is less well known. Palestine was then still a part of the Turkish Ottoman Empire, and along with a similar campaign in Mesopotamia (modern Iraq), the Allies were committed to beating the Turks in the Holy Land.

When Michael Fitzgerald arrived in Palestine, he soon found himself fighting

LITTLE GREY HOME IN THE WEST (2).
Far ahead, where the blue shadows fall,
I shall come to contentment and rest;
And the toils of the day will be all charmed away
In my little grey home of the west.

A postcard sent by the mother of Gunner
Thomas Wall – from Loughrea, County
Galway – to him at his station on Malta
during 1917. The message on the back reads:
'Dear Tommy, your letter of the 31 to Ciss
received today. Delighted at news it
contained. Am on the look out for my letter as
it has not arrived as yet. Will write when I
get it. We are all very well except Sept
[Concepta]. She is still very sick. Hope you
are tip top and that you got my last letter
telling you the money came all right after
all. Also Cissie's written some days ago and
papers. Kind regards from all the friends
and best love from us all, Mother.'

Studio photograph of Gunner Thomas Wall from Loughrea, County Galway, aged twenty-one. The image is stamped: Chretien & Co, Valletta, Malta, and was taken c1917.

for the 'grand prize', so to speak. As 25 December approached and the weather started to worsen, the British Army closed in on Jerusalem. The Turks fought bitterly to keep them back, but the British were determined to capture the city by Christmas. Then, on 9 December – the day after the Feast of the Immaculate Conception – word filtered down to the Irish troops of the 10th (Irish) Division – to men like Second-Lieutenant Michael Fitzgerald. Their comrades just a few miles away had achieved a victory that had not been won in combat for four hundred years. In 1517, the Ottoman Turks had captured it – now in 1917, the British were triumphant. For a thousand years, Christians had fought, sacrificed and died for this place, and whether those crusades had been just, or not, no one could deny their importance in history. The holiest prize in all of Christendom had just been taken by the forces of Britain and the Commonwealth. The Turks had been routed from one of the world's most fought-over cities. Jerusalem had fallen – and an Irish division had played a part in its capture.

Each battalion and regiment was invited to include a guard of a few officers and soldiers for the triumphal march through the city. For these soldiers entering Jerusalem, their minds could well have been spinning with Bible stories and sermons. King Solomon had built his temple here. The Ark of the Covenant had rested in its inner sanctum. Christ had walked these streets, fought with the moneylenders, been betrayed in the Garden of Gethsemane and crucified on nearby Calvary. Medieval kings had waged war over these buildings and towers.

Second-Lieutenant Michael Fitzgerald of 1st Royal Irish Regiment was one of the thousands of British troops to enter the gates of the city on 11 December. The Turks ultimately tried to retake the city but they never succeeded, and the rest of the war in Palestine saw the slow but steady defeat of the Turkish Army. On 4 May 1918, just before the battles of Megiddo, Michael Fitzgerald won a Military Cross for bravery. Promoted to lieutenant on 1 September, Fitzgerald left the fight not long after when he was hospitalised on 17 September with jaundice. On 2 October 1918, the city of Damascus fell to the British, and twenty-eight days later, an armistice was signed, ending hostilities between the Ottoman and British Empires in Palestine. The armistice was signed aboard the appropriately selected HMS *Agamemnon* in Mudros Harbour on Lemnos

Borton Pacha, the British Military Governor of Jerusalem, leads the Allied march through the town, followed by his two aides-de-camp and General Allenby further back. History records that General Allenby refused to enter on horseback because he did not want to appear as a victorious conqueror. Instead, he chose to humbly walk with his men. However, Second-Lieutenant Michael Fitzgerald recorded it otherwise. Apparently, Allenby had a large backside and did not cut a dignified figure in the saddle.

Island, the very place that both Agamemnon's conquest of Troy and the much more recent Gallipoli campaign had been launched. It had been four years since the Turks and British had first met in combat.

Michael Fitzgerald never fought in a battle again. However, he stayed in the army after peace was finally declared, and was still in Palestine in July 1919 when he fell ill again and was ultimately evacuated back to England. But that still was not the end of Fitzgerald's army service. As soon as he recovered, he returned to Palestine, where, on 19 December 1919, he was posted to 38th Royal Fusiliers, a Jewish unit.

The Zionist movement of the late nineteenth and early twentieth century – which supported the creation of a new Jewish homeland – had seen the British Army create Jewish battalions of the Royal Fusiliers during the First World War. Initially, these units had not been allowed to serve in Palestine, for obvious political reasons, but as the war dragged on, the Jewish soldiers finally got their wish.

When Michael Fitzgerald had shipped out to Palestine in 1917 it was with pro-Jewish leanings. However, when recurring bouts of sickness forced Lieutenant Fitzgerald to sit before an army medical board in Cairo in November 1920, Fitzgerald did not wait for the army to dismiss him on medical grounds. He made the first move and relinquished his commission on 1 April 1921. Michael Fitzgerald's political opinions had changed – the time he had spent in the Middle East had had a profound effect on him.

Ironically enough for a man who had travelled to the Middle East with a pro-Jewish opinion, Michael Fitzgerald ended up making Palestine his new home and joined their Defence Forces. In fact, he became a founder member of the Irish-Arab Society, and drawing on his experience as a former RIC constable, Michael Fitzgerald later rose to become Police Commissioner of Haifa.

In later life, he was always known for being a dashing, charming man – very handsome – and when Fitzgerald finally returned to Ireland from Palestine, he initially tried to set up a shooting and fishing retreat in Portumna, before abandoning the project and moving to Rathgar in Dublin to live with family. Unfortunately, he also had to suffer the loss of his wife and twin children. Both she and the babies died during childbirth. Michael Fitzgerald then spent his later years living in Balbriggan, where he remarried and had two sons. Looking back on an eventful life, he could always claim to be one of the honoured few who had marched in triumph through the gates of Jerusalem back in December 1917. Michael Fitzgerald – former lieutenant of the Royal Irish Regiment and Military Cross recipient, who had fought at the Battles of Messines Ridge and in Palestine – died in 1983. He was ninety years old.

The Palestinian campaign had been fought thousands of miles from home across arid deserts; it had been fought with mules, camels, horses and by sheer manpower. Christians and Muslims had once again killed one another over cities in the sand. After the Western Front, Palestine was the second largest theatre of operations, and the 10th (Irish) Division had been one of the units

which served there – Irishmen who must have wondered at being in the land of the Bible. However, their fighting and dying at Gaza, Beersheba, Jerusalem and Megiddo is even less known than their suffering and sacrifices made at Gallipoli. The First World War cemetery at Jerusalem is full of headstones bearing Irish names – men who made the pilgrimage to the Holy Land, men who never returned.

Opposite and above: *Christmas card sent by the British Red Cross to soldiers in late 1917. This particular card was sent to Gunner Thomas Wall from Loughrea, County Galway. The handwritten additions were made in 1979 by Thomas's younger brother, Raymond Wall, who served with the RAF during the Second World War.*

CHAPTER 4

THE SPRING OFFENSIVE

'Having rolled back the 66th Division on our right, he [the enemy] outflanked the right battalion of our brigade who were obliged to fall back – leaving our right flank exposed, and he was able to attack Malassise Farm from the right rear, it falling into his hands before the garrison had a chance of putting up a serious fight.'
Battalion War Diary, 2nd Royal Munster Fusiliers, 21 March 1918

B y the start of 1918, all eyes were on the Western Front. After Lenin and the Bolsheviks had come to power in Russia and made peace with Germany, 400,000 German soldiers (with a further 80,000 from the Italian front) started moving westwards to reinforce their beleaguered countrymen. America had entered the war on the Allied side, but the United States Army had no sizeable presence in Europe at this stage. So, as far as Germany was concerned, there was still hope – the plan was to strike a significant blow that would bring the Allies to the negotiating table before the Americans arrived *en masse*. If they failed, or if they waited too long and allowed the Americans to build up their forces, it would spell certain defeat for Germany.

Given the state of every army in the field by 1918 – British, French and German – this year would certainly see the end of the war. The men were shattered and each country was on the verge of starvation and economic ruin. The Allies kept praying for speedy large-scale American deployments, while the

Germans loaded more and more men onto westbound trains.

In fact, the Allies had no idea of the scale of the threat they were facing: 177 divisions of German infantry (seventy-three percent of the entire German Army worldwide), which meant that if you added up the total number of British and French soldiers available, the Germans still had 200,000 more men on the Western Front. The Germans also had superior numbers of artillery pieces and stockpiles of shells, and their morale was high, boosted by the arrival of so many Eastern Front units. Finally, the Germans had new specially trained assault troops – stormtroopers – who would be instrumental in the coming offensive.

Compare this with Allied morale – the Americans only had four divisions in France, only one of which was serving at the front, and they were only promising eighteen extra divisions by June 1918. Britain and France knew that this would be far too late.

German generals were well aware that this would be an assault truly deserving of the term 'monumental'. For most of the war, Germany had stayed on the defensive. Now, it was time to stop defending, it was time to attack.

Designed in 1907 for use with the Lee-Enfield No 1 Mk 3 rifle, this sword bayonet was made by Wilkinson Sword and measured twenty-two inches in length total (seventeen inches for the blade). To fit it into position, a soldier placed the bayonet over the muzzle and clicked it down onto a catch which held the bayonet firm. Once attached, it could not fall off accidentally or be pulled off. Soldiers were trained to holler at their enemies while charging them with the bayonet, in order to shock the enemy, and after lunging with force, they were trained to twist the blade in the wound to inflict maximum damage.

KAISERSCHLACHT – 'OPERATION MICHAEL'

LAWRENCE MOLLOY

The Germans fittingly called their upcoming offensive *Kaiserschlacht* (Imperial Battle), because that is simply what it was – the final showdown between the empires of old. The first phase was known as 'Operation Michael' and it was to go down in British military history as the German 'Spring Offensive'. The date for the attack was set – 21 March 1918 – and the target was selected. The British Fifth Army had recently taken over a forty-two mile sector of front from the French, centred on Cambrai and St Quentin, east of the old 1916 Somme battlefields. The poorly constructed defences were in desperate need of improvement. The problem was that the Fifth Army's battalions had been depleted by the Third Battle of Ypres and the Battle of Cambrai, and they simply had not the manpower or the resources to repair the local defences.

Towards the end of March 1918, these units were still awaiting refit – the arrival of new drafts – and had not undergone any recent period of training. They were tired, worryingly below strength, in an area that was strategically vulnerable – an area which the Germans had selected to punch through the British lines with fifty-eight divisions, forty-seven of which were stormtrooper divisions. Against these overwhelming numbers of enemy infantry, Fifth Army only had sixteen divisions. Furthermore, the standard layout for defensive fortifications in 1918 – a forward zone sparsely manned by snipers and machine guns, in front of a main battle zone, in front of a rear zone containing reserves – was non-existent in this former French position. All that was present were redoubts placed few and far between – easy for attacking troops to encircle and cut off. Worse still, the normal turnaround period for sending a division into the line before relieving it for rest was fifteen days, but one of Fifth Army's divisions had recently spent a mind-numbing fifty-eight days straight in the trenches. These men – the men of the 16th (Irish) Division – could barely stand, but they were about to come under attack from German artillery fire, followed by a tidal wave of elite enemy soldiers.

Private Lawrence 'Lar' Molloy from Rathangan, County Kildare.

One of the units in the 16th (Irish) Division was the 2nd Royal Munster Fusiliers, and in this battalion was Private Lawrence 'Lar' Molloy. A native of Kilthaun, Rathangan, County Kildare, at thirty-one years old, he was the eldest son of a widowed mother. Lar came from a farm-labouring background, and he was of the generation of Irish who knew what it was like to grow up in a crowded thatched cottage. When war broke out, Lar and a friend signed up together and were sent to the Curragh for training. However, the friend soon put a bayonet through his own foot to get out of the army.

It was while Lar was in training at the Curragh that he saw a soldier pick up a rifle, take aim at a coin balanced on a post in the distance, and put a bullet straight through it. Lar thought that that was not so hard, so he set up another coin – a tru'penny bit – took aim and fired. The shot was perfect and the coin was blasted off the post. And so Lar Molloy was drafted as a sniper. He served initially with the Royal Dublin Fusiliers before being transferred into the 2nd Royal Munster Fusiliers.

But not long before 21 March 1918, Lar's zeal for the army had faded away. When on leave to Monasterevan, to visit his wife Lucy and their son, Lar's family could not believe how black his skin was from all the dirt, smoke, and gunpowder. Worse still, he was terribly despondent. Nothing could lift his spirits – he had seen something, or done something, that was weighing heavily on his soul.

The severity of it was made clear to everyone when Lar's period of leave was up. Lar refused to go back to the front. Of course, the authorities had other ideas and men were sent to apprehend Private Molloy and return him to barracks. In the end, it took nearly every RIC policeman in Monasterevan to drag Lar kicking and screaming back to barracks.

'Please!' he begged them. 'If I go back, I'll die! I'll die! Please! Don't send me back! Please!'

However, on 21 March 1918, Lar Molloy *was* back in the trenches when the Germans released all hell on the British lines. The Germans initially targeted British command and communications – before swiftly changing aim to pummel their artillery. From Arras to St Quentin, British dugouts, communication trenches and artillery batteries vanished in a hail of dirt and steel and were shrouded in clouds of phosgene and mustard gas. Then the Germans swapped over to pounding the front-line infantry. For those that survived in the trenches, they were trapped in a chaotic deafening whirl of destruction. In five hours, 4,000 field guns and 2,600 heavy calibres fired a staggering 1.1 million shells at the British while 3,500 trench mortars added to the cacophony. When you take into account that there were only 2,000 guns involved in the pre-Somme bombardment of 1916, and that it took these guns a week to fire

1.5 million shells, the German barrage of 21 March 1918 easily becomes the most destructive display of artillery fire that the war had ever seen. Finally, after the shellfire had done its work, the German stormtroopers advanced.

As for Lar Molloy and the 2nd Royal Munster Fusiliers, the battalion war diary states that:

> At last the long expected enemy offensive commenced. The battalion was occupying a series of positions between Epéhy and Malassise Farm ... The enemy opened his bombardment at 4.30am, with gas shells on the batteries and ordinary heavy shells on the trenches. The bombardment lasted for six hours, and a heavy white fog hung over our positions.

Malaisse Farm fell to the Germans and Lieutenant-Colonel Herbert Ireland, commanding officer of 2nd Royal Munster Fusiliers, moved forward to take command but was wounded (he died a week later). His second-in-command, Major Marcus Hartigan, moved the battalion headquarters to the rear, but the Germans had now advanced beyond Lempire and were attacking along the Lempire-Epéhy road. 'They attacked Battn. Hdqrs. at 6pm and we were forced to move out after a short sharp fight, in which Maj. Hartigan became "missing".'

Meanwhile, three officers and '50 other ranks held on to the railway cutting S.E. of Epéhy. This party was pounded on the left by trench mortars, and a platoon of "C" Coy, on the left front cutting suffered terribly, 2Lt. M. Trecey being killed. The enemy now began to close in on the remnants of the battalion in the cutting ...' Luckily, however, night was falling, and so the survivors managed to slip away under cover of darkness.

But Lar Molloy was not amongst them. As a sniper, Lar would have been positioned in the front-line trenches of the 2nd Royal Munster Fusiliers' forward zone when the Germans launched Operation Michael. After the morning of 21 March 1918, Private Lawrence 'Lar' Molloy was never seen or heard of again. He died somewhere in the forward zone, aged thirty-one; his body was never recovered, and today his name is commemorated on the Pozières Memorial (Unfortunately, the Molloy family tragedy did not end there. Lar's only son later emigrated to Britain, where he joined the RAF. He was killed during the Second World War).

The scale and magnitude of the German attack simply cannot be underestimated. Tens of thousands of soldiers were launched against the British lines, but unlike previous frontal assaults made by the British, the Germans annihilated their enemies. Thousands were killed, thousands more were captured, miles of ground were taken and the British were routed in terror and confusion. The German officers leading the attack had been trained to be flexible, to adapt to the situation as it developed. There would be no time wasting, no sticking to a rigid battle plan if the conditions were not favourable. Above all, they had been trained to advance, exploit and disrupt – consolidation was for follow up waves to worry about. The attack struck the British front like a tidal wave and achieved its objectives – breakthrough, fear and panic.

Three *days* later the Germans had fought their way back to the old Somme battlefield of 1916, but then, when they tried to break through to Amiens on 5 April, they failed. The German infantry had gained considerable ground, but they were now expended, starving, and broken. There would be no Allied rush to the negotiating table.

When the German threat finally eased, the British had time to add up the long lists of dead, wounded and missing from each division – specifically those of the badly mauled Fifth Army. In total, the Allies – British, Commonwealth Forces, French and Americans – had lost over 250,000 men during Operation Michael (with German losses slightly lower; somewhere in the region of 240,000). However, the 16th (Irish) Division had been one of the worst depleted British divisions of the whole Spring Offensive. Having begun 21 March with roughly 9,000 men, a figure far lower than its proper establishment, it now numbered around 1,200 men. Exactly 7,149 men had been killed, wounded, or gone missing (which meant that they were either dead or POWs) since 21 March. It has been suggested that the Germans may have even targeted the 16th (Irish) Division because they believed that Irishmen, given the current climate back home, would not still stand and fight for Britain, but stand and fight they did. One unit – 6th Connaught Rangers – had suffered particularly badly. After they failed to receive an order to withdraw on the morning of 21 March, they were left alone to face two German *divisions*. They suffered 300 casualties on this day alone, which resulted in the disbandment of the battalion, its roughly 222 survivors being posted to 2nd Leinster Regiment.

In effect, the Spring Offensive reduced the 16th (Irish) Division to the point where it barely contained enough men to form a battalion. The pride of Home Rule MP John Redmond and so many Irish soldiers had been practically wiped out. Ironically, this came less than a month after John Redmond himself died in London on 6 March 1918.

DISMANTLING THE IRISH DIVISIONS

However, the 16th (Irish) Division was not the worst affected division of Germany's Operation Michael, although the divide between first and second place was not wide. While the 16th (Irish) Division was the second-worst affected division in the entire British Army, first place went to their northern Irish counterpart, the 36th (Ulster) Division, which incurred an equally irreplaceable 7,310 casualties. These two divisions had fought side by side at the Battle of Messines Ridge on 7 June 1917, and more recently they had symbolically stood shoulder to shoulder against the full ferocity of the German storm-troopers. Now, these units were divisions only in name, and soon, they were to be Irish only in name also.

The divisions bearing the name 'Ulster' or 'Irish' had never been one-hundred percent Irish-constituted in the first place – there had always been drafts of Scottish, Welsh or English – although in the early years of the war, the proportion of Irishmen in each Irish battalion was obviously in the majority and far higher than any other nationality. However, by 1918, due to the growing unpopularity of the war in Ireland (along with the fact that conscription had not been introduced in Ireland), there were fewer Irish recruits, and many Irish battalions had become visibly more multinational. However, while there were fourteen reserve battalions of the various southern-Irish regiments still stationed in Ireland or Britain – battalions that were full of men who could have easily been used to rebuild the Irish divisions – a decision was made in mid-1918 not to follow this course of action, one that was made for specific politically-motivated reasons.

Whereas the 36th (Ulster) Division was refitted as a cohesive division of Ulster

German infantry soldiers during the Spring Offensive in France in 1918. From his sniping position in the forward zone on 21 March, Private Lar Molloy would have had a good view of the masses of field-grey infantry as they advanced out of the swirling dust clouds of shellfire.

units, albeit with Englishmen filling the ranks of the regiments, the 16th (Irish) Division was dismantled. Irish battalions were disbanded, amalgamated, and transferred to other divisions, with only one or two token Irish battalions being retained in each of the division's brigades. This policy essentially destroyed the division's Irishness. By summer 1918, the 16th (Irish) Division contained battalions such as the 6/7th Royal Scots Fusiliers and 14th Leicesters – decidedly non-Irish units. The reason for this was that the British knew that the Germans were on the verge of defeat, and they simply did not want a large body of trained southern Irishmen returning home for a victory parade, not with the current political climate in Ireland. So while it was safe enough to leave the 36th (Ulster) Division in one piece, given its unionist heritage, the destruction of 16th (Irish) Division at the hands of the Germans gave the British the finest opportunity to take it apart, piece by piece, under the auspices of rebuilding it. It was not long before the same thing happened to the 10th (Irish) Division in

Palestine – their battalions were transferred to other divisions, and in their place, Indian units were assigned.

It must also be noted, however, that the 10th (Irish), 16th (Irish) and 36th (Ulster) Divisions had not been the only formations in which Irish units had served. The famous 29th Division – the men of the initial Gallipoli landings of 25 April 1915 – had included 1st Royal Dublin Fusiliers and 1st Royal Munster Fusiliers. Furthermore, thousands of Irishmen had also served in non-Irish regiments. However, while mid-1918 saw the end of the Irish divisions; it also saw the development of political tensions back home.

CONSCRIPTION

On 18 April 1918, the Military Service Bill became law. Instantly, there was outrage in Ireland. The bill made it decidedly clear that conscription was to be introduced in the country, and even though Irishmen had managed to avoid compulsory service up to now, things were apparently about to change. Of course, given the political situation and the popularity of achieving independence and a republic, this was like adding fuel to the fire. The British manpower situation on the Western Front was becoming desperate, but the idea of trying to force Irish nationalists into a khaki uniform was nothing short of madness. Logically, those that had no moral complaint with taking the king's shilling had either already enlisted or would do so of their own volition, so that meant that those who remained to be conscripted – those who refused on political or ethical grounds to fight for Britain – were going to be, for the most part, nationalists and republicans. The British might as well have tried to conscript the Germans.

In Ireland, Sinn Féin and the Labour movements quickly held a meeting. Conscription had to be resisted, and it had to be resisted throughout the country. Within two days of the Military Service Bill becoming law, the Irish Parliamentary Party was also discussing ways for Ireland to oppose conscription. The British had hoped to use Ireland to provide a fresh reservoir of men – they were only succeeding in uniting men and women of all political opinions against them.

23 April 1918 had seen a general strike take place which affected railways, docks, factories, mills, theatres, cinemas, trams, public services, shipyards, newspapers, shops and munitions factories. By May, a truly united front was presented in opposition to conscription when John Dillon – the new leader of the pro-Home Rule Irish Parliamentary Party – shared the stage with Sinn Féin's Eamon de Valera during a rally on 5 May in Roscommon. Both men and both parties set aside their political differences in order to voice their outrage at the British attempt to impose conscription in Ireland. The reason for de Valera's anger at the Military Service Bill is not hard to imagine – he was an Irish republican who disagreed with any British meddling in Irish affairs – but as for John Dillon, his frustration was fuelled by the fact that the British were attempting to make conscription a necessary concession in order to gain Home Rule.

The British reaction was predictable. Outspoken members of Sinn Féin were deported, and this prompted a special anti-conscription convention to be held in Dublin on 20 May which strongly condemned such acts. But conscription itself was not yet introduced in Ireland by the time the country received a new lord-lieutenant in May – Sir John French, the former Commander-in-Chief of the BEF. Tasked with pacifying the country, he banned Sinn Féin, the Irish Volunteers, the Gaelic League and Cumann na mBan on 3 July. Irish citizens everywhere were furious, and in the ensuing environment of enraged Irish resentment towards the British, Sir John told his superiors in England that imposing conscription in Ireland would be disastrous. He would need so many extra brigades to control the country that there would be almost no overall gain in soldiers for the war. Ultimately, the British backed down, deciding not to introduce conscription in Ireland.

But by then, it was too late – too late for the Irishmen already wearing khaki. They had never been held in high-esteem by those of nationalistic opinion, the British reprisals after the 1916 Rising had damaged their reputation beyond repair; two subsequent years of republicanism and nationalism being fermented in Ireland had distanced them from their people, their nation and their loved ones, but this latest British attempt to force Irishmen into uniform had shattered all hope of returning to even a neutral welcome. Whatever about after the Easter Rising, following the conscription crisis of 1918, Irishmen in the

British Army became a symbol of foreign dominance and authoritarian control. The individual soldiers may have been simple labourers looking for a better wage, naive youths in search of adventure, or those who thought that fighting under the Union Jack might actually have progressed Ireland's independence, but now, all that was meaningless. How could these Irishmen possibly be welcomed home?

However, it should be mentioned that, even with the conscription crisis still fresh in the minds of the Irish public, the number of voluntary enlistments in Ireland increased from August 1918 until the end of the war to levels not seen since before the Easter Rising. In these four months, 9,843 Irishmen volunteered for service in the British Army, and so it is perhaps ironic that at the same time that the British tried to force Irishmen into uniform, the Irish themselves were stepping up enlistments.

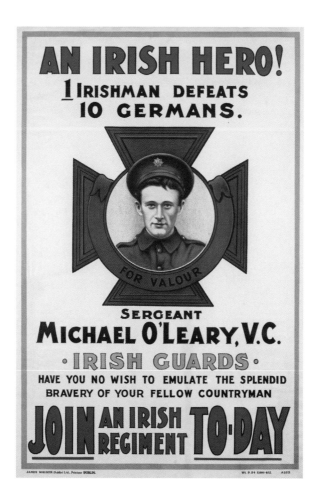

CHAPTER 5

IRELAND'S FLYING ACES

'A brilliant fighting pilot who has destroyed thirty-five machines and three kite balloons to date. He has led many offensive patrols with marked success, never hesitating to engage the enemy regardless of their being, on many occasions, in superior numbers. Under his dashing and skilful leadership his flight has largely contributed to the excellent record obtained by the squadron.'

Extract from Captain George McElroy's DFC citation, *London Gazette*, **3 August 1918**

The First World War was also famed for being the first war of technology and science – the first war that we could categorise as 'modern'. But aside from gas, tanks, and gigantic artillery guns, the war also saw the rapid development of a machine that would go on to revolutionise how we travel – the aeroplane.

The first sustained flight had taken place on 17 December 1903 when Orville Wright had flown the 'Wright Flyer' for twelve seconds in North Carolina. In the decade that followed, aeroplanes were flimsy constructions of wood, steel wire, and linen, and were predominantly viewed as toys for the rich. However, when war broke out in 1914, the aeroplane was adopted by the military and given a reconnaissance function. They might be flimsy, but the bird's-eye-view they could provide would be invaluable to commanders on the ground – that and they could carry a small payload of bombs, enough to unnerve enemy troops behind their own lines.

However, planes were not initially designed to fight each other. In the early days of the war, enemy pilots could only exchange waves, not bullets. Then, as the opposing armies started to see the need to keep their airspace free of enemy planes, pilots began carrying bricks and grenades to throw at their counterparts, and also rope – the idea being to get it tangled in the enemy plane's propeller, thereby stalling the engine. Soon enough, pilots were carrying pistols to shoot at each other, and by 1915, the machine gun was installed – creating the first dedicated fighter plane.

Although planes did not play a hugely significant part in deciding the outcome of the First World War – the way the famous Spitfire saved Britain during the Second World War – the battlefields of the sky are still a significant part of First World War history. They are significant because they preserved, for just that little bit longer, the old notion of heroic, glorious warfare. Opposing pilots went up against each other one-on-one, exactly like the dashing duelling gentlemen of old. The fighter pilots on both sides were worshipped by their respective infantry and revered like celebrities. Their exploits were followed, the kill-counts monitored with excitement, and their planes were cheered at when they swooped overhead.

However, flying was seen as extremely dangerous, the preserve of the thrill-seeker, and with good cause. Pilots constantly ran the risk that their engines might die beneath their feet, resulting in a fatal crash, or that they might be shot to ribbons by enemy machine guns. Even a wounded pilot was as good as dead

Webley Service Revolver: Primarily an officer's weapon, this pistol was also carried by airmen, naval crews and boarding parties, tank and machine-gun crews, and soldiers carrying out trench raids. Pilots often carried these revolvers to use on themselves rather than die slowly in flames.

if he could not still control his plane. If they ran out of fuel – they were dead. If the enemy came up behind them and they could not shake them – they were dead. Finally, they could also burn to death if their fuel tanks were hit. Jumping with a parachute was not an option, and many pilots carried revolvers to use on themselves if necessary – better that than die in flames. And yet, five confirmed enemy kills earned pilots the title of 'ace' and a place in the history books. For some, this was more than worth the danger.

'DEADEYE MAC'

GEORGE McELROY

At 10am on 21 February 1918, 15,000 feet up in the skies south of Honnecourt, a lone British SE-5 fighter plane was chugging through the air, armed with two machine guns – one Lewis gun and one Vickers gun – when far below him:

> [the pilot] saw 4 Albatross scouts [German aircraft] ... so dived east and got above and behind the most westerly. He opened fire at 400 yards, and then E.A. [Enemy Aircraft] dived vertically down. Capt. McElroy then got to 100 to 50 yards from the E.A., and put in 70 rounds. Pieces were then seen to fall off the E.A., which turned over on its back, and went down in a regular spiral, apparently upside down. Capt. McElroy then had to turn his attention to the other E.A., but no engagement ensued. The defeated E.A. was last seen out of control at 4,000 feet.

Satisfied that he had done his part for the day, the victorious pilot continued on his way.

The above extract is taken from a 'Combats in the Air' report from 24th Squadron, Royal Flying Corps, and the pilot mentioned is Captain George McElroy, a native of Donnybrook in Dublin. Age twenty-five in 1918, he was the son of the Donnybrook schoolmaster – Samuel McElroy – and was a Trinity College graduate and former civil servant. George McElroy had actually entered the army as a private when he enlisted in the Royal Engineers on

Officers and SE5a Scouts of No. 1 Squadron, RAF at Clairmarais aerodrome near Ypres on 3 July 1918. It was this particular type of aircraft that won Captain George McElroy his name.

13 September 1914, barely a month after the outbreak of war. He served as a dispatch rider with the motor-cyclist section of the Royal Engineers, was promoted rapidly to corporal, and served with the general headquarters' signal company in France. McElroy was singled out as officer material and sent to the cadet school in Ballieul – known as 'Ballyhooley' to most Irish troops after the town in County Cork where many of the 16th (Irish) Division had trained in summer 1915 – around the same time as the Second Battle of Ypres. On 8 May 1915, he succeeded in becoming an officer and was commissioned as a temporary lieutenant into the 1st Royal Irish Regiment. However, in October 1915 he was badly wounded by mustard gas and sent to Ireland for an extended period of home service, to recuperate.

It was during this time that he applied to join the Royal Military Academy

Woolwich (which was for training Royal Artillery and Royal Engineers' officers, unlike today when all British Army officers pass through Sandhurst), in order to gain a permanent commission. He was accepted and was due to relinquish his current temporary commission on 31 May 1916. However, with just over a month to go, the Easter Rising suddenly broke out on the streets of Dublin. Still stationed in Ireland and still a temporary lieutenant, McElroy was ordered to the capital to help put down the rebellion. While he did not agree with the principles of their uprising, George McElroy refused to fire on his countrymen. Frustrated by his pacifistic opposition, McElroy's superiors dismissed him from Dublin to a southern garrison.

Not long after, McElroy finally entered the Royal Military Academy Woolwich, which he attended for the rest of 1916. He left with special qualifications in French and advanced mathematics and was then commissioned into the Royal Garrison Artillery. So at this stage, he could claim to have served in the engineers, the infantry and now the artillery. However, this seems to have been simply a formality, as McElroy never once served as an artillery officer. It is very likely that he had to obtain a commission in another arm of the service before he could transfer into his desired role. McElroy's true goal was to join the Royal Flying Corps.

By the middle of the war, fighter pilots had taken on an almost mythical status as winged avengers, who appeared out of nowhere to fight off German aircraft. McElroy joined the Royal Flying Corps in March 1917 and was a flight officer by June. He served in two reconnaissance squadrons (14th and 6th) and then in two fighter squadrons (6th and 54th), and was posted to 40th Squadron in August 1917. It was here that he was mentored by none other than Major Edward 'Mick' Mannock, Britain's most famous air ace of the entire war – who was also Irish-born (Ballincollig, County Cork). McElroy had his first confirmed kill on 28 December 1917, and by February 1918, he had been promoted to flight commander and was now flying with 24th Squadron. This promotion and transfer happened just prior to the encounter with the four Albatross aircraft detailed above.

On 1 March 1918, Captain McElroy was back in the air, this time accompanied by Second-Lieutenants MacDougall and Hammersley over Beaurevoir. It was 10.45am and the British planes were flying at 5,000 feet on a routine patrol

Major Edward 'Mick' Mannock, Britain's most celebrated air ace of the war, born Ballincollig, County Cork. He was George McElroy's mentor.

when they spotted a DFW [Deutsche Flugzeug-Werke] two-seater German aircraft, another unidentified two-seater, and three Pfaltz fighters below them.

[McElroy] dived on a D.F.W. from left front and got to within 100 yards unobserved. He then fired 120 rounds and the two-seater went down in an irregular spiral. It was impossible to follow it down lower on account of the presence of other E.A [enemy aircraft], but it was obviously out of control. Lt. MacDougall confirms this. Lts. MacDougall & Hammersley attacked a Pfaltz but could not get nearer than 3-400 yards as the Pfaltz dived away vertically.

Five days later on 6 March, McElroy was flying southeast of St Quentin, this time only accompanied by Second-Lieutenant MacDougall. It was early in the morning – 7.05am:

Capt. McElroy observed 3 E.A. scouts approaching our lines. He flew towards and east of them apparently unobserved by E.A., and dived on to the highest, firing from 150 to 50 yards range. E.A. immediately dived and Capt. McElroy continued to fire. At 3,000 feet E.A. began to spiral on his wing tip and was seen to hit the ground N.E. of Bellecourt.

Forty-five minutes later:

2 D.F.W.s were seen on Cavalry Corps front. Capt. McElroy and Lt. Mac-Dougall dived at separate machines but Lt. MacDougall was unable to get his gun to fire. Capt. McElroy fired about 50 rounds, the E.A. diving east. He then pulled off to clear gun trouble, which recurred on again opening fire and E.A. retired east returning at 8-10 when a similar fight took place with same result owing to gun trouble.

In fact, later the same day, McElroy and his two wingmen – MacDougall and Hammersley – downed a plane each when they came across a group of four Albatross scouts and one DFW two-seater aircraft. The enemy planes were painted in a black and white chequered pattern, but for a moment, it looked as though MacDougall was in trouble. One Albatross got directly beneath him while another headed straight for him from the west. However, he managed to climb and then race down out of the sun, machine guns firing at the German planes. As for McElroy:

[he] dived on an Albatross scout which dived away, and got in 200 rounds at extremely close range. E.A. went down smoking and before reaching the ground burst into flames.

Two days later, McElroy attacked another DFW two-seater. But after firing on the enemy aircraft and putting it into a spin, 'Capt. McElroy was attacked at this juncture from above by 2 Albatross scouts and had to turn around.' McElroy climbed towards the sun to escape before turning his attention back to the two-seater. He dived at the enemy, firing in bursts, when at fifty yards range 'the Vickers gun jammed and Lewis drum was empty, so he had to pull off to correct.' By the time everything was fixed, the enemy had fled the scene.

However, the real battle of the day came at few hours later at 2.55pm on 8 March, southeast of La Fère. Again in the air with MacDougall and Hammersley, although this time also accompanied by Lieutenant Barton, McElroy saw anything from a dozen to fifteen enemy planes – Fokker triplanes, Albatross scouts and Pfaltz's – being fired on by Allied anti-aircraft fire. He moved in to join the battle.

> Capt. McElroy got on the tail of a triplane on his level, firing short bursts. The E.A. went down in a steep dive, which Capt. McElroy followed, firing both guns at very close range (250 rounds). Pieces were seen to fall, and the left wing collapsed, and the E.A. crashed in a field.

Meanwhile, back in the air, British planes ducked and dived in amongst the Fokkers, Albatross' and Pfaltzs. MacDougall attacked an Albatross, Hammersley dived on a Fokker, while Barton engaged and shot down another triplane, having shaken an enemy aircraft that was tailing him. McElroy too had to escape from an enemy plane after Hammersley uselessly came to his rescue with jammed machine guns. The score at the end of the day: British 2, Germans 0.

Finally, on the morning of the next day – 9 March 1918 – McElroy and three lieutenant comrades encountered five enemy Albatross scouts northeast of La Fère. The Germans turned and ran when they saw the British planes coming, but the British managed to catch up and a general engagement followed. Two German planes were shot down, the other three escaped and McElroy and his men suffered no casualties.

By now, McElroy was acquiring the legendary status that pilots like

Mannock had already become familiar with. He had earned the nicknames 'McIrish McElroy' and, perhaps more in keeping with his combat skills, 'Deadeye Mac'. On 26 March 1918, McElroy's citation for the award of a Military Cross appeared in the *London Gazette*, the award being:

> For conspicuous gallantry and devotion to duty. He has shown a splendid offensive spirit in dealing with enemy aircraft. He has destroyed at least two enemy machines, and has always set a magnificent example of courage and initiative.

McElroy was to the men of 1918 what an astronaut was to the people of the 1960s. Like his mentor, Mannock, McElroy had also developed a reputation for flying incredibly dangerous missions, yet somehow always managing to send the Germans down in flames while he flew home victorious. But how long would he be able to keep it up?

On 29 March 1918 – while the German Spring Offensive was steamrolling along – Donnybrook's air ace was back in the skies above France, having recently been awarded the Military Cross for his outstanding acts of bravery. Flying in his SE-5, Captain George McElroy:

> ... saw 5 E.A. behind their lines, west of Foucaucourt and below clouds. I climbed above clouds and got over gaps in same, apparently unobserved. I dived on an Alb. scout and fired about 100 rounds at a range from 100 yards to 20 yards. Saw bits come from E.A.s fuselage. E.A. went down completely out of control, crashing between Foucaucourt and River Somme.

Fifteen minutes later, now west of Warfusée and 2,000 feet up:

> [McElroy] saw a D.F.W. approaching our lines. Dived and got in position under tail and opened fire. E.A. immediately dived followed by [McElroy], which continued to fire, and E.A. went into a slow spiral, and was still in same state at about 200 feet from the ground. [McElroy] pulled up into clouds, and lost sight of E.A. About 100 rounds fired.

This act earned McElroy a bar to his Military Cross.

That was the last mission McElroy ever flew with the Royal Flying Corps. The reason for this was that when the Irish captain flew his next mission on 1 April 1918, he was now a pilot in the newly-created Royal Air Force (RAF). On that day, in the air above a wood north of Moreuil, McElroy fired on a new-model enemy two-seater with 150 rounds, but the aircraft escaped to the east. Twenty minutes later, 5,000 feet above Marcelcave, he encountered three Albatrosses and climbed above them until he was high enough to dive on the last one in formation. He raced out of the skies, ripped up the target enemy plane with 100 rounds from both his Vickers and Lewis machine guns, and then continued on his patrol.

Only another twenty minutes later, McElroy encountered one of his greatest challenges to date when he sighted seven enemy planes diving and strafing British forces north of Moreuil. The Irish pilot was alone and outnumbered, but undaunted:

> [he] dived steeply from 10,000 feet and fired about 200 rounds at each of the two nearest E.A. The whole formation fled east. I followed, firing at long range, about 3 miles over.

McElroy's daring boosted his already substantial reputation as a dashing, danger-loving champion.

The amazing thing is that the following day, 2 April, Captain McElroy encountered another seven Albatross scouts, except this time, they were being escorted by a secondary patrol of four more flying 4,000 feet above the first group. Unperturbed, McElroy attacked the lower formation, gunning down one aircraft with both machine guns at close range. Suddenly, the RAF captain realised that a German plane was under his tail. McElroy pulled up, shot into the air, performed a stall turn, and rushed down towards the pursuing German Albatross. He fired fifty rounds, but with the group of four planes above about to descend on him, McElroy was forced to withdraw from the area before he saw what happened to his latest target. Two days later, he shot down an enemy Pfaltz fighter (one of a group of seven) returning from a raid against British ground troops. Of course, with McElroy, no matter what the odds, if there were other enemy planes in the area, he had to engage them. Against the six remaining machines, he ducked and dived around them, swooping and firing until he was forced to withdraw – the reason: he had run out of ammunition.

Unfortunately, Captain George McElroy was not on hand to help during the Battle of the Lys. After failing to capture Amiens on 5 April 1918, the Germans launched another offensive only four days later. Having rested and re-organised as quickly as possible, the stormtroopers advanced once more on a front running from Dixmude, through Ypres, on to La Bassée. But McElroy could not take to the air. On 7 April, he had flown a mission in which he had downed three enemy planes, but after this mission, McElroy was sent to England to convalesce from an unspecified injury. But he did not stay out of the air for long. His total score of enemy machines destroyed was now twenty-seven, and by the time he returned to action in June, McElroy would have a second bar to his Military Cross. The citation, which appeared in the *London Gazette* on 26 July 1918, read:

> For conspicuous gallantry and devotion to duty. While flying at a height of 2,000 feet, he observed a patrol of five enemy aircraft patrolling behind the lines. After climbing into the clouds, he dived to the attack, shot down and crashed one of them. Later, observing a two-seater, he engaged and shot it down out of control. On another occasion he shot down an enemy scout which was attacking our positions with machine-gun fire. He has carried out most enterprising work in attacking enemy troops and transport and in the course of a month has shot down six enemy aircraft, which were seen to crash, and five others out of control.

Two hundred thousand Americans arrived in France between March and April 1918, and another 250,000 in June. The balance of power started to shift to the Allies, but the Germans still refused to give up. Having tried to break through to Amiens and failed, having tried to break through to Paris and failed, the Germans launched one last offensive. This would be the last sizeable battle of the war, but where would this final showdown be fought? To both sides, the location was obvious – Reims.

As the new offensive approached, Captain George McElroy was posted to 40th Squadron on 14 June 1918 and took to the air again on 1 July – the second anniversary of the Battle of the Somme. That day over Harnes and back in his SE-5 aircraft, McElroy shot down a German observation balloon, the observer leaping out of the basket and opening a parachute as the balloon went up in flames above him.

The following day, he was forced to land at Mazingarbe due to air pressure trouble, and then took off, to fly a solo low-altitude patrol. He spotted an enemy working party gathered around the wreckage of a downed German plane and scattered them with his machine guns, before shooting down an enemy two-seater near Lestrem. On 5 July, the Irish air ace sent another enemy machine crashing into the earth, but the fight had brought him so close to the ground that German infantry raked the sky with machine-gun tracer bullets. McElroy escaped, but encountered the same problem later on over La Bassée when his patrol dropped down low to pursue two enemy planes.

Day after day during July, McElroy was in the air, and day after day, he shot down enemy aircraft. He frequently attacked groups of four or five enemy fighters by himself, following a tactic of getting behind the last in formation, riddling that plane with bullets, before either racing after another target or flee-ing into the sun. However, ground fire was becoming more and more of a prob-lem, with enemy planes using flares to signal German troops, and with McElroy's dives constantly being fired on by enemy infantry. Somehow, though, he always made his escape, and for this incredible display of coolness under fire and heroism, he was soon awarded the Distinguished Flying Cross.

On 15 July, both the Allies and Germans suddenly rushed into battle, and as the Allied infantry stormed across no-man's-land and bayoneted and bombed the enemy northwards around Reims, Captain George McElroy of 40th Squad-ron RAF was flying over Pont à Vendin-Carvin on 25 July when he encoun-tered an enemy plane over the *métallurgique* works.

> [McElroy] got east of E.A. and dived down from right rear firing a few short
> bursts at fairly close range, but had to pull off owing to fuel pressure trouble.
> Changed onto emergency tank, then followed E.A. who was now making east.
> [McElroy] secured position behind tail of E.A. and fired 100 rounds from 200

down to 100 yards range. E.A. went into a steep dive, pulled out temporarily at about 1,000, but then seemed to stall and spin, and finally crashed just west of Bois d'Epinoy.

By now, he had been awarded a bar to his Distinguished Flying Cross, the citation for which (*London Gazette*, 21 September 1918) read:

> In the recent battles on various army fronts this officer has carried out numerous patrols, and flying at low altitudes, has inflicted heavy casualties on massed enemy troops, transport, artillery teams, etc., both with machine-gun fire and bombs. He has destroyed three enemy kite balloons and forty-three machines, accounting for eight of the latter in eight consecutive days. His brilliant achievements, keenness and dash have at all times set a fine example, and inspired all who came in contact with him.

When McElroy took off at 8.15am on 31 July 1918 on a solo offensive patrol in his SE-5, everyone expected him to return with more valiant tales of aerial acrobatics and heroic victories. But he did not. In fact, the Donnybrook-born Captain George McElroy never returned to British lines. Perhaps the increasing strength of enemy ground fire was an omen, or the air pressure or fuel pressure trouble that had plagued his aircraft on and off for the past few weeks should have been taken as a sign, but when a German plane flew over British lines in early August and dropped a note, all hope was lost. The note stated that Captain McElroy had been killed by ground fire on 31 July 1918.

A Distinguished Flying Cross. This medal was the Air Force's equivalent of the Military Cross, and was established on 3 June 1918. In the Air Force bravery medal hierarchy, it was junior to the Conspicuous Gallantry Cross, which was itself junior only to the Victoria Cross.

Captain George McElroy died aged only twenty-five. He had managed to bring down forty-seven enemy aircraft in his short but illustrious flying career, when destroying five German machines was enough to officially earn the title of 'ace'. McElroy had taken countless risks. He had actively sought out the enemy, attacked formations that outnumbered him, and fired at German aircraft with machine guns at close range – there was only so many times he could swoop and dive his way to safety. Today, his body lies in Laventie Military Cemetery.

To this day, Captain George McElroy is still considered the third most successful British pilot of the First World War (forty-seven confirmed kills), with first place held by his mentor, Edward 'Mick' Mannock (seventy-three confirmed kills), and second going to James McCudden (fifty-seven confirmed kills). Not far behind them in overall fifth places was another Irishman, the aptly named Thomas Falcon Hazell from Roundstone, Clifden, County Galway (forty-three confirmed kills). A former infantry officer with the 7th Royal Inniskilling Fusiliers, Hazell survived a bad crash in June 1916 after joining the RFC that year. He earned a Military Cross, Distinguished Service Order, and Distinguished Flying Cross during the war, and served as both a flying instructor and a squadron leader. He died in Ireland in 1946, aged fifty-four.

When you take into account that Mannock, McElroy and Hazell were Irish, another unknown aspect of Ireland's First World War involvement emerges – the forgotten legacy of our flying aces. Irishmen hold first, third and fifth place

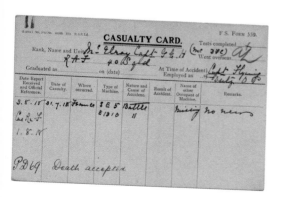
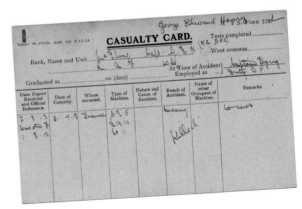

Casualty Card for Captain George McElroy.

in terms of most successful British pilots of the war. And if you broaden the scope to include pilots from all combatant countries, an Irishman is still in the top three. After Germany's famous Red Baron, Manfred von Richthofen (eighty kills), and France's René Fonck (seventy-five kills), Edward 'Mick' Mannock comes in overall third place.

Captain George McElroy outlived his mentor by only five days – Major Edward 'Mick' Mannock was killed on 26 July 1918, aged thirty-one, and has no known grave. He was awarded the Victoria Cross, the Distinguished Service Order with two bars, and the Military Cross with one bar, and today his name is commemorated on the Arras Flying Services Memorial.

Other famous Irish pilots include Joseph Creuss Callaghan and William Robert Gregory. A former Royal Munster Fusilier, Callaghan was from Kingstown (now Dún Laoghaire) in Dublin. A pilot since 1915, he earned five kills to his name, and became an aerial gunnery instructor in 1917, earning the nickname the 'Mad Major' for his aerial acrobatics. Living up to his nickname, he attacked twenty-five German aircraft all by himself on 2 July 1918, but was shot down in flames by German air ace Franz Büchner. Today, the Mad Major lies in Contay British Cemetery. He was, like George McElroy, only twenty-five years old. As for Major Gregory, he was a former Connaught Ranger and also an ex-Ireland international cricketer. He was the son of Lady Augusta Gregory of Galway, and on 23 January 1918, aged thirty-seven, he was shot down accidentally by an Italian pilot. Today he lies buried in Padua Main Cemetery.

CHAPTER 6

BOY SOLDIERS

'How old are you? Sixteen, eh? Well, take a walk for about an hour, and be nineteen when you come back.'

First World War recruiting sergeant

It was long believed that John Condon from Waterford had been the youngest soldier killed on the Western Front, that he was killed in action age fourteen. Using contemporary census records, this has turned out to be untrue. John Condon was actually eighteen when he died on 24 May 1915, a fact that is slowly starting to achieve more widespread acknowledgement. However, while the youngest casualty has since turned out not to be an Irishman, an Irishman was certainly the youngest officer on the Western Front. On 20 April 1915, Michael Joseph Aloysius Sheehan from Skibbereen, County Cork, left St Finbarr's College in Farranferris to join 7th Leinster Regiment. On 25 September that year, he joined the Royal Munster Fusiliers as a second-lieutenant and entered the war. What no one knew, however, was that Sheehan was only sixteen years old. He was promoted to lieutenant in July 1917, was wounded twice – once on 3 September 1916 during the Battle of Guillemont on the Somme when he was diagnosed, aged seventeen, with shell-shock – but ultimately survived the war. He went on to join the British Indian Army in 1919, make captain in 1920, and serve in the Second World War as a brigadier-general in Burma.

Sheehan was by no means an exception. An unknown number of underage soldiers enlisted during the war, many for the same reasons as their adult

The minimum enlistment age was initially nineteen, so many teenagers lied in order to sign up. Also, recruiting sergeants often had no problem with taking on underage soldiers, and when these boys were asked their age and answered 'sixteen' or 'seventeen', they were often simply told to 'take a walk for about an hour, and be nineteen when you come back'.

counterparts – the wage, the escape from poverty, the perceived heroism and adventure of it all. Notions of glory and valour drove much older men into the army, so it is not surprising that many young boys were keen to enlist after seeing proud soldiers march through their town, or after they heard the military recruiting band with its pipes, drums, flags and pomp.

Of course, we cannot do these young men the injustice of referring to them as immature. In early twentieth century Ireland, a boy might be learning a trade or working fulltime as a labourer or a field hand by age twelve, once he had finished primary school, if he even managed to stay in education this long. Very few went on to second level, and university was the preserve of the rich. The boys of old Ireland grew up much faster than the children of today. Also, given the poverty, disease, hardships and death that were common in most Irish towns, these boys were wiser and tougher than their modern counterparts – proved by the fact that quite a few of these young soldiers became NCOs and won medals for bravery even before they were out of their teens. They were helping to support their families financially at ages when modern boys would be still in school, with exams – not survival – being the most pressing concern of their near future.

But, in common with modern young men, the young men of old Ireland possessed the same feelings of invincibility and a craving for adventure. So when war broke out, many saw it as their chance to 'get some action', to 'slay the Hun', and perhaps become the envy of people back home. Curiously, some of these men returned home with a neutral, sometimes positive view of their time in the trenches, but it is also likely that these young Irishmen, when they were still in the mud, filth and blood and not separated from it by years of retrospection, often wished, prayed and begged that they could just go home. Some of these young men never came home, and others returned with injuries that would plague them for the rest of their lives. They were the Irish boy soldiers of the First World War.

NOM DE GUERRE

JAMES MANLEY

Although not still a boy by the time that war broke out, the story of James Manley from Roundwood, County Wicklow, is a good example of what inspired men such as him to enlist. He joined the Royal Munster Fusiliers in July 1904 because he wanted to do his bit and make a difference. As his great-niece, Mary Kennedy, later recalled, he saw the army as giving him the chance to defend his country, and 'fight the good fight', so to speak. So, with glorious idealism swimming in his head, James Manley went down to the local recruiting office to sign up. But he was only fourteen years old, and with his family known locally, James decided that he would have to serve under an assumed name. If he lied about his age but gave his real name, the recruiting sergeant might know the Manley family, and if that happened, James knew that he would probably be sent home to his parents. So, he enlisted under the name James Doyle, and set off to be trained as a soldier.

He fought throughout the First World War – though obviously in his twenties by then – but James Manley was never sorry about his decision to enlist and always said that 'I was glad to have done my bit,' the youthful enthusiasm having apparently never left him. The only thing he did regret, though, was not enlisting under his own name. But, of course, he knew that if he had tried that, he might not have been able to enlist at all. James Manley, aka Private James Doyle, died in 1961. He was seventy-one years old.

SPIRITUAL COMFORT

JEREMIAH FITZGERALD

As for Jeremiah Fitzgerald from Cork city, another young soldier, he *was* still underage when the war broke out. Fitzgerald, like James Manley above, enlisted in the Royal Munster Fusiliers before the war and was sent to France upon the outbreak of hostilities with the 2nd Battalion, but unlike James

Above: *A Princess Mary Christmas gift tin, issued to all soldiers of the BEF in December 1914. Each tin contained a greeting card, with tobacco and cigarettes, or sweets and a pencil for non-smokers.*

Manley, Jeremiah Fitzgerald enlisted just a few months before the war and so had only just completed his training by the time he was called up for active service. He was only sixteen, and had run away from home to enlist. He fought at Mons, and then at the First Battle of Ypres where he, along with every other man in the BEF, received a brass Christmas gift tin from Princess Mary.

Fitzgerald always carried a picture of the battalion chaplain – Father Francis Gleeson of the Dublin archdiocese. Father Gleeson was a beloved member of the Royal Munster Fusiliers, and he is famous for ripping off his parochial badges during the First Battle of Ypres and organising the Munster survivors of a German attack to hold the line after all of their officers had become casualties. Father Gleeson is also well known in Royal Munster Fusiliers' history for giving absolution to A Company, 2nd Battalion just before the Battle of Aubers Ridge in 1915. Out of twenty-two officers and 520 men who made the assault, only three officers and 200 men came back.

Jeremiah Fitzgerald was still only a young man when he left the war. He was evacuated home after his leg was blown off in France. Having run away to escape his old life, he returned home a permanent invalid. But he still hung on to the picture of Father Francis Gleeson, the priest so beloved by the 2nd Royal Munster Fusiliers. Jeremiah Fitzgerald never forgot the man who gave comfort and spiritual support to him and his comrades in the trenches.

THE 'NOTORIOUS' STOKER

MICHAEL WHELAN

Then there was Michael Whelan from Dungarvan, County Waterford – a young man who was one half of a pair who could only be described (with good humour) as 'notorious'. The other half was his brother, Thomas Whelan – a pre-war regular and artillery gunner whose conduct sheet is full of run-ins with military authorities, drunk charges, fines, field punishments and even a demotion. He served in Gallipoli, the Western Front, and then had a leg blown off on 28 April 1918 which resulted in his discharge.

Stokers shovelling coal into the enormous boilers of a British battleship.

So Michael Whelan had quite a reputation to live up to. And in that respect, he certainly did not disappoint. Michael was a 5'2" farm labourer and, when war broke out, he decided that he wanted to be a stoker in the Royal Navy. This was appalling, backbreaking manual work, shovelling coal into roasting hot boiler furnaces – a real man's job – and although Michael had successfully enlisted, there was just one problem. He was only fifteen.

Michael was sent to Devonport, to the shore establishment *Vivid II* – the stokers' training ship. Shore establishments, or 'Stone Frigates' or 'Hulks' as they were known, were outdated and decommissioned warships used for training purposes. Within a few weeks, however, an exhausted Michael Whelan was admitted to the Royal Naval hospital in Plymouth. He had contracted the measles, and his condition worsened when he developed pneumonia. Doctors took one look at him and realised Michael's age. Working as a stoker was not a job for a boy, and Michael had already proved that he had not the strength nor the stamina for it. On 1 January 1915, he was discharged and sent back to his family in Waterford. However, that was not the end of his military career.

Three years later Michael Whelan turned eighteen. And so, now legally eligible to enlist, Michael Whelan insisted on realising his old plan of joining the Royal Navy. In September 1918 – just before the end of the war – he enlisted again, only this time he was smart enough to join as a seaman. He stayed in the navy after the war ended and, from the 1920s onwards, Michael served aboard various battleships, light cruisers, shore establishments, minesweepers, and destroyers, sailing around the world to stations in India and China.

During the Second World War, he served aboard the famous HMS *Warspite*, and by then had amassed enough complaints on his conduct sheet to rival his brother as the most 'notorious' of the Whelans. He had been punished for using abusive and threatening language, for frequently going absent without leave, and for being drunk. In fact, during the Bombardment of Tripoli, Seaman Michael Whelan was actually in the brig for being caught drunk onboard ship. But when general quarters was sounded, even prisoners had to man their stations, and so Michael raced to his post, only to return to his cell once the fighting was done.

On 17 September 1945, the Second World War over, Michael Whelan was discharged from the Royal Navy. He was suffering from pulmonary tuberculosis. At this stage, it had been a long time since Michael had lived in Ireland, and he finally returned to his native Dungarvan. Six years later, in April 1951, the TB finally got the better of him and he passed away in the family home. He was only fifty-one years old, but had amassed nearly twenty-eight years of military service in that time.

TO SEE THE WORLD AT HIS MAJESTY'S EXPENSE

ANTHONY DOYLE

Another young man who lied about his age to fight in the First World War was Anthony Doyle. One day in August 1914, he stole out of his house and travelled to Portobello Barracks (now Cathal Brugha Barracks) in Dublin to enlist. He came from a wealthy family, and when Doyle had been born in 1898, his father had owned a guest house in Rathmines, a tea and coffee merchant shop at 9 Lower Camden Street, and the family had been residing at 36 Wexford Street. However, Doyle's father had subsequently sold these properties and returned to his native Shillelagh, only to move back to Dublin in the early years of the twentieth century. By 1911, the Doyle family were living on Charlotte Street, Dublin, and Anthony's father was working as a commercial traveller.

Anthony Doyle, along with two friends, had decided to join the army in order to 'see the world at His Majesty's expense', according to Doyle's great-nephew – Peter Doyle. He lied about his age, he was only sixteen, and was posted to 7th Royal Dublin Fusiliers. After training in the Curragh and Basingstoke, he was sent to Gallipoli in 1915, along with the rest of 10th (Irish) Division.

Thankfully, however, for Anthony Doyle, he did not land on Gallipoli with the rest of 7th Royal Dublin Fusiliers on 7 August. On that day, as the Dubliners rowed towards the southern beaches of Suvla Bay, men already ashore were being blown apart by landmines and Turkish artillery. Some confusion with regards to orders had resulted in some battalions being diverted from their designated beachheads and redirected elsewhere, meaning that in any one place, the number of attacking Irish troops had been thinned out. British warships pounded the Turkish hills with salvos, and as the first waves of Dublin men leapt ashore, the beach around them was already full of the dead and dying, along with broken rifles and scattered equipment. The 11th (Northern) Division had landed at Suvla not long before the 10th (Irish) Division, and their corpses were already littering the sand.

Royal Dublin Fusiliers' cap badge: This regiment went by many nicknames – 'The Blue Caps', 'The Old Toughs', 'The Lambs', and 'The Dubs' – and was formed in 1881 by the amalgamation of two old East India Company regiments – the 102nd (Royal Madras) Foot and 103rd (Royal Bombay) Foot, with a tradition stretching back to 1662. Although it was named after a city and not a province, it recruited from Dublin, Kildare, Wicklow and Carlow, with the regimental depot at Naas.

Greeting card made by Private Anthony Doyle from Dublin.

Now, so far from their original target (the Dubliners were supposed to land to the north of Suvla and assault the Kiretch Tepe Sirt Ridge), the men of 7th Royal Dublin Fusiliers were ordered to attack the closer enemy position of Chocolate Hill. But instead of attacking it from the rear, where its defences were weaker, they assaulted it from the north and ended up charging straight uphill into a network of Turkish trenches. However, since the Turks had already fallen back to the summit of the hill, the Dubliners were able to climb the slopes. The Turks were bayoneted and shot down, and the hill was soon captured by the Irishmen. There was a cost to pay – 100 men were killed or wounded in the process. If Anthony Doyle had landed on Gallipoli on 7 August, he might not have survived beyond that day. He was most likely left behind on Lemnos as part of a detachment.

Anthony Doyle joined his Dublin comrades two days later. Attempts were made to press on from Chocolate Hill over the following days, but to no avail. The Turks had responded quickly to the British invasion and had been swift to identify and garrison any vital areas of high ground that their enemy had not yet reached. Also, the British soldiers were completely parched, but since many of them had thrown away any 'extra' equipment that they had been carrying once the fighting started, they had no water canteens to drink from. Worse still, their throats were swollen so badly that they could not even eat, and those that finally gave into the maddening thirst and ran to one of the sparse few wells nearby often ended up as victims of the ever-vigilant Turkish snipers. The Turks had eyes on the wells, and they were not going to let their Irish enemies drink without a fight.

Doyle and the 7th Royal Dublin Fusiliers were finally relieved from the front on 11 August when they were marched down to B Beach at Suvla for rest. However, two days later they were sent north from B Beach to the Kiretch Tepe Sirt Ridge – the place that they had originally been supposed to assault. Other Irish units had managed to secure a foothold on the ridge, and as the Dubliners scaled the slopes – heading over the summit to take up positions facing north – they would have been greeted with a sight of the ridge dropping down into the expanse of the beautiful Aegean Sea.

On 15 August, young Anthony Doyle and the rest of 7th Royal Dublin Fusiliers were ordered to attack in an attempt to relieve pressure from the crescent of hills around Suvla and finally take the Kiretch Tepe Sirt Ridge. A British destroyer came as close to shore as possible, to support the advancing infantry, and pounded the hills with its heavy guns. It was, literally, an uphill struggle against a dug-in enemy who fought bitterly to drive the Irishmen back. Anthony Doyle and his Dublin comrades, along with men from the Royal Munster Fusiliers, had to bayonet the Turks off the high ground and then cling to it for all they were worth, while on the southern slopes, more men of the 10th (Irish) Division moved to attack the Turks over ground that was, according to fellow Gallipoli veteran Edward King, 'undulating, criss-crossed with gullies, thickly over-grown with scrub – a veritable maze. Every landmark, every tree, every open patch of ground had been ranged by the Turks.' Enemy artillery observers could easily pick out the British soldiers struggling inland, and they were picked off by machine-guns, keen-eyed snipers, and wave after wave of shells. This was the battle recorded by Edward King in which the 5th Royal Inniskilling Fusiliers returned with only three officers and 200 other ranks.

That night and on into the next day, the Turks counter-attacked on the Kiretch Tepe Sirt, in an attempt to drive the men of Dublin and Munster back down the ridge towards Suvla. Seventeen-year-old Anthony Doyle spent the night of 15 August 1915 fighting for his life. The Irishmen gave ground slowly, but many were cut off and surrounded. These poor souls fought on alone or in little groups, visible to their comrades down the slopes, but completely unable to break out and reach them. Many ran out of ammunition and, with bayonet, the butt of their rifle, or with their bare hands, they fought the enemy in close quarters. These encircled soldiers were all killed – blown to pieces by enemy grenades, bayoneted, or shot as they tried to defend their little bit of hillside. Those watching below were powerless to help them. At the end of the day, the Battle of Kiretch Tepe Sirt was over. Anthony Doyle was still alive, only now he knew what war was really like.

He survived the Gallipoli campaign and was redirected, along with the rest of the 7th Royal Dublin Fusiliers and 10th (Irish) Division, to Salonika in October 1915. After the Serbs begged the Allies for assistance against a new build-up of German and Austro-Hungarian forces, the Allies agreed and made moves to transport their troops through Salonika in northern Greece to Serbia. However, due to Greek political issues, and the fact that Bulgaria suddenly attacked Serbia without even a declaration of war, the Serbs were beaten before the Allies could even reach them. In a massive invasion by three enemy armies – Germany, Austria-Hungary and Bulgaria – seventeen percent of Serbia's entire population were killed. The Serb people were routed from their homeland, and only 150,000 of them made it to the refuges of Albania and the Greek island of Corfu.

It was then that the French and British turned their attention to setting up an advanced line of defence north of Lake Doiran. Serbia could not be saved, but the enemy might be stopped from

Men of the 5th Connaught Rangers manning the trench line on Kosturino Ridge during the harsh Balkan winter, 1 December 1915. Clothes went solid and the soldiers had to beat their coats to make them soft enough to put on. In some instances, the greatcoats actually shattered and fell to pieces.

advancing further. Trainload after trainload of troops chugged through the mountains of Macedonia towards the new front and here, Anthony Doyle, along with other Gallipoli veterans and new recruits alike, dug in to prepare for the inevitable – the arrival of the enemy.

At the Battle of Kosturino that soon followed in December, the Allies in Serbia were forced to retreat back towards Greece but managed to stop short of being chased all the way into Salonika. Eight miles north of the city they erected a new line of defence and as the Bulgarians dug in on the Doiran and Struma hills to the north, the French and British constructed trenches and rows of barbed wire to keep their enemies back.

What followed for Anthony Doyle was an appalling winter of bitter ice and snow. Conditions were miserable and men were forced to huddle in their dug-outs to escape the slicing winds. The Balkan winter of 1915 was harsh. Ration supplies were not always adequate and snow and frost ravaged the freezing men. Frostbite was common. Roads and tracks glazed over with ice, men could not get their footing and slipped whenever they moved. Moving carts and guns became treacherous – the wheels could not grip the ground.

But the winter did pass, only for Anthony Doyle to be wounded in early 1916 and sent home to recover. While back in Ireland on leave, he visited home with one of the friends he had joined up with, but this friend now had terrible facial scars from being caught on barbed wire. When the time came to return to duty, the friend went illegally absent and was never heard from again.

Also while on leave, Anthony had a visit from his brother Lawrence. This was around the time of the Easter Rising and all of Anthony's brothers would soon be involved in the IRA. Lawrence was hardcore anti-British; he would go on serve in IRA Intelligence, and he tried to convince Anthony to leave the army and fight the 'real war'. But Anthony was having none of it, and on 10 June 1916, he returned to the trenches in Salonika and his Dublin comrades. By now, the summer heat was worsening and Gallipoli veterans were remembering the sand, flies, and blight of last year's summer against the Turks. Soon enough, the 10th (Irish) Division was being plagued by malaria. Thousands began to fall ill.

September opened with the 7th Royal Dublin Fusiliers – now positioned along the Struma River front in Macedonia – having to mount a rescue mission

A British patrol entering a village under shellfire, during a typical small-scale operation in the Struma Valley, 1917.

across the river into Bulgarian territory, to retrieve comrades from the 6th Battalion, men who had been wounded and left behind during a previous patrol. The plan was to ultimately cross the river and establish a foothold on the far bank, and this is exactly what Anthony Doyle and his fellow soldiers did on the night of 9 September.

The following day, 31st Brigade pressed through this new British line and, as the war diary records:

> ... about 14.30 ... engaged the enemy driving him back to the line of the villages [Karadzakoj-Zir-Bala and Jenikoj] where he had a strong line of trenches from which they were unable to dislodge him. The enemy artillery from this on till dark was heavy and accurate on our trenches, the bridge, and river, but owing to it being nearly all shrapnel, a great many blind shells, and the fact that our men were well dug in we only sustained two casualties (both wounded) ... we understand that the 31st Brigade casualties amounted to about 160 killed, wounded and missing. It was

estimated by the staff that the steel helmets which were only issued the previous day saved about 40 casualties.

Two years in and the soldiers were only receiving protective headwear now. The British were forced to withdraw back across the river and continued attempts to press forward failed until, on 23 September 1916, the 7th Royal Dublin Fusiliers were ordered to try again:

Major D.E. Wilson is ordered to attack, take, and burn the village of K. Bala and retire with 250 men of the Battn. supported by flank parties of 100 6th R.D.F. on right and 50 6th R.M.F. on left, each with 2 Lewis guns ... Major Wilson moved out in two lines of 100 and 150 men at a distance of 100 yards on a front of about 350 yards at 16.00. The attack was not opposed till the advance had proceeded about 800 yards, and was about 700 yards from village when heavy rifle and machine-gun fire was opened on them from trenches in front, and on either flank of village. The line advanced by rushes for another 300 yards but were becoming enfiladed by machine-gun fire from the right which must have been well concealed as the flanking party of 6th R.D.F. do not appear to have engaged it. The F.O.O. [Forward Observation Officer] tried to get the artillery on to it but firstly their instructions that their use of shells was limited, and later the breaking of the [telephone] wires, foiled the attempt.

Major Wilson and later Capt. Fletcher having been wounded [Wilson died the following day] the command devolved on Capt. Le Cocq who, just prior to being hit himself, finding it impossible to cope with the fire directed on them from an estimated force of 100–200 men and 6 machine guns all well concealed, ordered the retirement about 17.15. ... [Battalion casualties] comprised 50% of officers and 25% of the men ... The Brigadier congratulated the Battalion on the work it accomplished in locating the positions and testing the strength of the enemy. He stated his opinion that the force was quite inadequate to take the village.

Total casualties in the 7th Royal Dublin Fusil-iers were seven missing, five officers and forty-six other ranks wounded, and seven other ranks killed. Private Anthony Doyle was one of the latter. His family later learned that as his battalion retreated towards the river, Anthony had been shot by a Bulgarian sniper and killed outright. Having enlisted at sixteen, served in Gallipoli age seventeen, he was killed at only eighteen years old. He was still not legally old enough to enlist, even though he had been fighting for two years.

It would take two months for news of his death to reach his grieving parents in Dublin, and his body now lies in the Struma Military Cemetery. Mirroring the rapidly changing political climate back in Ireland, his death split the family right down the middle and Anthony Doyle's mother had a complete falling-out with her son Lawrence – the brother who had tried to convince Anthony to join republican forces. When she died years later, Lawrence was not even informed of his mother's death until after she had been buried. Unfortunately, events like these were to happen much more frequently after the Civil War in Ireland, when brother fought against brother, and sons against fathers.

THE STRENGTH OF THE YOUNG

LUKE COOTE

While youth was also responsible for young lads naively joining up, youth was also what saved some boy soldiers from wounds that might have killed older men. While serving with the Royal Munster Fusiliers, Luke Coote, the eldest of Michael and Mary Coote's five sons, from Ennis, County Clare was shot in the

Above: The 'Widow's/Dead Man's Penny' for Private Anthony Doyle.

arms, the stomach, and the chest on 16 June 1917 – just after the Battle of Messines Ridge. Miraculously he survived. He had enlisted, only sixteen years old, had already been promoted to corporal, and remembered afterwards that he had been surrounded by bits of other people's bodies on the battlefield. After recovering from these incredible injuries, he returned home to Ireland only to apply his military skills to the republican cause and fight alongside none other than Michael Collins during the War of Independence. Luke Coote then went on to work on the railways, but after the army discovered that he was working while in receipt of disability payouts, they reduced his pension significantly. Luke Coote lived on long after he received his collection of severe wounds. He died in 1968.

ESCAPE TO WAR

EDWARD DOWLING

Some lads, of course, signed up to escape the misery of life in Ireland. One such young man, Dan Connolly from Nenagh, enlisted at age sixteen, to

Leinster Regiment cap badge: The unit could trace its heritage back to the 100th Foot (Prince Regent's County of Dublin Regiment), which was formed in 1804 to fight in the Napoleonic Wars – although the unit fought exclusively in Canada during this time. In 1818 the regiment was disbanded but later reformed in Canada in 1858, which explains the Leinster Regiment's full title – The Prince of Wales' Leinster Regiment (Royal Canadians). In 1881, the old East India Company regiment – the 109th (Bombay Infantry) Foot – was absorbed into the unit. By the time of the First World War, the Leinster Regiment recruited from Longford, Meath, Westmeath, Offaly and Laois, with the regimental depot in Crinkell near Birr. The unit motto was Ich Dien *– German for 'I serve'.*

escape the terrible poverty of the town. He survived the war, but his family never spoke of him again. He was erased from history, a black mark that was not to be remembered.

Another boy who enlisted to escape a horrible existence was Edward Dowling – Longford-born but who grew up in Athlone. After his father had died while Edward was still young, Edward's mother had sent him and his eldest siblings to Artane Industrial School in Dublin in the hopes of getting an education. She simply could not afford to keep and feed so many children in her tiny home in Athlone.

According to Joe Dowling – Edward Dowling's nephew – Edward hated Artane Industrial School. The children of abusive parents often wound up here; children who, due to what they had seen growing up, often turned out just as violent themselves. Edward would have been educated alongside those who had been sent to Artane for stealing or other petty theft – desperate street children who had perhaps stolen food and been unlucky enough to get caught. In 1914, after years of such harsh school discipline, Edward ran away and joined the army.

Aged seventeen, Edward enlisted in the 7th Leinster Regiment. He landed in France in December 1915 in preparation for the Big Push of 1916, fought throughout the Battle of the Somme, and by 1917 – now aged twenty – Edward was a lance-corporal and a recipient of the Military Medal for bravery. Then on 31 July 1917, Edward Dowling found himself advancing in the Ypres sector. This was only a few weeks after the Battle of Messines Ridge, and the Third Battle of Ypres was beginning. But on that same day, twenty-year-old school-escapee Edward Dowling was killed in action while his battalion put in an attack on German positions east of Ypres. His body now lies in Potijze Chateau Lawn Cemetery.

**

Ultimately, the war killed or maimed the young Irish volunteers the same as it did to everyone else – indiscriminately. And as for the reception that these young veterans received when they returned home, they were equally shunned and made to feel ashamed as much as every other survivor. True, they could avail of the excuse that 'I was young, I didn't know what I was doing', but men like James Manley refused to choose this path. To his dying day, he never regretted enlisting in the army. Even the boys who died were forgotten, often erased from family history. In some instances, grieving mothers were too distressed to speak of their dead sons; while some proud fathers put politics before family. Of course, the reason why the stories of so many of the underage war dead of Ireland are not preserved is the simple fact that they never lived long enough to have children who might remember the tales of their father and pass them on. The war simply cut these young men down and ended their family history on the battlefield.

However, the death of a young man in the trenches often had a particularly profound effect on one specific member of their family; the soldier's brother – especially an older brother – often took it very badly. He felt that he should have been there to protect his younger sibling. In other cases, where it was unclear if a sibling had been killed or was just missing in action, the brother often enlisted in the naive belief that he could find and retrieve the lost sibling.

This is exactly what happened in the case of the Grey brothers from Tallow, County Waterford, and although one signed up to find the other, many Irishmen enlisted with their brothers for the same varying reasons that drove individuals to the recruiting offices. Enlisting with your brothers made the idea of going to war that little bit more bearable; men felt safer with their family surrounding them, and with their trustworthy brothers at their side. Of course, with several members of the one family fighting in the same regiment, Irish parents were often cursed with two or three sad telegrams all at once.

Opposite: *A First World War period (King George V) example of a Military Medal for bravery, identical to the one that Edward Dowling would have earned. Established on 25 March 1916, this medal ranked joint third and lowest (along with the Military Cross, which was the officers' equivalent of this medal) in the bravery medal hierarchy. The other two were, in ascending order, the Distinguished Conduct Medal/Distinguished Service Order (other ranks/officers respectively), and then the Victoria Cross.*

CHAPTER 7

BROTHERS-IN-ARMS

'O God help me, help us all to bear it. O my Son, my Son. Genesis 43.14. – "If I am Bereaved of my children, I am Bereaved."'

Diary entry of John Busteed Fowler from Cork, 25 October 1916

In the case of the First World War, sibling rivalry often extended to the trenches. Some men did not want their brothers to claim all the glory and so they too enlisted. In other cases, brothers signed up together as a way of supporting and taking care of each other. There were also some pro-British Irish families who saw the war as a call to arms to serve King and Country. Then there were the families in which poverty and hunger were rampant, where the army was a decent choice on so many levels – it fed you, clothed you, housed you, paid you, trained you, and allowed you to work alongside your brothers.

With infant mortality common in Ireland at the time, death was no stranger to families, but during wartime, parents were now being faced with the violent deaths of adult sons. These parents had managed, through hard labour and personal sacrifice, to feed their sons, school them, and keep a roof over their heads. Now, a collection of little telegrams arrived to let a father and mother know that they no longer had a family.

THE 'MISSING' BROTHER

EDWARD AND WILLIAM GREY

After the Battle of Mons had been fought and the BEF had been forced to retreat, one of the Irishmen who found himself on the road to Paris was Private Eddie Grey from Barrack Street, Tallow, County Waterford. Back in December 1912, he had joined the 1st Irish Guards, aged eighteen, having previously worked as a farm labourer.

Eddie certainly took to the army with difficulty. Three months after joining his regiment, in March 1913, he was awarded ten days of confinement to barracks for being 'extremely idle on parade' and for 'not moving when spoken to by a NCO'. Before this punishment was even up, Eddie secured himself a further fourteen days' confinement for 'bad order for parade'. He then earned seven days' detention for 'breaking out of barracks when [a] defaulter between the hours of 9.45pm & 6.15am and remaining absent until apprehended by the Civil Police at Croydon at 8am', and for being 'improperly dressed' during this time.

Eddie then behaved himself for a few months before being awarded seven days' confinement to barracks in June 1913 for 'bad order for parade', eight days for 'idle and laughing on parade ... very dirty rifle ... badly folded coat for 2pm parade ... sitting down at commanding officers' orders', eight more days

Above: Irish Guards' cap badge: At the time of the First World War, the Irish Guards was the youngest Irish infantry regiment in the British Army. It had been formed in 1900 by order of Queen Victoria – who had been impressed by the bravery shown by Irishmen in the Second Boer War. Nicknamed 'Bob's Own', after their first honorary colonel – Field Marshal Lord Roberts – the Irish Guards started out the war with only one regular battalion, but raised another regular and another reserve battalion during the course of the fighting. They recruited from across the island of Ireland and their unit motto was Quis Separabit – 'who shall separate us'. In 1914, they were based in Wellington Barracks, Westminster.

for 'bad order for Bn. Pde. when for presentation of Colours', followed by seven days of detention for 'late answering defaulters' call' and 'refusing to double [time] when ordered'. Eddie always just barely completed the punishment before he somehow earned himself more and, on most occasions, he was still in the process of being punished when a new round was handed to him.

When war broke out in 1914, Eddie was stationed in Wellington Barracks. He had only been punished once so far that year; in May he had been awarded seven days of confinement to barracks for 'firing on the wrong target' during shooting practice. After sailing to France aboard a crowded ship, Eddie and his comrades then had to march through a raging thunderstorm and endure an eighteen-hour train journey. The 1ˢᵗ Irish Guards only arrived at Mons on the day of the battle – 23 August 1914.

Part of the original BEF, the 1ˢᵗ Irish Guards prepare to leave Wellington Barracks for France in August 1914. Private Eddie Grey from Tallow, County Waterford was with them.

The following day when the retreat from Mons began, Private Eddie Grey found himself heading for France with the 1ˢᵗ Irish Guards. The march was down hot and dusty roads with the Germans constantly on the tail of the British. That night, the battalion war diary records that they rested south of La Longueville:

> Arrived about 9pm & bivouaced for the night in an orchard having been 44 consecutive hours under arms without any rest.

Exhausted nights of no sleep followed, and along with frequent German harassment, the men found themselves continually marching. It looked as if the Germans would never stop coming, and it frustrated the soldiers that their officers would not let them make a stand. Soldiers' feet got so swollen that they did not dare to take their boots off in case they could not get them back on again.

Before the army, Eddie Grey's life had revolved around his family and working in the fields. Now, his world was full of machines, guns, airplanes, artillery, and bombs – all of which were designed to kill him.

The British did fight rearguard actions – at Le Cateau and Villers-Cotterêts – in an attempt to slow the Germans down. But each time they suffered terrible casualties and each time, they were forced to retreat once again. Now, with the entire BEF falling back towards Paris, the columns of exhausted, marching men were made up of mixed together groups from different units. They were usually woken up at 3am every morning to move on. There was no food getting to the troops as transport was simply not available. The occasional cup of tea had to suffice. Men grumbled and complained, and the officers quietly expressed their concerns to one another; there was no news or information reaching them, they had no idea what was going on.

Beside the soldiers on the roads trudged the refugees, the poor Belgian country people and townsfolk mingled together with the French as they travelled further south. Carts were packed high with possessions, with a cow or a goat sometimes tied to the side. Children were seen walking alone, crying in French, the soldiers unable to understand. One man saw an old Belgian being pushed along in a wheelbarrow by another old farmer.

The roads were cobbled, the heat was unbearable, and the dust was extremely uncomfortable. It got up your nose, in your eyes, in your hair, drove men mad, and only made the fact that they were retreating feel a thousand times worse. As for the marching infantry, the men's feet soon starting bleeding in their boots, they started to stagger, and as the kilometre stones kept counting down to Paris, they became more and more despondent.

However, after the Germans made some fatal tactical errors, the Allies turned and attacked at the Battle of the Marne. With the enemy in sight of Paris, the British and French managed to push the Germans back the way they had come. Eddie Grey and his comrades were heading north now, the retreat was over. The soldiers finally had their purpose again.

The Irish Guards started to pursue the Germans back towards Belgium, but the enemy managed to stay just out of their reach, until, on 8 September 1914 near Rebais, Eddie Grey and 1st Irish Guards came under fire from the German rearguard. Now, catching up with the retreating enemy:

> The Battalion was ordered to support the advanced guard [3rd Coldstream Guards], and make good the crossing of the River Petit Morin, the objective being the village of Boitron. No's 1 and 2 Coys advanced ... over the high ground and down into the valley through very thick woods. On the river line the Battalion reinforced the 3rd Coldstream Guards, but the advance was checked by heavy infantry and machine-gun fire. The 3rd Coldstream Guards and 2 Coys Irish Guards were ordered back to the high ground, and the guns were ordered to shell the river valley and the village of Boitron. When the position had been well searched by the artillery, the Brigade was ordered to attack ... the enemy were now seen retiring, and the Battalion crossed the bridge at Le Gravier and occupied Boitron.

After reorganising, the pursuit was continued, but the Irish Guards soon came under renewed German fire – from a wood on their left flank. The battalion charged the wood and destroyed a German machine-gun company of six guns that had remained behind to try and slow the British advance. But this was not the worst of the day's events. The battalion was soon being shelled, but there were no enemy in sight. Then the Irishmen realised they were being targeted by their own artillery. The mistake was soon corrected, but, over the course of the war, events like these would happen too regularly for comfort.

The following days were spent reorganising, handing over prisoners, evacuating the wounded, and pursuing the Germans back towards Belgium. The BEF had gone from being an army in retreat, to an army on the advance.

On 12 September 1914, having survived the Battle of Mons, the retreat from Mons, Villers-Cotterêts, and the Battle of the Marne, Private Edward Grey from Tallow, County Waterford was killed in action near Courcelles. Aged twenty-two, exactly how he died is not known and his body was never found. With no known grave, his name is recorded on the La Ferte Sous Jouarre Memorial. Within days, the Germans managed to construct a defensive line along the River Aisne that the British could not penetrate, and the horrors of trench warfare began.

Back in Tallow, however, Eddie Grey's family soon received a telegram that he was simply missing. Since this telegram does not survive, we do not know the exact wording, but the telegram instilled some hope that Eddie might still be alive. And so, in a tragic and needless move to try and find his lost older brother, William Grey enlisted in the army at Youghal, County Cork on 18 May 1916. He asked to be posted to the 1st Irish Guards, in the hope of finding out what happened to Eddie.

William Grey, aged twenty-two, arrived into the war on 23 December 1916, two days before Christmas. The 1st Irish Guards were in the Somme sector – the battle there having quietened down for the winter. Irish Guardsmen were chewing on meagre icy bits of food, biting down on bread that had to be sawed through because it was so frozen, while all around them, the cold was so intense that their heating stoves often simply went out from the drop in temperature. At the front, machinery and vehicles seized up from the ice, while boots and clothes went so rigid from the frost that they had to be pummelled to make them pliable enough to put on.

Ultimately, William Grey went on to participate in the British pursuit of the Germans on the Somme – when the enemy started to withdraw to the Hindenburg Line in early 1917. He was then redirected to Belgium in preparation for the Third Battle of Ypres. However, after weeks of intense training, William

Grey was hit in the right arm by a lump of shell while withdrawing from the front under heavy fire on 15 July 1917. He was evacuated to hospital in Rouen, but was then shipped back to England to undergo surgery. The shrapnel was successfully removed, but so was a length of bone. A year later, on 3 July 1918, William was discharged from the army. As his granddaughter, Assumpta Murphy, recalls, he had enlisted in the innocent hope of finding his 'missing' brother. Now, he was a casualty himself, and he had still not learned what had happened to Eddie.

William Grey suffered terribly after the war. He returned home, and the fact that he had never managed to find out what had happened to Eddie tore him apart. His wife often found him sitting in a corner, crying and shaking, saying 'Where is Eddie? What happened to him? Is he still alive?' Years turned into decades and still William wanted to know what had happened to his brother. Sometimes, his wife would even wake up in bed at night to find William missing. She would find him under the bed, wide-eyed and shivering, clutching a brush as though he was clinging to his rifle in a shell hole.

William Grey suffered from shellshock for the rest of his life, and was known to many as the Tallow postman. He died, never knowing what had happened to his brother, and this led his family to follow Eddie Grey's trail many years later. They managed to trace him to the battlefields of France, and find his name engraved on the La Ferte Sous Jouarre Memorial. They learned that he had died on 12 September 1914, long before William had even joined the army.

IN SEARCH OF JUSTICE

CORNELIUS AND DANIEL CORKERY

A similar story is that of the Corkery brothers. On 23 November 1914, Private Cornelius Corkery of the 1ˢᵗ Connaught Rangers – a pre-war regular from West End, Millstreet, County Cork – was killed at Ypres. He has no known grave and today is commemorated on the Le Touret Memorial. Nearly one year later on 4 September 1915, his seventeen-year-old brother Daniel was aboard the

Hesperian on his way to Canada. Daniel was planning to emigrate when suddenly the *Hesperian* was torpedoed by *U20* off Fastnet Rock – the same German submarine that had sunk the *Lusitania* four months previously. Daniel Corkery survived the tragedy, and as soon as he was able, he lied about his age and enlisted – perhaps to seek revenge for both his brother and the *Hesperian*. However, on 21 March 1918 – day one of the German Spring Offensive – Daniel was serving in the 2nd Royal Munster Fusiliers when they were overrun by enemy stormtroopers. Daniel was killed, aged twenty, and today his body lies in Tincourt New British Cemetery.

SOLDIERS OF THE COMMONWEALTH

GEORGE, HUGH, ISAAC AND WILLIAM STEWART

While Eddie and William Grey and Cornelius and Daniel Corkery did not serve at the same time, a set of brothers that did were the Stewarts – a Presbyterian family from Ballyness, Dungiven, County Derry. There were four brothers in all; they were well educated, and each one had named their mother – Margaret Stewart – as their next-of-kin. However, they did not all serve in the same army.

In 1915, Private George Stewart entered the war. He was twenty-seven years old at this point and had enlisted in September 1914, right after the outbreak of war. George had emigrated to Canada in May 1913 to work as a clerk, and since Canada had declared war on Germany as soon as Britain had, George felt it was his duty to enlist. He was posted to 14th Battalion (Quebec Regiment), Canadian Expeditionary Force, and set foot on French soil on 15 February 1915.

On 21 May 1915, he took part in an attack on the infamous Vimy Ridge, and in early 1916, George spent a few weeks serving as an officer's batman at a training school. He then returned to the front, and while the build up continued in the Somme sector for this year's Big Push, the 14th CEF was still centred on Ypres.

The Stewart family from Ballyness, Dungiven, County Derry. (Hugh Stewart, back row, first from left; William Stewart, back row, second from right; George Stewart, back row, first from right; Isaac Stewart, front row, first from left; Margaret Alice Stewart, front row, first from right).

Then, on 2 June 1916, the Germans launched an assault on Tor Top Ridge. The British front line was destroyed. The following day, the Allies prepared to mount a counter-attack. Along with his Canadian comrades, George Stewart found himself struggling through the trenches past files of wounded from the previous day's attack. He was due to take part in the counter offensive. At 07.10am, the Allies rushed out of their positions to drive the Germans back and recapture lost territory. However, within six hours, the attack had failed, and somewhere on the battlefield lay George Stewart's body. He was twenty-eight years old. His body was never recovered, and today his name is commemorated on the Menin Gate Memorial in Ypres.

In his will, he left everything to his mother, and she soon received just under £190 from George's solicitors. Although a decent sum of money in 1916, it must have done nothing to relieve Margaret Stewart's grief.

Meanwhile on the Somme, only a couple of weeks later, George Stewart's younger brother Isaac went into action. Isaac, a former bank clerk and the only one of the four brothers to actually fight in the British Army, fought with the 14th Royal Irish Rifles as part of the 36th (Ulster Division) on 1 July 1916. He was twenty-six years old, had enlisted in Belfast on 12 September 1914, and had been on the Somme since 5 October 1915. In the bloody fighting during which the Ulstermen captured the Schwaben Redoubt, Isaac Stewart was shot in the right hand and badly wounded. He survived the battle and was evacuated, but the injury never allowed him to serve at the front again. He spent the rest of the war in various reserve battalions of the Royal Irish Rifles, and went on to become a bank manager in civilian life. He died in 1968.

The youngest Stewart brother entered the war not long after Isaac left it. On 26 July 1916, Private Hugh Stewart arrived on the Somme. Like his late brother George, Hugh had emigrated to Canada before the war and had enlisted in June 1915 while working as a clerk for the Canadian Bank of Commerce. He served with the 31st Battalion (Alberta Regiment), CEF but was badly wounded and evacuated within two months. On 26 September 1916, Hugh was hit in the left knee and right thigh by lumps of shrapnel. The thigh wound was so bad that it had to be cleaned by drawing rags soaked in carbolic acid straight through the hole from one side to the other, and as for the knee, even after it healed Hugh could never flex it properly again. The Canadian Army gave him a desk job and he served out the rest of the war in England. He finished the war as an acting staff-sergeant and soon returned to Canada where he went on to become a bank manager. However, it was the eldest of the four Stewart brothers who arguably travelled the most, rose in rank the most, and suffered the most.

On 21 August 1915, Private William Stewart arrived on the Gallipoli peninsula. However, he was not serving with the British, he was serving with the Australians. Back in September 1912, twenty-six-year-old William went to work in Sydney, Australia, having completed an apprenticeship as a draper with Marshall and Snellgrove of London. In March 1915 he enlisted in the 19th Battalion Australian Imperial Force and sailed from Sydney with his battalion on 25 June, landing at Alexandria in Egypt on 23 July. Within a month he found himself in Gallipoli.

At this stage, the campaign against the Turks was winding down as attempt after attempt to press inland had failed. William would have come ashore at ANZAC Cove, the famous beach where the AIF had landed and sprung into action. But it looked as though all of that effort, and all of the suffering and fighting and dying had been for nothing.

By September 1915, William Stewart was promoted to lance-corporal and found himself defending Pope's Hill. He had already encountered the ferocity of the Turks – his position had been shelled, bombed, mined, machine-gunned and charged several times. Many of his Australian comrades had been killed, but when the order was given to withdraw from Gallipoli, William was still alive.

His unit was redirected to the Western Front and on 1 August 1916, by then a sergeant, William Stewart entered the trenches below Pozières on the Somme. Pozières was the highest point on the Somme battlefield and capturing the high ground is a staple of military strategy. Previous attacks on Pozières by the British had failed. The town had been flattened by repeated artillery barrages, but on 23 July – after a severe artillery pounding and with help from phosgene gas (deadlier than chlorine gas, with no colour and only a trace odour) – Australian soldiers of the 1st Division had secured the German trenches to the south of the town, forcing the enemy to withdraw to the north and the east. But the Germans had been determined to retake their lost positions. They had pummelled the Australian lines with several days' shellfire and continually counter-attacked across no-man's-land, while the Australians had cut them down with machine guns and laid waste to advancing enemy soldiers with artillery. When Sergeant William Stewart arrived on 1 August, Pozières Ridge was a blasted landscape of craters, dotted with corpses, German dugouts and machine-gun emplacements. Furthermore, his comrades in the 1st Australian Division had just suffered over 5,000 casualties in just under ten days and 2nd Division another 3,500 killed and wounded.

The Australians ultimately managed to capture Pozières, but a subsequent assault at night to capture the German positions north and east of the village had ended in confusion and failure. Therefore, another attack was planned to take place at dusk on 2 August, so that the attacking infantry could actually see what they were doing. But for this attack, new trenches would have to be dug for the Australian soldiers to hide in during the day before going over the top at dusk. William Stewart suddenly found himself digging. However, every time the Germans heard the work parties shovelling away, they called down heavy thunderous barrages on the Australians and so, on 2 August, the trenches were still nowhere near ready. It was not until dusk on 4 August that they were finally considered acceptable. Sergeant William Stewart led his men into position and got ready for the sun to set.

The infantry charged the German positions north and east of Pozières on the Pozèries Ridge at dusk as planned. The attack was a remarkable success and the Australians advanced well beyond their target objectives. In the distance were the green fields of untouched open country. But like before, the Germans were not about to let this strategic high ground fall into Allied hands. In their newly-captured trenches, William Stewart and 19th AIF tried to make themselves as small as possible when the enemy started shelling them from every direction on 5 August. The ground was churned and men were buried alive by earth and shellfire. But the line had to be held and so they stood firm. The following day, the Germans launched a counter-attack in an attempt to push back the exhausted Australians, but they were cut down by machine guns and forced to withdraw. Finally, William Stewart was relieved from Pozières on 6 August, the ridge exploding in a terrific hail of shells as he marched away. He bivouaced at Tara Hill near Albert and got what rest he could. The next day, the Germans counter-attacked again on Pozières and drove the Australians back, but the dogged Australians mounted a fierce resistance – severe hand-to-hand fighting took place and the Germans were bayoneted back the way they came. Once again, Pozières was secured, but at a cost of nearly 7,000 casualties in the Australian 2nd Division.

Two weeks later, on 19 August 1916, when 19th AIF re-entered the trenches around Pozières, William Stewart was not with them. In fact, he had been sent away from his battalion for training in order to receive a battlefield commission. William had been selected to become an officer, and so when he returned to the fight later in the year, he was now Second-Lieutenant William Stewart.

On 14 November, with the harsh winter weather starting to freeze the Somme solid, Second-Lieutenant William Stewart found himself standing in a trench north of Flers. He was the last of his brothers left in the war. George was dead, and Isaac and Hugh had been evacuated due to severe injury. The statistics were not looking good.

Along with other units, 19th AIF had been tasked with assaulting a German-held position known as 'The Maze' and the battalion had a complement of 451 men with which to mount the attack. At 7am in the morning, William found himself waiting to scramble over the top and lead his men in the advance. But suddenly, a German shell exploded near his position, killing him instantly. He was only thirty years old.

His limp body dropped to the ground; his comrades were ordered to move to another section of trench and after the battle they were unable to locate where William Stewart had fallen. Out of 451 soldiers, William was one of 381 men killed or wounded in 19th AIF on 14 November 1916. Four days later, the Battle of the Somme officially came to an end. He had survived Gallipoli and Pozières, the two great graveyards of ANZAC soldiers, but never survived the war. Today, his name is commemorated on the Villers-Bretonneux Memorial.

And so, back home in Derry, Margaret Stewart had now lost two sons to the war – a conflict which had badly wounded her two remaining boys. However, in this family, it was not only Margaret Stewart's sons who had joined the war effort, but her daughter as well. Margaret Alice Stewart, a Trinity College Dublin graduate, joined the Women's Royal Naval Service and was successful in receiving an officer's commission. She worked in the department's coding section, and after she was demobilised in 1919, she married and settled in England. While still serving, two stained-glass windows were installed in Dungiven Presbyterian church as memorials to those who had served in the First World War and Margaret was invited to unveil one of the two brass plaques listing the names of those who served and those who died. This she did, wearing her WRNS uniform – one of the plaques bearing the names of her two dead brothers.

FOR KING AND COUNTRY

DICK, BILL, GERALD AND FRANK FOWLER

From the far end of the country, the four Fowler brothers of Cork also fought together. They shared a lot in common with the Stewarts mentioned above. They were all former bank clerks, and three of the four had emigrated to Canada before the war. Their progress through the war was chronicled by their father – John Busteed Fowler, a stockbroker from Sidneyville, Bellview Park, Cork – in his diary, and it records that by 1914, his sons Dick, Bill and Gerald were all working as clerks in Canadian banks, while the youngest, Frank, was still at school in Ireland.

On 4 August 1914, John Fowler wrote a short entry in his diary: 'War declared against Germany, 11pm.'

Far away in Canada, it did not take his three sons long to enlist. Dick went straight to his local recruiting office in Ottawa and enlisted on 20 August. He was twenty-three years old, the eldest of John Fowler's sons, and had previously served in the Officer Training Corps back in Ireland. Bill and Gerald signed up

Irishmen were not just recruited for the British Army. Here is a Canadian Army poster calling on Irishmen to enlist in an Irish-Canadian regiment.

together on 23 September at Moosejaw. Bill was twenty-one and Gerald was nineteen. The youngest of the three, Gerald also had the most prior military experience. Like Dick, he was a former member of the Officer Training Corps, but he had also been serving in the 60th Canadian Rifles since arriving in Canada.

The three brothers were all posted to various regiments and on 4 October 1914, as the first waves of the Canadian Expeditionary Force were sailing from Gaspe Bay to Plymouth – a convoy of thirty-two liners and six battleships full of men, horses, and artillery – the Fowler brothers from Cork found themselves heading back across the Atlantic.

All three sons managed to visit their father at the end of October, before returning to their camps in England. Bill and Gerald were stationed on Salisbury Plain and Dick was in Winchester. Then on 28 November, they all received word that Dick's regiment was due to depart for France. Bill and Gerald managed to get down to Winchester to spend some time with their brother, and, on 20 December 1914, Dick sailed away to the war.

He went straight into billets in a small French village, fifteen miles behind the front line at Ypres, where he spent Christmas and New Year's. He wrote a letter to his father on New Year's Day saying that the men were all delighted at being treated to plum pudding, and that everyone was in good health and in the best of spirits. This was not true for long, for within a few days, Dick Fowler was suffering from severe diarrhoea and was starting to pass blood. The newly-arrived Canadians were learning about all the delights of the Western Front, including dysentery. Dick was carried off to hospital and had to remain there for the next two weeks. By 16 January 1915, however, he was on his way back to the trenches.

On 10 February 1915, it was Gerald's turn to join the front. Promoted to lance-corporal, he travelled to France and in mid-March, he wrote to his father, saying that he had undergone his 'baptism of fire', alluding to his first taste of the war. But he said no more than that.

Bill was the last of the three Fowler brothers to depart for France, and left his station at Lark Hill for the Base Training Depot, in preparation for embarking. He entered the war on 12 March 1915. Within a week of landing in France, Bill was posted to 7th Battalion (1st British Columbia Regiment) CEF and found himself in the trenches. On 14 April, he met up with his brother Dick at

Vlarmertinge for a few hours, before returning to the front.

And so on the night of 24 April, two days after his unit had been called on to help fill the gap caused by the first Western Front German gas attack, Bill was trying to get some sleep. It had been an exhausting couple of days, and that morning, after the Canadian Division had moved to a position west of St Julien, the Germans had launched another gas attack. To try and negate the effects of the gas, soldiers had been told to urinate on their handkerchiefs and then hold them to their noses.

That night, 24 April 1915, while trying to rest in his dugout, Bill Fowler was killed. He was twenty-one years old. A German shell had slammed into his position.

On 12 May, his father, John Fowler, learned of Bill's death and wrote in his diary:

> O God help me to bear it. Oh what an outburst of grief was here today when we read this letter and realised that dear good affectionate Bill was gone, and yet he died to save Belgium, and for his King, his country and his God – He sleeps in Jesus.

Above this entry in John Fowler's diary was another of loss and tragedy. On 7 May, he recorded:

> S.S. *Lusitania* sunk off Kinsale by German submarine. 1400 lives lost. Dreadful scene in town.

Three days later, just before hearing of his own son's death, John Fowler met three children in Cork – they had lost their father, mother, and two brothers in the sinking.

Opposite: *Excerpts from the diary of John Busteed Fowler from Cork, concerning the death of his son Bill in the trenches and the wounding of his son Gerald, 1915.*

1915

May 7   S.S. Lusitania sunk off Kinsale by German Submarine
         1400 lives lost — Dreadful scenes in Queenstown.

10   Went to Queenstown & spent some hours with Tommy & Mrs
         Chater & 3 little Mainwarings — Mollie Bessie & Beddy
         who lost a father mother & two brothers in Lusitania.

12   A letter from Gerald in which he tells us of
         dear dear Bill's noble death — O God help
         me to bear it —   It was on 27th April.
         Oh what what an outburst of grief was here today
         when we read this letter & realize that dear good
         affectionate Bill was gone, & yet he died to save
         Belgium, & for his King, his country and his
         God. —   He sleeps in Jesus.

18th   Dick writes —   " I am glad to know so he never
         " knew what hit him — death must have been
         " instantaneous —   Sleeping peacefully in his 'dug out'
         " — a shell — and still he sleeps — Dear old Bill,
         " how we shall all miss him; but, oh, how proud
         " we all are of him.   He gave his life fighting
         " for the right — doing his duty to his King, his

1915

" Country & his God!"
May 22nd   About 3. am this morng I opened my eyes &
         distinctly saw our dear Bill standg at the side of
         my bed. He looked so well & happy, & so nice, &
         I said out loud, "Oh Bill is that you? My dear
         dear Son"   And then he disappeared!

John Fowler soon received a letter from Dick, saying:

> I am glad to say he [Bill] never knew what hit him. Death must have been instantaneous – sleeping peacefully in his dug out – a shell – and still he sleeps.

Another letter followed from a man named Bob Crouch – a twenty-four-year-old former carpenter from Ottawa – who had been in Bill's battalion when Bill had died. Bob wrote:

> I was right there when it happened, and I buried the poor boy myself. Hadn't time to do very much, but did all I could for the bullets were flying all round us. But I wrapped him in a blanket first, I am sure he will be all right, and put a cross up. I do not like having to tell you about it, for we thought a lot of one another. He did not suffer at all. Well, I know he is in the presence of God and we will meet again.

Bill's personal possessions were also soon sent to his father in Cork. Sadly, they arrived on what would have been Bill's twenty-second birthday. Bill Fowler's grave was later lost. Today, his name is commemorated on the Menin Gate Memorial in Ypres.

A month later at Festubert, Gerald Fowler was involved in an attack. But again, as in the previous battles of 1915, shell shortages were a serious problem. During the Battle of Festubert, British batteries often completely ran out of ammunition. Yet still the infantry had to go on in, and Gerald Fowler advanced as ordered. However, while advancing up a pummelled communication trench, struggling to reach the front, a shell detonated to Gerald Fowler's right and a large chunk of shell fragment ripped through his jaw. He was knocked unconscious and rushed to a dressing station. Gerald was alive, but part of his face had been destroyed. He was only one month away from his twentieth birthday. In the space of two months, John Fowler in Cork had suffered the death of one son and the disfigurement of another.

With massive trauma to his jaw, Lance-Corporal Gerald Fowler was initially brought to Wimereux Anglo-American Hospital, where he was operated on three times to remove shrapnel, pieces of bone and teeth. Transferred to a dental surgeon in London, Gerald had another operation to remove more teeth. It quickly became clear that he would need major surgery to help repair his face. Along with the horrific jaw injury, there was damage to the bone surrounding his right eye. Once the teeth and bone fragments were removed, the fractures to what was left of his jaw necessitated a splint to keep his upper and lower jaws together while they healed. While this was installed, he could not open his mouth or eat solid food.

Next, along with chronic rhinitis – large quantities of mucus running from a nasal inflammation – there was fluid discharge from the various wounds that had to be dealt with, and when a piece of shell fragment in his nose started to cause him breathing difficulties, he had to be operated on again. His nose was effectively scalped, with the shell fragment and bits of damaged nasal bone

Canadian Army medical document outlining the injuries sustained by Lance-Corporal Gerald Fowler.

being removed to help his breathing. When the splint was finally removed in December 1915, Gerald was only able to open his mouth about a half an inch. And by the time he was discharged from hospital on 30 March 1916, he had been in hospital for ten months, been operated on six times in total, and now had severe difficulty chewing. Although the open wounds had healed, Gerald Fowler was still in pain and terribly scarred.

He was granted a furlough in April 1916 and travelled home to see his father in Cork. A week later and Gerald returned to London. He was no longer considered fit to serve as a combat infantryman, but his prior experience as a bank clerk secured him a role in the Canadian Pay and Records Office. He stayed in this role for the rest of the war, although he was always in and out of hospital. On one occasion in March 1917, he required treatment for a case of scabies, having failed to cure himself with sulphur baths. Assigned to permanent base duty because of his injuries, he was soon promoted from acting corporal to acting sergeant. Unfortunately, he reverted all the way back down to lance-corporal by the time the war ended. When he was finally discharged, he chose to stay in England rather than return to Canada. He got work with the Canadian Bank of Commerce branch in Lombard Street, London and did part-time work for the Canadian ex-Forces Association. Gerald Fowler later married, had a son and a daughter, and died age seventy-seven in March 1973.

Meanwhile, back in October 1915, Dick Fowler was still in the war when he suffered another attack of dysentery while stationed in the trenches at Bray on the Somme. He had had terrible diarrhoea back in January for two weeks, but the condition had not troubled him since. Now it was back and Dick had to be stretchered to hospital in Rouen. He found it hard to breathe, was coughing a lot, and his face and ankles were swollen. Dick remained in Rouen for over two weeks and was soon diagnosed with nephritis, caused by exposure and a subsequent infection. The conditions in the trenches were definitely bad. Dick had just recently lost two teeth when they broke as he bit down on a biscuit. Evacuated back to England, he had to stay in hospital for over a month until there was no longer any blood in his urine. Even then, he was still suffering from breathing difficulties and headaches when he was discharged, and so it was decided that he was unfit to return to France.

Like his brother Gerald, Dick was assigned to permanent base duty and, again like his brother, Dick's former job as a bank clerk was to prove very useful. As soon as he started his new office job with the Canadian Army medical office in London, Dick was finding himself on the promotions list every couple of months. He was quickly promoted to lance-corporal, and when he was promoted to corporal, he was made acting sergeant the same day. Granted permission to marry in April 1916, in February 1917 he was again admitted to hospital with rubella, but by the end of the year he was acting company quartermaster sergeant. Unlike Gerald, Dick never reverted to a lower rank, and when the war finally ended he was on a superintending clerk's pay with the rank of regimental sergeant major (warrant officer class one). However, Dick did decide to go back to Canada, and in October 1919, he sailed with his wife and infant son from Liverpool to Quebec, returning to his job in the Canadian Bank of Commerce. Cork-born Dick Fowler lived out the rest of his life in Canada. He died in 1968, aged seventy-seven.

1916 saw the fourth and last Fowler brother enter the war. Having lost one

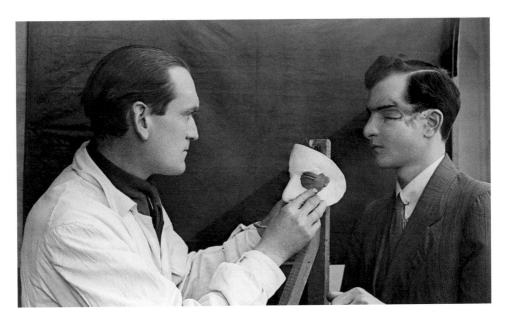

Captain Francis Derwent Wood RA puts the finishing touches to a cosmetic plate and compares it to the face of the disfigured patient, for whom the plate is being made. Derwent Wood was a sculptor who had joined the Royal Army Medical Corps. However, the facial injuries suffered by Lance-Corporal Gerald Fowler from Cork were far more severe that those of the patient pictured.

brother during the Second Battle of Ypres in 1915, and with another brother terribly facially disfigured from a shell burst – both of which had served in the Canadian Expeditionary Force – Frank Fowler, the youngest of all the Fowler brothers and the only one who had not emigrated to Canada, succeeded in being appointed as a second-lieutenant to the 3rd (Reserve) Leinster Regiment stationed in Cork on 5 November 1915. He started his training eight days later.

Frank stayed in barracks in Cork until March 1916 when he moved to Kilworth Camp. If he remained with a reserve battalion, he would not be sent overseas, but all this changed when it was decided that he should be attached to a battalion in the field, and, soon enough, Frank Fowler was sent to England in preparation for joining his new unit in France. On 20 July 1916, nineteen days after the start of the Battle of the Somme, he met with his two surviving brothers for dinner in London – Gerald, who had had half his jaw blown away, and Dick, who had also fought at the Second Battle of Ypres but who had been invalided out of the Canadian Army due to severe recurring bouts of dysentery. After dinner, Frank stood up, said goodbye to his brothers, and left to catch the boat to France. He landed at Boulogne later that day and went into base at Étaples. That day, his father wrote:

> May God preserve him in this awful war and may he trust in the living God who alone is able to keep him from harm.

Frank was posted to the 2nd Royal Irish Rifles and joined them on 24 July 1916 at 8pm. The battalion had just relieved the 1st Royal Inniskilling Fusiliers in the trenches at Mailly-Maillet Wood on the Somme. That night, the war wasted no time in introducing itself to Frank Fowler. He soon wrote a letter to his father describing how it was 'simply hell last night'. The newly-arrived second-lieutenant was forced to hunker down with the rest of his comrades for a troubled night of shellfire and explosions. But the next morning he was still alive, and a 4lb cake and some chocolate soon arrived from his father.

Within a month, Second-Lieutenant Frank Fowler was starting to get into the routine of trench life. He made regular inspections of the trenches and defences, detailing his men to fix and repair anything that needed attention.

He reported frequently to his superiors, and when the 2nd Royal Irish Rifles were moved to camps at Acheux and Hédauville in mid-August, he organised training and parades for his men.

Then on 19 August, the day after the Battle of Delville Wood, the battalion:

> ... marched to dugouts at Northern Bluff, relieving 7th West Riding Rgt. ... The Battalion had to provide numerous carrying and working parties ... In dugouts at Northern Bluff, in early morning, [the] following casualties were suffered by one of the fatigue parties: 2/Lt. F.R. Fowler ... wounded. Other ranks 3 wounded. [Fowler] remained at duty.

Six days later, on 25 August 1916, the army sent Frank's father, John Fowler, a telegram stating:

> 2/Lieut. FR Fowler ... was wounded 20th August but remained at duty.

John Fowler soon received a letter from Frank clarifying everything and was relieved to hear that his son was safe, but this near miss made him start to worry. *'Oh God preserve him,'* he wrote.

On the day that Frank received his wound, 20 August, the German artillery had opened fire at 9pm on the Bluff and the Ancre valley below

Second-Lieutenant Francis 'Frank' Fowler from Cork, 1916. Only eighteen years old, Frank had previously been a cadet while attending the Cork Grammar School, and he had only finished his schooling in 1914. Like his brothers, he also had some experience working in banking.

with artillery. High explosives and shrapnel shells began detonating all around. Although the enemy barrage lasted only an hour and a half, over 450 men of the 2nd Royal Irish Rifles spent the rest of the night frantically digging and repairing the damage, and over the following few days, these working parties continued, with the Germans frequently shelling the battalion's position. Sometimes the shells would fall into the Ancre River and rumbling geysers of water would erupt into the air.

After the Battle of Pozières Ridge and the subsequent action around Mouquet Farm in early September 1916, Second-Lieutenant Frank Fowler from Cork and the 2nd Royal Irish Rifles found themselves in reserve positions on 8 October. The companies were spread out between Mouquet Farm, Pozières cemetery and other trench positions, and the weather was miserably wet. This did not change the fact that working parties were still needed, and that these men had to operate in mud-logged positions that were intermittently shelled by the enemy. The mud stuck to their uniforms, to their weapons, to their packs and equipment. It made the soldiers feel like they weighed a ton, and it made walking exhausting and painful.

The battalion was still in reserve during the capture of Stuff Redoubt on 9 October, but Frank Fowler and his comrades moved forward into the trenches again on 13 October. The 2nd Royal Irish Rifles were not engaged in any major operations, and to the men, it seemed like they were being perpetually ordered to do three things: carry, work, and suffer enemy shelling. The mood in the battalion was certainly not high-spirited, and still every day, men were being killed and wounded. Sometimes they were even ordered to crawl out into no-man's-land and cut the enemy wire.

Then on 16 October, British artillery started bombarding the German lines. The bombardment continued on into the following day, and while Frank and his battalion were happy that the enemy was finally being shelled for a change, they were less than happy at what the extremely wet weather was doing to their trenches. Winter was now arriving on the Somme and all that the soldiers had built and prepared seemed to be melting all around them. The rainwater soaked into everything, and the sides of the trenches collapsed. The soldiers were tired of working, tired of being used as German target practice. Mental exhaustion started to set in. Life was monotonously dangerous and repetitive.

But officers like Frank Fowler had to keep their troops going; the working and the carrying simply had to be done.

The next day, 18 October, the 2nd Royal Irish Rifles received orders to prepare to assault the German positions across no-man's-land. The reason for the long British barrage was suddenly made clear. An attack had been planned. The war diary records that the battalion started off the day:

> In trenches. Wet weather. Usual shelling continued. The front line was slightly reorganised as an assault from our lines (Hessian trench) on to the German line (Regina trench) was intended to take place on the morrow. In consequence the battalion extended to the west, taking over almost 200 [yards] more of the line. 2/Lt F.R. Fowler, 3/Leinster Rgt. attached 2/R.I. Rifles was killed while reconnoitring the new part of the line to be taken over. Casualties: O.R. [Other Ranks] 1 wounded.

A week later on 25 October 1916, Frank's father received another telegram from the army. We 'deeply regret to inform you that Second Lieutenant F.R. Fowler, Leinster Regt., was killed in action 18th October. The Army Council express their sympathy.'

John Fowler wrote in his diary that day:

> O God help me, help us all to bear it. O my Son, My Son.
> Genesis 43.14. – 'If I am Bereaved of my children, I am Bereaved.' His [Frank's] last letter was dated 17 Oct, the day before he fell, and in it he wrote. 'Any more of the children's birthdays at hand? I would not like to pass them by. Remember me to H. Eason, Mrs. Dent and W. Farrel ... I am in the best of health.'

This was the second son that John Fowler had lost to the war. On 23 November 1916 he received a letter from a Lieutenant George Jones, a friend of Frank's, who wrote that:

> When your son met his death he was, as usual, doing his duty bravely and cheerfully. He was inspecting trenches with another Officer who was some distance in

front when he was hit by a shell and unfortunately killed. Through his death I have lost one of the very few friends I ever had, and feel his loss so keenly that I do not like to think about it. Still I trust we shall meet again.

A former school friend of Frank's, PR Mack, also wrote to John Fowler:

I was indeed greatly grieved to hear that Frank had been killed. He was always such a splendid fellow in every way, and I feel that I have lost one of the very best friends of my schoolboy days.

Then, on 18 November, a pen and a book belonging to Frank were sent home to Cork – they were the only possessions of his son's that John Fowler received from the army, suggesting that Frank had taken a direct hit from the shell that killed him. Normally, items like clothing, a watch, or other items that an officer or soldier kept on his person would be sent home, but there was nothing but the pen and book left to post.

Frank Fowler had only been nineteen years old. Today, his name is recorded on the Thiepval Memorial on the Somme. Like Margaret Stewart in Derry, John Fowler in Cork had two sons killed and two sons badly wounded. Similarly, three of his four boys had fought in the army of another country, and while three had served in the ranks, one had been an officer, exactly like in the case of the Stewarts. Both families also had strong links to Canadian banking. These similarities are bizarre, but, at the end of the day, all they really equate to is that, by 1916, two families at either ends of Ireland were suffering the exact same grief.

EVERY SINGLE ONE

JOHN, HUGH AND JAMES SHINE

From Abbeyside, Dungarvan, County Waterford, Colonel James Shine was fifty-five when war broke out. He was a surgeon in the Royal Army Medical Corps, and was already a veteran of both the Third Burmese War (1885) and

Surgeons tending wounded at a dressing station near Hill 60 in the Ypres Salient,
August 1917. Colonel James Shine from Dungarvan, County Waterford would have
found himself working in similar conditions.

the Boer War. He was also a Companion of the Order of the Bath. Colonel
Shine, of all men, knew what war really meant, and he ended up spending most
of the First World War in the Ypres sector, treating horrendous wounds, ampu-
tating shattered arms and legs, removing lumps of shrapnel from bone, standing for hours on blood-stained floors, and watching young men die by the
thousand.

However, on 25 August 1914, two days after the Battle of Mons, his twenty-
five year old son – Second-Lieutenant John Shine of the 2nd Royal Irish Regiment – was killed in action. Today he is buried in Mons (Bergen) Communal
Cemetery. The following year, another son, Second-Lieutenant Hugh Shine of
the 1st Royal Irish Fusiliers, was killed in action on 25 May 1915. He has no
known grave and is commemorated on the Menin Gate Memorial in Ypres.
Finally, on 16 August 1917, just after the start of the Third Battle of Ypres –
during the disastrous assault on Frezenberg Ridge by the 16th (Irish) Division –
Colonel Shine's last surviving son, Captain James Shine of the 9th Royal Dublin
Fusiliers, died aged twenty-six. Also with no known grave, he is commemorated on the Tyne Cot memorial. When Colonel James Shine returned home

to Dungarvan after the war, now aged fifty-nine, he left every single one of his children behind him.

JEREMIAH, PATRICK, EDWARD AND RICHARD LONERGAN

Ordinary working-class families had to suffer this pain as well. In 1914, John and Mary Lonergan were the parents of four sons from Fethard, County Tipperary. Then, on 10 January 1915, the first of successive tragedies occurred. On that day, their son – Private Jeremiah Longeran of the 1st Irish Guards – was killed in action. Today he lies buried in Rue-des-Berceaux Military Cemetery, Richebourg-L'Avoue. Just over two months later, forty-year-old Private Patrick Lonergan of the 1st Royal Irish Regiment – a veteran soldier who had previously served on the northwest frontier of India in 1897–98, and who was married and living on Thomas Street in Clonmel – was killed on 16 March. With no known grave, his name is commemorated on the Menin Gate Memorial in Ypres. Just over three weeks later, Private Edward Longergan – 1st Irish Guards – was killed on 1 April. He is buried in Guards Cemetery, Windy Corner, Cuinchy. Three brothers in the space of four months, but then, on 7 June 1917 – the day of the Battle of Messines Ridge – Private Richard Lonergan of the 6th Royal Irish Regiment was killed in action. Today he lies buried in Irish House Cemetery. By 1917 – three short years – John and Mary Lonergan no longer had any sons.

'MICK AND DICK'

MICHAEL AND RICHARD FLYNN

On 22 March 1918 – day two of the German Spring Offensive – it was the turn of Richard Flynn from Castlepollard, County Westmeath, to try and stop the advancing Germans. A former Royal Dublin Fusilier, Richard was now a Pioneer in J Company, 3rd Battalion, Special Brigade, Royal Engineers. As part of the Special Brigade, he would have been in charge of releasing gas from cylinders to try and halt the onrushing enemy. But the German shock troops came on so fast that Richard's position was quickly overwhelmed. In the chaos of charging field-grey infantry and hammering shellfire, Richard Flynn was killed. He was twenty years old. His body was never found, and today he is commemorated on the Arras Memorial.

Exactly seven months later on 22 October 1918, Richard's brother – Private Michael Flynn of the 2nd Leinster Regiment – was peppered with shrapnel during a German shelling. He was rushed to DuHallow dressing station just north of Ypres and tended by a nurse named Cox, who as it happens, was also from Castlepollard. But Michael did not last long and he succumbed to his wounds later that day. He died, aged twenty-three, and today his body lies in DuHallow ADS (Advanced Dressing Station) Cemetery.

After the war, Nurse Cox returned home to Castlepollard and told the Flynn family how Michael had died. When the armistice finally came, the boys' father, who was already a widower, received a letter from the army. As next of kin to both men, he was entitled to collect his dead sons' war pensions. The pair had been known jokingly as 'Mick and Dick' in Castlepollard, but now they were both dead. It must have been a sad task for their bereaved father, collecting compensation for the loss of two children.

THE IRISH NEW ZEALANDERS

MICHAEL AND PATRICK FINN

Irish brothers even came from as far away as New Zealand to fight. In early June 1918, Patrick Finn entered the line with 12th Company, 1st Canterbury Regiment, New Zealand Expeditionary Force. Having emigrated to New Zealand in 1913 with the promise of land and work, Patrick had enlisted along with his brother Michael in 1917. Originally from Ballyduff, County Waterford, Patrick was the younger of the two brothers – and the shorter one, only 5'1" – a timber-mill hand employed by the Parker Brothers of Hangatiki.

He joined up in June 1917, but during training, for whatever reason, he refused to make out a will. Soldiers enlisting for war service were not stupid – they knew what could happen – and most men made out wills to make sure that if they died, that their affairs would be in order. Patrick Finn simply chose not to. He sailed for Liverpool on 13 October 1917, spent the winter stationed in England, and only arrived in France on 14 February 1918 – St Valentine's Day.

However, on 2 June 1918, while Patrick Finn and his New Zealand comrades were suffering under a terrific enemy bombardment, a shell screamed overhead and exploded beside Patrick. Injured by shrapnel, Patrick collapsed, bleeding heavily. Stretcher-bearers picked him up, dressed his wounds, and rushed him to the No. 2 New Zealand Field Ambulance. But the damage was just too great and Patrick Finn succumbed to his wounds. He died aged twenty-six. Today, his remains lie in Sailly-au-Bois Military Cemetery.

Three months later in September 1918, Patrick Finn's older brother Michael – a twenty-seven year old who had previously worked as a farmer in Waimaha, New Zealand on leaving Ireland – was serving with 2nd Wellington Infantry Regiment, NZEF. Unlike his brother, Michael had been sent to France in 1917 and had fought during the tail end of the Third Battle of Ypres. But Europe in the depths of winter put a fierce strain on Michael Finn's health. On 7 December 1917 he was admitted to hospital with influenza and bronchial difficulties, and for the next three months, he was bounced around from hospital to hospital and from depot to depot until he was well enough to return to the front.

Then, on 14 September 1918, in an event that mirrored Patrick Finn's death, a shell landed near Michael. But this was not an explosive or shrapnel shell – it was a gas shell. Michael's breathing and chest had suffered greatly over the winter, and now creeping, noxious fumes were pouring into his lungs. Michael Finn collapsed. But despite his previous winter illnesses, he survived, and was evacuated to hospital in England. Fortunately, he ultimately survived the war.

'OVER THERE'

STEVE AND JERRY CREGAN

Some Irish brothers even fought in armies outside the British Commonwealth. Serving in France in 1918 were the Cregan brothers – Steve and Jerry – from Tarbert, County Kerry. They were both US Army soldiers, and a third brother

Corporal Jeremiah 'Jerry' Cregan, US Army, from Tarbert, County Kerry around the time of the First World War.

– Patrick – was also in the army but was serving stateside. Private Steve Cregan was the younger of the two and had arrived in France in April 1918 with the 308th Infantry Regiment in the US 77th Infantry Division – America's first division comprised entirely of draftees, men from New York who had been trained in Camp Upton in Yaphank, NY (now the Brookhaven National Laboratory). Steve, along with his brothers, was one of those thousands of Irishmen who had left the land of their birth to create a new life in America. In fact, he was not the only Irishman in the 308th – there were plenty of emigrants or second-generation Irish alongside him – and his was not the first generation of Cregans to wear an American uniform. His uncle, Michael P Cregan who was also from Kerry, had fought with the Union Army during the American Civil War.

As for Steve's older brother, Corporal Jeremiah 'Jerry' Cregan, Jerry was in France serving with the 524th Engineers. He was thirty-six years old, a man who had worked as a coal tender aboard ship to pay for his passage from Ireland to New York in 1898, aged sixteen at the time. After living on the Westside of New York City and working on the trolley cars, before moving to Jersey City, New Jersey and taking up a job with the Department of Public Works, Jerry enlisted in the US Army at Fort Slocum, New York on 24 May 1904.

By 1918, Corporal Jerry Cregan had various claims to fame. Having served at several duty stations, he was posted to the Philippines where he served under

General Arthur MacArthur Jnr. – the father of the famous American General Douglas MacArthur. Also, while on his way back home to Ireland in April 1912 for a furlough, Jerry's ship – SS *Carpathia* – was steaming through the black, ice-filled waters of the north Atlantic when it received word that a nearby vessel had struck an iceberg and was going down. The *Carpathia*'s captain ordered full steam ahead to reach the stricken ship, and the passengers and crew were alerted to be ready for receiving survivors. Of course, the story is a well known one, and when *Carpathia* reached the scene of the distress call, the only survivors she found were the ones in the lifeboats – the lifeboats with *Titanic* written on the side of them.

In this seemingly endless war, Jerry had promised his mother that he would look after Steve. He was so close to keeping his promise, but, on 9 November 1918 – two days before the armistice – Private Steven Cregan and the 308th Infantry Regiment were advancing on Sedan. Intermittent German shellfire opened up on them and claimed the life of Steve Cregan. Along with seven other men of the regiment killed in the last days of November, Steve was one of the last ever casualties suffered by the 308th in the First World War. Today, his body lies in Suresnes Cemetery, five miles west of Paris.

After the war, his brother Jerry served in the 8th Infantry Regiment as part of the army of occupation in Germany. However, the army soon granted Corporal Jerry Cregan an extended furlough. But instead of returning to his newly-adopted home of New York, Jerry travelled back to the land of his birth – Ireland. Yet he did not give up the soldiering while he was back in Kerry. In fact, he joined the IRA.

Jerry Cregan fought in the War of

Master Sergeant Jeremiah 'Jerry' Cregan, US Army, c1930s.

Independence against the British with, as his son – Jeremiah 'Jerry' Cregan Jnr. recalls – 'those great Kerry footballers, Con Brosnan and John Joe Sheehy'. He was an American soldier for fifteen years at this point, had just finished fighting a world war, and now, here he was, taking to the Kerry hills to fight against foreign oppression. Years later, he would be awarded a War of Independence medal with 'Comrac' bar – a rare enough find amongst the medals of any contemporary US soldier.

With the War of Independence having ended in 1921, Jerry Cregan returned to the US and the American Army. While stationed at Camp Pike, Arkansas, he was recommended as a candidate for officers' training camp. However, he had only recently returned from a tour of duty in the Philippines and unfortunately developed dingy fever – a tropical disease that causes severe headache, muscle and joint pain, high fever and rash. When Jerry was finally discharged from hospital, the officers' training camp had come and gone.

He retired from the US Army as a master sergeant in 1931 while stationed in Schofield Barracks, Hawaii, and decided to return home to Kerry in 1935. He built a home in Carhoonkilla, Tarbert, not far from where he was born in Ardmore, before marrying a local girl in 1937. The couple had eight children, but Jerry simply could not sit still. The desire for adventure and travel brought the family to move to Baldoyle in Dublin, Listowel in Kerry, Glin in Limerick, Tralee in Kerry and then back to Tarbert.

When one of Jerry's sons – Jeremiah 'Jerry' Cregan Jnr. – followed in his father's footsteps and emigrated to New York in 1958, aged seventeen, Jerry Snr. wrote his son a letter, with the pages sewn together with thread. It is an interesting insight into the values of an old soldier:

Jeremiah, a few reminders that you or anyone should put into practice immediately in any walk of life that you may daily find yourself:

1. Don't take a low, mean advantage of anyone regardless of who they may be.

2. Be above board in your dealings with everyone that you may happen to come into contact with.

3. Don't tell a lie, regardless of consequences. The Americans detest a person that tells a lie, and rightly so.

4. When called upon to do a certain work, do it immediately. Do it whole-heartedly. Do it to the very best of your ability. In other words, leave your trade-mark after you.

5. If you done something that is wrong, own up to it, and tell the truth, and everyone concerned will think a thousand times more of you.

6. Be a man amongst men.

7. Don't have a chip on your shoulder.

8. If you definitely know that you are in the right, don't take back-water.

9. Don't allow anyone to make a lackey or fool of you.

10. Always be courteous towards everyone.

11. Be ready to give a helping hand to anyone, especially women, the old and infirm when boarding a bus, train, or any passenger vehicle. All women, the old and infirm to get on first, and a helping hand will certainly show courtesy. Politeness of manners, an act of civility. Opposite to this you find impoliteness, disrespect, rudeness.

12. Be always on time. It is better to be an hour too soon than a minute too late.

I served thirty years in the US Army, and never missed or was late for roll call, and we may have sometimes from ten to twelve roll calls each day. I have nine excellent discharges from three different branches of the service, namely infantry, coast artil-lery and engineers. I held every rank in the army, from private to master sergeant.

I was highly recommended to attend the Officers' Training Camp, but at that time, we were just after coming from the Philippine Islands. I and several others had dingy fever. We had to go to hospital. When I returned to duty, the Officers' Train-ing Camp was over.

In addition to holding the rank of sergeant, I was supply sergeant – infantry. At other times I was drill-instructor-sergeant in coastal artillery. I was sergeant and gun-commander. I was also, at other times, the provost sergeant.

When I retired, the regiment (complete) turned out, paraded, and passed in review in my honour. Colonel Ward and myself stood at attention, his staff officers in rear. After the parade, all the officers assembled at headquarters and shook hands with me. Immediately after, my company gave a big turkey dinner, drinks, cigars, and presented me with a gold watch. The colonel made a speech. My company commander made a speech. At dinner, I was sitting between the colonel and my company commander. I asked my company commander for permission to say a few words. He said, 'By all means, we know we will hear something good.' I had my speech typed out myself. Colonel Ward said it was a great speech and gave orders to type it out, frame it, and hang it in his office.

Jeremiah, all those things are not hearsay, they are positively true facts. I could tell you a good many of my exploits in the army.

Best wishes, Dad.

In December 1972, Jerry Cregan passed away in his home in Tarbert, County Kerry, where he is now buried. He was ninety years old.

***

Ultimately, Irish brothers fought and died in nearly every Allied army of the war. Covered in this chapter are Irish brothers in the British, Canadian, Australian, New Zealand, and US Armies, but it must not be forgotten that South Africa also had an Irish regiment.

Any former soldier will tell you that brotherhood in the army is not limited to those who share the same blood. Soldiers in war form a strong bond. A trust is born out of shared suffering and looking out for one another in the most desperate of situations. The war made brothers out of many Irishmen who were normally divided by class, politics and religion.

For some, these war experiences were of mass slaughter and senseless waste – of living a feral existence, surviving only from day to day – while for others, their experiences revealed something about themselves, or about those around them. Some men discovered amazing inner resources. Others found true support and affection from friends and family. There were those that had such unbelievably lucky escapes that they could not help but wonder if God was looking out for them, and there were men who literally had spiritual experiences in the trenches.

For the men of the next chapter, each soldier went through something that was not typical of all First World War veterans. These men experienced the bizarre, the lucky, the unknown. And sometimes, even in the middle of hell, they encountered the compassion of the enemy.

CHAPTER 8

AGAINST ALL ODDS

'For conspicuous gallantry and devotion to duty during an attack and an enemy counter-attack which followed. His portion of the trench was heavily bombed ..., but he stationed himself as near to the enemy as possible and continually caught their bombs in mid-air and threw them back. His courage and daring during several very critical hours contributed materially to the final defeat of the enemy.'

Private Kieran White's DCM citation, *London Gazette*, 28 March 1918

War stories are often full of inexplicable events – quirks of fate and million-to-one happenings. Surviving in the First World War was so often down to chance, but some Irishmen had such extraordinarily lucky escapes that fate, or God, could almost be evoked. In the case of one of the men in this chapter – who was found by his best friend in the middle of a cratered battlefield – the odds of such a rescue are almost too impossible to ascribe it to chance. And then there were the Irishmen who saw things in the war that they just simply could not explain.

A 60-pounder Mk. II gun, firing from an open position near La Boisselle during the Battle of Bapaume, 25 March 1918. It was a gun like this that Gunner John Mangan from near Ballina, County Mayo had to load and fire by himself for hours after the rest of his gun crew were killed by enemy fire.

SUPERHUMAN RESOLVE

JOHN MANGAN

During the incredibly stressful and unbearable moments of war, the true nature of who we are often surfaces. One man who discovered just how determined he could be was John Mangan from outside Ballina in County Mayo. A gunner with the Royal Garrison Artillery, Mangan was a 6'6" ex-policeman. On one occasion, during a German attack, he was manning a sixty-pounder heavy gun with several comrades when an enemy shell landed in the middle of the group, killing everyone except John Mangan. But Mangan knew he had to fight on. The Germans were attacking and they had to be held back. So, alone, he loaded and fired his gun for hours, until reinforcements arrived. When you take into account that each shell weighed 60lbs (or 27.3kg), which Mangan had to load by himself over a period of several hours, while he was under constant enemy fire, it shows the reserves of strength that a man could call on when he had absolutely no other choice.

LUCKY ESCAPES

JOHN O'ROURKE

On a dark night, Private John O'Rourke from Roscommon town was in the Ypres sector. O'Rourke was not living in Ireland when he joined the British Army. He had been living in Chester in England, close to the Welsh border, and that is probably how he wound up in the Royal Welsh Fusiliers. At this stage in the war, O'Rouke was already familiar with, 'rats as big as dogs, and lice as big as grains of corn', as he later told his son, Michael O'Rourke. But on this dark night, the disgusting nature of war was about to be replaced with terror and panic.

O'Rourke was out on a patrol in no-man's-land, and along with several comrades, they were navigating their way over a slag heap when O'Rourke became separated from the others. Trying to catch up with his comrades, O'Rourke slipped and fell, in an avalanche of coal dust and dirt, into enemy barbed wire. Worse still, his patrol had been tasked with bombing an enemy trench and O'Rourke had seventeen grenades strapped to his uniform. Snagged on the wire, frantically trying to free himself, he looked down and realised that the pins of several of the grenades were caught on the barbs. If he pulled away from the wire, he would blow himself to pieces.

The poppy, which grew abundantly on the battlefields of the Somme before the guns churned the earth, became the everlasting symbol of the First World War. Men used to pick the flowers by the roadside and pop them into their tunic buttonholes. Ironically, the poppy has always been a symbol of death. In Greco-Roman myths, they were given as offerings to the dead and poppies on tombstones were taken to represent eternal sleep. However, the scarlet colour was also a reminder of the guarantee of resurrection after death, which in the context of First World War soldiers signifies our eternal remembrance of them.

O'Rourke's comrades could not find him and so he had to hold still in a terribly uncomfortable position. He simply could not free himself. Hours went by, O'Rourke's muscles cramped up, and the dawn got closer and closer. If he was still out there when the sun rose, he would be in full view of the German lines and a sitting target. Then he heard shuffling nearby. He froze. Other soldiers of the Royal Welsh Fusiliers sneaked out of the darkness and unhooked the grenade pins from the barbs. Sweating heavily and trembling, Private John O'Rourke finally made his way back to friendly territory. But this was not his greatest escape of the war.

Months later on the Somme, O'Rourke found himself racing across no-man's-land during an attack with his Welsh comrades. He had recently picked a poppy from the battlefield and it was sitting in his buttonhole. Suddenly, a shell-burst blasted pieces of shrapnel into his ear, arm and knee – all on his right side. O'Rourke collapsed and passed out. When he woke up, dazed and disorientated, he was staring up at a smoky sky. He looked around and realised he was surrounded by dead and wounded. None of the other wounded were moving or making a sound. Suddenly, two stretcher-bearers leapt over John O'Rourke. As shrapnel shells burst overhead, they looked around quickly and one yelled to the other, 'Let's take a chance on this lad.' Out of all the wounded on the battlefield, the two stretcher-bearers picked John O'Rourke. They heaved him up onto the stretcher and rushed off with him over craters and ditches.

When a doctor looked over O'Rourke's wounds, he told the Roscommon man that his right arm would have to be amputated. 'If only to fill my coat sleeve,' said O'Rourke. 'Leave it.' He made the doctor do everything he could to save it and refused to accept amputation. In fact, the doctor did manage to save O'Rourke's arm and, although it was three inches shorter after the operation, it was still able to fill his coat sleeve.

John O'Rourke went on to survive the war and return to his native Roscommon, and at the time of writing, the family still have the poppy that O'Rourke was wearing in his buttonhole when he was injured, the exact one – pressed and framed – to remember the day that John O'Rourke nearly died, and to remember the men that did.

TOM LALOR

Then there was Tom Lalor from Mountmellick, County Laois – a man who overcame impossible odds and had his fair share of amazing escapes. Having claimed that he was nineteen when he was really only sixteen, Tom Lalor succeeded in enlisting in 1914. He was initially posted to the 6th Leinster Regiment, where he served in Gallipoli and Salonika. It was in Salonika that Private Lalor took part in a grenade attack on a Bulgarian machine-gun emplacement. Along with a Sergeant Chester from Portlaoise, they charged up to the gun, hurled their bombs, and silenced it for good.

Lalor was also aboard a ship that was torpedoed in Alexandria port, an event which left him clinging to a cork-float for a day, before he was rescued. On another occasion he contracted malaria and, while in hospital, a Gurkha in the next bed decided to show Lalor a gruesome item that he was keeping as a souvenir – allegedly, it was a severed Turkish head. Given the Gurkhas reputation for fierceness in battle, this story could very easily be true.

Tom Lalor's father and his brother Pat were also serving in the Leinster Regiment. However, Pat Lalor was captured by the Germans and interred in Limberg POW camp. He killed a sentry and was subsequently sent to labour in Belgium as punishment. It was there that Pat Lalor met a Belgian girl and fell madly in love. They both survived the war and married soon after.

Not long after Salonika, Private Tom Lalor found himself transferred into the 2nd Leinster Regiment and sent to the Western Front, but not before spotting Kitchener at Tilbury Docks as he set sail to France. In 1916, Lalor took part in the Battle of the Somme, where he had a lucky escape from a German gas cloud. The gas was approaching and Lalor had no gas mask, but he managed to find one on a dead French soldier and get it on just in time. However, he was subsequently buried alive by shellfire for three suffocating days along with six other comrades – surrounded by heavy, black earth and stinking corpses – an event which was one of the most terrifying experiences imaginable. When he was dug out by comrades, Tom Lalor was finally sent back to Ireland and posted to the 4th (Extra Reserve) Leinster Regiment in late 1916.

He decided to stay in the British Army after the war. Sent to India in 1921, Tom Lalor served in Malabar, where he and twelve other soldiers were surrounded for several days by enemy forces. Lalor and his comrades fought desperately to resist the siege, and erected defences using tin cans and string in order to warn them when the enemy was approaching.

When the Leinster Regiment was disbanded in 1922, upon the formation of the Irish Free State, Tom Lalor returned to Ireland, but, before leaving India, he could also claim to have seen Gandhi on his travels. Lalor decided that sol-diering was what he knew best and so he joined the National (Free State) Army, serving during the Irish Civil War. He married in 1933, got some local work as a gardener, and it finally looked as though fighting and sacrificing were over for Tom Lalor.

But as the years passed, Lalor began to succumb to the effects of shellshock. He started to shake terribly, so much so that the bartender in his local had to serve Tom his drink in a jug so he would not spill it. He soon earned the nick-name 'Mad Tom' and, to annoy him, people constantly asked him what he would do if he ever met any 'Japs' again (this was the name Lalor and the locals gave to the Indian enemy of 1921). These questions drove him crazy and brought back memories of the siege in Malabar, where he and his comrades had struggled bitterly to stay breathing.

The worst of Tom Lalor's latest troubles came when Mountmellick received a new parish priest – a man who was an ardent nationalist. His first act was to remove the war memorial plaque from the local church, a plaque which had the names of all the men from Mountmellick who had gone to war but never come home. Tom Lalor became enraged when he learned this and refused to go to Mass ever again.

In 1991, all those years after being shipwrecked, gassed and buried alive, Lalor – aged ninety-three – was interviewed by the *Leinster Express,* because of both his First World War service and also because he was now Mountmellick's oldest citizen. He recalled that a friend once shot two of his own fingers off to get discharged, and also remembered that, on the Somme:

> You would sink up to your neck in the mud ... You daren't light a fire to boil up
>
> some tea, otherwise a whizzbang [shell] would drop on you. To boil up tea we had
>
> to dig in deep into the mud at night.

Regarding the fear of death, Lalor said:

> You just never thought about it. You just accepted it. You never became friendly with the soldiers you were fighting alongside. It would affect you too much it they were shot ... My own father fought in the Leinster Regiment too. I never liked fighting alongside him in case something happened. You were always better off beside strangers.

Of the winters that Tom Lalor experienced in the trenches, he said:

> It was so cold you could get frostbite. If you had it, they'd cut off your toes and send you home ... Then they came out with a heat rub which was supposed to stop the frostbite when you wore it on your feet. Some lads who wanted to be sent home

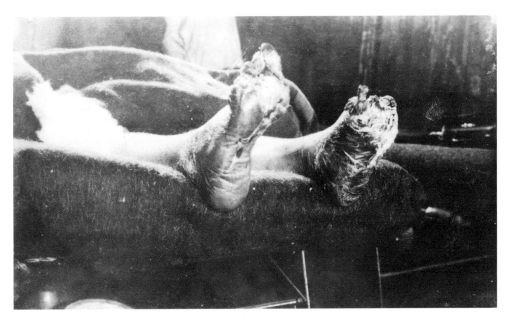

Caused by as little as eleven hours of exposure to damp, unsanitary and cold conditions, trench foot started with numbness in the feet. Swelling followed and as blood flow was cut off, the feet began to rot. Blisters, sores and fungal infections could also occur, and gangrene and amputation were often the end result. During the First World War, officers regularly inspected their men's feet for the condition and soldiers were given whale grease to protect their feet, but the grease only served to make their feet sweat and absorb more moisture. This picture shows a Canadian soldier suffering from an extreme case of trench foot in France, 1917.

wouldn't put it on, so they'd lose their toes. To stop that, an order came down that if you didn't put the rub on, you'd be shot. That soon ended that way out.

The ninety-three-year-old also remembered the debut of tanks on the battlefield:

> We thought they were great. They went straight through the barbed wire and we followed. Of course the Germans were terrified of them. It didn't take long before they had tanks of their own.

When asked if, given the choice, he would have lived his life any differently, Lalor replied, 'I would go through it all again ... I've no regrets. None at all.' Soon after giving his newspaper interview in 1991, Tom Lalor passed away.

A FRIEND IN NEED

PADDY KENNELLY

One of the most miraculous stories of the First World War has to be that of Paddy Kennelly from Ballybunnion, County Kerry. Kennelly was a seaweed vat farmer. When he joined the British Army on 11 February 1915, he was posted to the 9th Royal Munster Fusiliers. After initial training in Cork, Private Kennelly was sent to Blackdown, near Aldershot in England, and then, on 17 December 1915, he entered the war. The 9th Royal Munster Fusiliers formed part of the 16th (Irish) Division and were due to fight in the Big Push of 1916 on the Somme.

On 27 April 1916, Kennelly was at Hulluch, during the infamous German gas attack which left 538 men of 16th (Irish) Division dead and another 1,590 wounded. However, his battalion were not in the front-line trenches and so they did not suffer the gas, but they were ordered forward soon after, to drive back the German attack that followed. In amongst the gas-blackened dead and the dying men with foam spewing from their mouths, Paddy Kennelly came face to face with the enemy.

Three months later on 19 July – just after the start of the Battle of the Somme – Paddy Kennelly was now serving with the 8th Royal Munster Fusiliers and was involved in a failed raid on enemy lines. The next day he and his comrades were ordered to try again. On 20 July, as the war diary records:

Following an intense bombardment at 11.50pm ... which lasted 3 minutes, A, B, C & D [raiding] parties again left the trenches to raid the enemy line ... As before the enterprise was covered by repeated salvoes of rifle grenades. A & B parties again failed to penetrate the enemy wire, but cleared the fire trench behind it with bombs. C party under Lt. O'Brien penetrated into the fire trench ... & bombed it successfully ... All dugouts met were bombed & a party of the enemy driven off ... Party D under 2 Lt. Maher reached the enemy fire trench ... when 8 Germans who had taken cover under a shelter were killed. The party then worked onwards inflicting several other casualties, until the resistance became too strong when they withdrew. The party were subjected to severe machine-gun fire when returning, the guns being trained on a [point of] fire the enemy had lighted by some mechanical means just outside the gap in his entanglement [wire]. An [enemy] officer surrendered himself to one of the section leaders of C party, but wounded this NCO with his revolver after his surrender had been accepted & was shot. A prisoner taken by D party endeavoured to break away from his escort while pushing through the enemy wire & was shot. Our casualties were 5 OR killed & 23 OR wounded, officers 2 being killed & 5 wounded.

One of the wounded soldiers was Private Paddy Kennelly. He had been shot in the right leg and was taken to 33rd Casualty Clearing Station and then to 112th Field Ambulance. Kennelly survived, and was finally sent to the base hospital at Étaples to recover.

However, he returned to the war only one month later when he rejoined his unit on 25 August. Then, on 3 September 1916, Kennelly and the 8th Royal Munster Fusiliers formed up at a location known as the 'Gridiron' and waited for the order to launch an attack on the town of Guillemont. For the previous two days, the Munster men had been suffering terrible gas and shell bombardments

German dead scattered in the wreck of a machine-gun post near Guillemont on the Somme, September 1916. Private Paddy Kennelly from Ballybunion, County Kerry, was involved in the Battle of Guillemont, and, during the fighting to take the town, 8th Royal Munster Fusiliers suffered 265 casualties in a single day.

while positioned in Bernafay Wood, but now at 3am on 3 September, they went on the offensive. The battalion had been tasked with capturing enemy positions east of Guillemont, and they advanced on a sunken road that was their designated target. However, while Guillemont itself fell to the British, the battalion came under heavy counter attack. By the time the 8th Royal Munster Fusiliers were relieved in the early hours of the following morning, they had suffered 265 killed and wounded.

Paddy Kennelly was not among the dead or injured, and, over the next few days, he found himself resting and refitting with his battalion in Carnoy Camp. However, on 7 September he was sent back to the sunken road east of Guillemont. Ginchy had to be taken, and, after listening to British artillery pounding the German lines and enemy sniper bullets whizzing through the air all day on 8 September, Kennelly exited the trenches again the following day with his comrades.

At 4.40pm the Battalion left its trenches on Sunken Road to attack enemy line. As their trench at this point had not been touched by our artillery & was held by over 200 men & 5 machine guns it was impossible to carry it by a frontal attack. The leading companies of the Battalion never penetrated into this position. The Battalion was relieved at 3.30am by 3rd Grenadier Guards. Casualties 76 OR & the following officers. Killed: 2 Lieut. F. Brown. Wounded: Capt. J. Watts-Russell, 2 Lieuts. F. Arnold, C.L. Sweeney, E.J. Keane.

Second-Lieutenant Francis Brown was twenty-two when he died. From Bangor, County Down, he has no known grave, so today his name is commemorated on the Thiepval Memorial. Paddy Kennelly, however, was still alive. He was turning out to be a very lucky man indeed.

But this was nothing compared to what happened to him in 1917. On 7 June 1917, Private Paddy Kennelly – now in the 1st Royal Munster Fusiliers – was advancing up Messines Ridge. The 16th (Irish) Division and the 36th (Ulster) Division were fighting side by side, nationalists and unionists suffering and dying beside each other. Nearing the town of Wytschaete, Paddy Kennelly was pressing forward with his battalion – pushing the Germans back, securing objectives – when the Kerryman suddenly felt like he had been kicked in the chest. Kennelly had been shot straight through the body. He collapsed to the ground while the rest of his Munster comrades kept advancing. Kennelly started fading in and out of consciousness, his body going numb. Then Kennelly's eyes focused on a soldier running by. Kennelly could not believe it. He recognised the man. It was his friend from back home in Ballybunnion – Mikey Collins.

By sheer coincidence, Paddy Kennelly's friend Michael 'Mikey' Collins, a Boer War veteran who had served under Kitchener in South Africa, and who lived only five miles down the road from Kennelly in Ballybunnion, had re-enlisted in the Royal Munster Fusiliers and had been in the trenches below Messines not far from Kennelly that morning. Neither man had known that the other was in the Royal Munster Fusiliers, and as far as Paddy Kennelly was concerned, Mikey was an ex-soldier – he had not re-enlisted or been recalled to the army. It was a miracle that the two men encountered each other on the battlefield, and Kennelly seized his only chance at survival.

'Mikey,' he called out. The running soldier stopped. 'Mikey Collins,' he called again. Mikey turned round and could not believe his eyes. He sprinted over to Kennelly and glanced down at Paddy's wound. Before he could say anything, Kennelly passed out. Mikey had been 'put on the spot' so to speak. He could not leave his friend there to die, so he knew what had to be done. Mikey Collins dropped his rifle, hauled his friend up onto his shoulders, and then struggled to bend down to pick up his own weapon. He knew that he had to get Paddy Kennelly to a dressing station, but Mikey also feared that he would be shot by his own officer, if he returned without his rifle. So, as fast as he could, Mikey trudged back across no-man's-land lugging Kennelly on his shoulders, along with his immensely heavy pack, equipment, and rifle. He navigated his way around motionless, shell-torn tanks – tanks that had been supposed to support the infantry attack but had been knocked out – and he managed to get back to safety with Paddy Kennelly. Mikey Collins had only enough time to deposit his friend at the dressing station before being ordered back to the fight. Their chance meeting had been brief, but it saved Paddy Kennelly's life.

Even though the bullet had gone right through him, and even though Kennelly subsequently caught pneumonia in hospital, his constitution was strong enough for him to survive. He recovered, but he was still not discharged from the army. The army continued to have a role for him, though he would no longer have to serve as a combat infantryman.

In March 1918, the indestructible Paddy Kennelly was sent to Palestine. He travelled overland from Cherbourg to Taranto, Italy before sailing to Alexandria and then continuing on to the Holy Land. He was posted to 518th Company, Army Services Corps, attached to 60th Division's supply train. Kennelly stayed in this role until the end of the war and then returned home to his seaweed vats in Ballybunnion, County Kerry. Since leaving Kerry in 1915, he had been to France, Belgium, Italy, Egypt and Palestine, but now he was finally home. Kennelly's friend – Mikey Collins – the man who had saved his life during the Battle of Messines Ridge, also survived the war. However, Mikey had beaten Kennelly home to Ballybunnion – after fighting at Messines, Mikey had gone on to fight in the horrific Third Battle of Ypres where he had been wounded and subsequently discharged. When Kennelly returned home, he found Mikey suffering from terrible shellshock and hitting the drink hard, living a rough life in the pubs.

Mikey became an alcoholic, but Paddy Kennelly refused to let his friend waste away. Kennelly was no counsellor or therapist, and was not trained in how to deal with shellshock, but he visited Mikey regularly, spent time with him, talked to him, and took care of him as best he could. In fact, Paddy Kennelly looked after Mikey Collins until Mikey died an old man. Mikey Collins had saved his life in 1917, and Paddy Kennelly never forgot this debt. Paddy Kennelly also lived to be an old man. He ultimately died and, like his old friend, was buried in his hometown of Ballybunnion.

BERNARD FLOOD

While some Irishmen survived against impossible odds or were saved by their comrades, some Irishmen survived the war thanks to their Allies. One such man was Bernard Flood of the Royal Irish Rifles from Drogheda, County Louth. A Gallipoli veteran, Bernard was now serving on the Western Front and after advancing across no-man's-land during an attack, he was shot and his body dropped to the muck. He had two young children and Bernard's wife soon received a telegram stating that her husband was missing, presumed dead. Days turned into weeks, and weeks turned into months. It looked as if Bernard had certainly been killed, until that is, two months after initially disappearing, he turned up in a French hospital. Apparently, back on the day of the attack, his regiment had been serving at the end of the British line, just next to where the French lines began. During the attack in which he had been involved, Bernard had been wounded, and had somehow found his way to the French hospital.

Bernard's wife then received another telegram, letting her know that her husband was safe and sound. In one brief moment, she suddenly had her husband back, and Bernard's children had their father back. Bernard was sent on to a hospital in Edmonton, London, before being discharged from the army on 31 July 1918 – now aged thirty-three – and sent for further treatment to Leopardstown Hospital in Dublin.

After being ultimately released from hospital after the war had ended, Bernard Flood returned to his native Drogheda but found it hard to get work. He

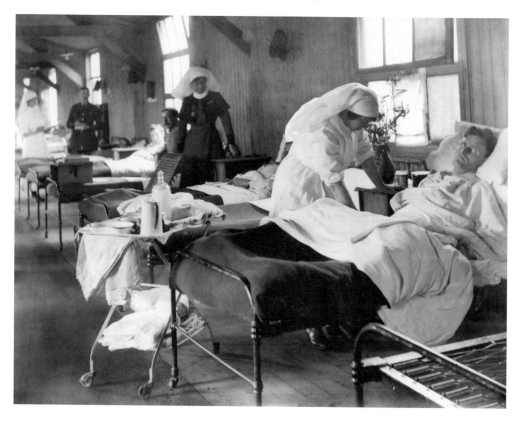

Nursing staff tending to bed-ridden patients on a ward in No. 6 General Hospital, Rouen. Private Bernard Flood from Drogheda, County Louth, spent two months in a similar French hospital. Meanwhile, his wife back home believed he had been killed.

worked for a while in a mill run by an ex-army major, then his old wounds worsened and he could not work at all. So, with a large back garden, he started growing vegetables and sometimes he would go shooting for rabbits. Every Wednesday, as reliable as could be, his army pension would arrive, even during the Second World War when there was fierce strain on the British treasury.

Unfortunately, his son died fairly young, leaving Bernard's grandson with no father, so Bernard raised the boy himself. Bernard's grandson used to ask about the war – like all boys, he was fascinated by the perceived adventure of it all – but Bernard would never speak of it. He hated any events or days of commemoration. He could not understand why such a nightmare was remembered. However, each year, he would go by himself to the war memorial in Drogheda and place a wreath in memory of his fallen comrades – his friends that are now just names on a plaque. Bernard Flood, who smoked eighty cigarettes a day, died aged eighty-nine and is buried in Drogheda. Currently, he has no tombstone – unlike his former comrades, his name is not engraved on stone. There is no plaque that commemorates his life.

RISKING LIFE AND LIMB

KIERAN WHITE

The story of Private Kieran White – born in Cloghan, County Offaly but raised in nearby Banagher – is also one of remarkable survival. On 20 November 1917 – day one of the Battle of Cambrai – he found himself fighting with the 6th Connaught Rangers at Bullecourt to the north of the main battlefield. His battalion and their supporting units had been tasked with making a diversionary attack away from the main assault, in order to tie up German troops to the north. Kieran was one of seven brothers and three nephews who had all enlisted.

Private White's objective on 20 November was the capture of Tunnel Trench at Bullecourt. After a four-minute artillery bombardment at 6.20am, B Company led the way and Kieran and A Company followed. They poured into the enemy trench and found that the quick British bombardment had smashed it to pieces and turned it into a blasted ditch. Bombing parties pressed on and over 150 Germans surrendered. However, it was not long before the enemy launched a counter-attack to re-take Tunnel Trench and surrounding positions. At 7.10am, they stormed the 6th Connaught Rangers.

The battalion's right flank was soon badly exposed and soldiers of C and D Companies were becoming casualties of German machine guns. A Company and Kieran White, on the far right of the line, were hit worst and the situation was chaotic. Enemy troops were hurling grenades and pouring murderous fire onto A Company as they flooded towards the attacking Irishmen, desperately trying to drive them back. A group of Royal Engineers rushed forward with a mine, in order to blow up and seal the tunnel that the Germans were using to advance towards the 6th Connaught Rangers, but the mine was hit by a bullet and it exploded, killing the engineers. Now there was nothing stopping the enemy and they just kept coming.

Soldiers of the 11th Royal Inniskilling Fusiliers in a captured German trench near Havrincourt on the first day of the Battle of Cambrai, 20 November 1917. To the northwest, Private Kieran White from Banagher, County Offaly and the 6th Connaught Rangers were mounting a diversionary assault.

Machine-gun bullets bit into the earth around Kieran White and his comrades. Germans kept charging up the tunnel and into the trench and then, suddenly, a fresh enemy counter-attack arrived. For hours, Kieran and his fellow soldiers fought hand-to-hand with the Germans in a desperate struggle to stay alive. Soldiers were bayoneted, shot, blown to pieces and clubbed to death as the Irishmen fought bitterly for their lives. A Company were quickly running out of bombs and while Irish machine gunners were plastering their German counterparts with fire, if the men in the trenches ran out of bombs, they would be massacred.

Down the trench from where he was huddled, Kieran White saw German bombers, just behind a traverse, flinging bombs down at him. He waited until they hurled a grenade and then suddenly charged straight at them, catching the bomb in mid-air and flinging it back at the traverse in the trench before it exploded. He used the chaos and confusion following the explosion to position himself on the other side of the traverse to the enemy bombers – just around the bend – and when they threw another grenade, Kieran caught it and hurled it back. He stayed as close to the enemy as he humanly could and repeatedly caught their bombs and flung them back, over and over and over. With A Company soon completely out of grenades, Kieran and his comrades were forced to withdraw, leaving a trench clogged with dead behind them. For his display of incredible bravery, Private Kieran White was soon awarded the Distinguished Conduct Medal.

Kieran White ultimately survived the war and returned to his home in Banagher, County Offaly – along with his seven brothers and three nephews who all came back safe without a scratch. But it was not long before the ex-British soldier came to the attention of local republicans, and so, in order to assert himself and defend his honour, Kieran arranged a fight with the main IRA man who was giving him trouble. The former Connaught Ranger battered his opponent, proving that he was a force to be reckoned with and best left alone. He did it, in his own words, as his grandson – also Kieran White – remembers, 'so that I could always hold my head high'.

Kieran White later got work with the local council on the roads, and used to boldly attend war commemoration ceremonies in Birr, even though many of the locals frowned upon it. He died in November 1975 – aged eighty-nine.

An example of a First World War period (George V) Distinguished Conduct Medal, identical to the one earned by Private Kieran White. Established on 4 December 1854 during the Crimean War, this medal (along with its officers' counterpart – the Distinguished Service Order) was only junior in the bravery medal hierarchy to the Victoria Cross.

JOSEPH MULLEN

On 2 October 1918, Gunner Joseph Mullen of 74th Brigade, Royal Field Artillery from Portarlington, County Laois, was in the vicinity of Noyelles. Mullen was a member of the trench mortar-battery – a job which had never endeared him to the regular infantry. Whenever he and his mortar crew fired a round, the Germans would fire back, and the British infantry were the ones pounded by the explosions. As a result, infantrymen went to great lengths to keep mortar-men away from them, often using trench mortar pits as latrines – anything to try and keep soldiers like Joseph Mullen from manning their posts.

While positioned in the front line on 2 October 1918, an enemy machine gun opened fire near Mullen's position. The German gunners had managed to find a vulnerable and exposed section of the British line. British soldiers were pinned down.

An officer came charging down the trench. He wanted a volunteer to go and take out the machine gun – preferably someone 'young and single', no one who was going to leave a widow and children behind if they died. The German

A group of Irish artillerymen during the First World War. These gunners are soldiers of either the Royal Horse or Royal Field Artillery. Gunner Thomas Wall from Loughrea, County Galway is identified, sitting front row, second from the right.

A British 9.45-inch trench-mortar crew stand with their weapon in an old German trench in Pigeon Wood, Gommecourt, March 1917. It is snowing, and one of the men appears to be placing a cover over the end of the barrel. Gunner Joseph Mullen from Portarlington, County Laois, would have had to operate mortars such as these.

machine gun had a clear field of fire over no-man's-land; there was only sparse cover – shallow shell craters and mounds of dirt – and whoever went out there was almost bound to be chewed up by the gun.

'I'll go,' said Joseph Mullen. The officer handed him a grenade and off he went. Mullen dived over the parapet and scrambled for cover. He made it, took a few deep breaths and darted again, and again. Each time, the German machine gun was trained on him and each time, he managed to make it from cover to cover, constantly moving closer to the enemy. When he was near enough, he pulled the pin, flung the bomb, and hoped for the best.

The bomb went off. Grenade fragments split through the air and the German machine gun stopped firing. Very carefully, Joseph Mullen crawled back to the British trenches to be congratulated on a job well done. He was soon awarded the Military Medal for bravery.

After the war, Joseph Mullen returned home to work in the local Odlums' factory in Portarlington as caretaker. He lived in the mill house, and went on to serve in the FCÁ during the Emergency. He retired quite early in life, and when asked in an interview about the day he won his Military Medal, he simply said, as his granddaughter – Geraldine Murphy – recalls, 'I just had to throw a hand grenade and come back. It sounds more impressive than it actually was.' The modest Joseph Mullen died age eighty-eight in 1985, described by his family as 'a gentle soul', who made it his business 'never to say a bad word about anybody'.

SAVED BY THE ENEMY

MATTHEW CROWE

Then there were those that owed their lives to the enemy. One Irishman who found himself in this unusual position after the war was Matthew Crowe.

After the Easter Rising in 1916, the Germans decided that they could not let such a fantastic propaganda opportunity pass them by. And so, in front of Irish regiments all along the line, placards written in English started to appear above German parapets with slogans like 'Irishmen! Heavy uproar in Ireland. English guns are firing on your wives and children.' Signs like these were witnessed by Matthew Crowe of the Royal Irish Fusiliers, and his son – also Matthew Crowe – remembers that, although his father dismissed them at first, they started to burrow into his mind after a while. Crowe decided to try and get home to see what was happening for himself. One day, along with a friend, he slipped away while in a rest camp and tried to bluff his way home to Ireland. But whoever he encountered saw right through the bluff and Crowe was found out, disciplined, and ordered back to the trenches.

Matthew Crowe was originally from Thomas Street in Dublin, and so he was familiar with the poverty and squalor of the inner-city tenements. Years before the war, to escape this miserable life, he enlisted in the army, along with his three brothers – only it nearly took him years to do it.

On the day that Crowe went down to the recruiting office to join there was an army band outside playing and marching up and down. 'F*** it,' he said, 'if

I'm going in there with the band outside.' So Crowe went home, refusing to let anyone say that he had joined the army because of the hype. He had made up his mind, he wanted to do it, but he was not going to be accused of enlisting because some marching band had got his blood up. Day after day, Matthew Crowe went back to the recruiting office, and day after day he cursed and went home – the band still parading on a recruitment drive. Then finally, the drummers and pipers were gone. Inside a now much quieter recruitment office, Matthew Crowe joined the British Army.

He served in India, where the humidity and the heat were a shock to a lad from Dublin, and, on one occasion, he was packed onto a sweltering, overcrowded train for a three-day journey across the country. In fact, Crowe was still in India – stationed at Quetta – with the 2nd Royal Irish Fusiliers when the war broke out. The battalion sailed for Europe and Crowe arrived on the Western Front on 19 December 1914. He was now a lance-corporal.

It was not long before he found himself in a column of men marching to the front. The men were all fairly silent, wrapped up in their own thoughts, so Crowe pulled out his harmonica to play a tune – he was a very good player. But as soon as the first few notes hit the air, a young second-lieutenant, recently graduated from Sandhurst, came storming up to him. 'You, lance-corporal, shut up! Do you want the enemy to hear us coming!?' Crowe brought the harmonica away from his lips. He stared at the young officer and then glanced at the massive column of advancing British troops. 'There's thousands of us!' he said. 'I think they f***ing know we're coming!'

The officer was not impressed. After the march, Crowe was ordered to present himself before the provost sergeant. He marched up to the sergeant and was immediately berated. 'How dare you speak to an officer like that! You should …' Suddenly, a burst of red exploded from the sergeant's skull. The sergeant dropped to the ground like a stone and Lance-Corporal Crowe was sprayed with his blood. German sniper. That was Matthew Crowe's entry to the war.

After entering the trenches, Matthew Crowe quickly learned the tricks of the trade. At night, he would stand on the fire step and stare out into no-man's-land on watch. Things would move in the dark, and it was hard to make out what they were. Of course, Crowe had to be careful firing a shot. If he fired his rifle, the muzzle flash would pinpoint him for the Germans and if he reappeared in the same place, they would have him in their sights. So Crowe started sticking forks in the parapet as reference points. Wherever he saw something moving, he would jam in a fork pointing it that direction. When he knew it was a German raiding party, he would take aim in the dark and fire, drop down, pop up, quickly find his aim again thanks to the forks and fire. Those forks probably saved his life.

Crowe's experiences in the trenches were certainly varied. He once went three months without changing his lice-ridden shirt, and being the joker that he was, he once ran the Union Jack up the flagpole upside down. If an army runs its flag up the pole upside down this means 'distress', but the Union Jack looks so alike either way up that nobody noticed. On that occasion, Crowe escaped the sergeant's wrath. However, after the German placard propaganda incident, when Crowe tried to make it home to Dublin, he was demoted to private before he was returned to the trenches.

Later in the war Private Crowe was to have his lucky escape – only he did not have his comrades to thank. When Crowe was shot in the leg during an enemy attack and left behind while his battalion was forced to retreat, he found himself lying out in no-man's-land with a severe knee wound. Taken prisoner by the Germans, he was brought to an enemy clearing station and, contrary to some of the anti-German propaganda, was treated by a German doctor. In fact, when the doctor realised that Crowe's knee wound needed surgery and that wire had to be inserted to repair the joint, the doctor chose to use gold wire to prevent any infections from rust. The operation was a success, and thanks to the enemy, Matthew Crowe's leg was saved. Years later, whenever his son brought a girl home, Crowe would always make the joke that, while the girl's legs might be pretty, his leg was worth a fortune.

After the war, Matthew Crowe was released from captivity and he returned home to Dublin where he began working for Guinness's. The company had a reputation for supporting workers who enlisted, holding their jobs open for them. Of course, not all of these men came home, and one of the vacant positions was filled by Matthew Crowe.

Every morning, Crowe would bring his two children to school on a pushbike before cycling off to the brewery. On one icy winter morning, he was passing the canal when he saw a horse trapped out on the ice. The poor beast was slipping and sliding and could not get to the bank. Crowe cycled on into work, but the image of the horse on the ice kept gnawing at him. So, against the protests of his foreman, who he referred to as a 'freemason bastard', Crowe cycled back to the canal, stripped down to his long johns, climbed over the railings and pencil-dived into the ice beside the stranded horse. The idea had been to break the surface of the ice and force the animal into the water. It could then swim to shore. The problem was that Crowe sliced open his stomach in the process and nearly killed himself. He was rushed to hospital, but insisted that saving the horse had been the right thing to do. 'I saved that mare because it does more work than the bloody Lord Mayor!'

Crowe might have been more of a rogue than a rebel, but during the War of Independence, he did his bit for the republican cause. One night, Crowe was playing cards with some friends during a blackout when the Black and Tans burst in. They grabbed one of Crowe's friends and started to beat the man. This scene deeply affected Matthew Crowe, and, even though he was not particularly nationalistic, he decided to do something about it. The IRA was having trouble with some of the Black and Tans' defences – namely wire-mesh walls that were erected around buildings to make grenades bounce off. Crowe decided to help them out. He suggested to the IRA that they attach fish hooks to grenades, so that the explosives would catch on the wire-mesh fences of the Black and Tans defences and blow them apart. This was Matthew Crowe's small, but useful, contribution to the War of Independence.

EDWARD MONKS

After the war, Private Edward Monks from Nenagh, County Tipperary would have a similar story to tell. A labourer and shoemaker by trade, Monks had joined the army after walking from Nenagh to Birr with a friend to enlist. But by the time that Monks first entered the war on 5 November 1915 when he arrived in Salonika to join the 6th Leinster Regiment, his friend had already been killed in the trenches.

Monks lasted only a month, before he was hospitalised in Salonika. He was suffering from frostbite. Further complaints soon developed, namely asthma and influenza, and so, on 1 February 1916, Edward Monks had to be evacuated

Wounded Allied POWs; note the distinctive striped dressing gown worn by wounded men in Germany. The five men in peaked caps are British soldiers, while the man on the far right and the black man in the centre are French. The latter is certainly a soldier from one of France's African colonies. This image comes from a picture postcard, evidently sent by one of the photographed prisoners, and is marked Wiesbaden, Germany, 1916, which means that these men were most likely captured during the Battle of the Somme.

back to England – the harsh Balkan winter having taken its toll. Fit for duty by March 1916, he was sent to the 3rd (Reserve) Leinster Regiment in Cork to await his return to the war. While in Cork, he absented himself from duty in April, earning himself three days of confinement to barracks. Two weeks later he absented himself again. For this infraction, he was awarded seven days of Field Punishment No. 2. This was similar enough to Field Punishment No. 1 – where the soldier was forced to undergo hard manual labour while shackled and tied to a heavy object – except that, with Field Punishment No. 2, the soldier was not tied to anything or restrained. It looked like the war was already starting to leave a lasting impression on Edward Monks.

By June 1916, Monks was back in the war, and, on 18 August, his battalion – 2nd Leinster Regiment – was ordered to support the attack on Arrow Head Copse at Delville Wood (nicknamed 'Devil's Wood') by entering the British front lines after the 13th Middlesex Regiment had gone over the top. However, due to intense enemy shelling, this was almost impossible to achieve. The battalion suffered heavy causalities, simply trying to get from the reserve trenches to their *own* front lines, but still the men struggled on, managing to reach the front before being relieved in the early hours of the following morning.

By the time they had withdrawn from the front, crawling back to the shelter of craters around Carnoy, over 150 men of the 2nd Leinster Regiment had become casualties. Private Edward Monks was uninjured, and he was still serving with the 2nd Leinster Regiment on 31 August when the battalion was attacked by the enemy. British counter-attacks followed and by the end of the next day, Edward Monks from Nenagh had been shot in the knee and wrist. He was once again evacuated back to England. The wounds in his arm soon healed but the injury to his knee caused fluid to build up. Monks began to complain of tenderness around the calf muscles and he suffered from bad swelling which prevented him from flexing his knee properly. By 20 September, however, only nineteen days after being shot, Monks was discharged as fit for duty. His knee was still in pain, but the army deemed that he was ready to return to service. When he arrived back with the 3rd (Reserve) Leinster Regiment in Cork he was fined six days' pay on 26 September for absenting himself yet again. He had been hospitalised twice so far during the war, and now he was to prepare himself for returning to the front once again.

On 22 March 1918 – day two of the German Spring Offensive – Monks was exhausted from the previous day's tremendous German attack but was still alive. He had spent 21 March with his battalion standing firm under cover of an embankment while German shells tore Irishmen to pieces all around him. The 2nd Leinster Regiment had suffered badly and, by the afternoon, they had been forced to retreat, with four enemy companies attacking them as they fell back on a line of defence. By nightfall, however, the German troops had been successfully repulsed. The Leinster men had been lucky, but they were worn out. That was only day one.

On the morning of 22 March, as the war diary records:

[at 7.30am] the 66th Div. apparently retired exposing Right Flank. Enemy worked through Gap and inflicted heavy casualties on Right Companies.

The battalion was subsequently forced to withdraw time and time again. By 11.30am they had managed to establish themselves in some shallow trenches, but then:

> By 12 noon this position was rendered untenable not only by the enemy but by our own guns whose barrage was coming down on the ridge and trenches. The two Right Coys ('A' & 'B') had suffered severe casualties mostly from infilade [sic] fire from right rear.

By the evening of 22 March 1918, after a further retreat, the survivors had managed to form some sort of a temporary defensive line, but, somewhere, out there on the battlefield covered in Germans, was Private Edward Monks. He had been hit in the head by a lump of shrapnel. However, while he was bleeding profusely from a severe head wound, he was still alive. He had been left for dead by his comrades, but who could blame them – the German push was so swift and strong that food depots and ammunition dumps were being abandoned fully stocked, so it was inevitable that the wounded and the fallen would be left where they lay. Monks was found unconscious, barely alive, by German soldiers and brought to a German dressing station like Matthew Crowe had been previously. Here, his wound was treated, but not by a German. In fact, it was a Russian surgeon who saved Monks' life by installing a metal plate in his skull – presumably this man was in the service of the German Army due to the recent peace treaty between Germany and Russia. Monks, again like Matthew Crowe, became a POW.

Monks was released after the armistice and then, just after Christmas 1918, his case was reviewed by an army medical board and Monks was deemed no longer fit for military service. Finally, he was discharged and free to return home to Ireland. But the scars of war never left him. Aside from the physical chunks of metal that were visible in his leg and arm until the day he died, and the chronic bronchitis that was a legacy of being gassed, Monks suffered terrible flashbacks for the rest of his life. They would come on him without warning, and he would suddenly go very quiet. When his children were still young, they did not know what was wrong with their father, and the family knew that at times like these, it was best to simply leave him alone.

This is unfortunately indicative of what veterans suffering from shellshock, or post traumatic stress disorder, went through in Ireland. The men did not know how to deal with what they were feeling. Their families did not know how to comfort them. Communities ignored them and did not want to know, and so the men spiralled into a pit of depression and guilt.

On one occasion, not long before he died in the early 1960s, Monks told his daughter that, during the war, he and his comrades had all been sent miraculous medals by the Pope. Years later, Edward Monks' son moved to Australia, where, each ANZAC day, he would wear his father's medals in order to commemorate his part in the First World War.

THE HAND OF GOD

DAVID O'SULLIVAN

However, while there are some stories that could be called lucky or even miraculous, there are some that defy explanation.

By 1918, German U-Boats had been wreaking havoc on Allied shipping in the North Atlantic for years, and Zeebrugge in Belgium was one of their bases of operation. U-Boats were coming and going from the port, unmolested, and while Admiral Jellico of the Royal Navy had argued back in 1917 for support for a raid against Zeebrugge, it was only in April 1918 that he finally got the go ahead for his plan.

A plan was devised. The British filled three old cruisers – *Thetis, Iphigenia,* and *Intrepid* – with concrete and mines, the idea being to sail the old ships into the narrow Zeebrugge canal, detonate the mines, and sink the ships creating a very effective dam to U-Boat traffic. Simultaneously, in order to cover the operation, the cruiser HMS *Vindictive* would come up alongside the Zeebrugge 'mole' (a heavily-fortified, crescent-shaped jetty that protected the harbour) and offload infantry, whose job it was to attack German gun emplacements. However, HMS *Vindictive* would need help in manoeuvring itself into position alongside the mole, and so two Liverpool Merseyside tugboats were enlisted for

The Mersey ferries HMS Daffodil *and HMS* Iris *at Dover soon after the vessels returned from the Zeebrugge Raid, 24 April 1918. Private David O'Sullivan from Ballymoe, County Cork had been killed aboard the* Iris.

the operation – the *Daffodil* and the *Iris*.

On the night of 23 April 1918, twenty-year-old David O'Sullivan from Ballymoe, County Cork, was on board the *Iris*. He was the eldest of a large family, and having joined the Royal Marine Light Infantry, O'Sullivan had been detailed to take part in this amphibious landing.

The operation began about fifteen miles out to sea. HMS *Vindictive*, which had been towing the two ferries up to this point, released them and they followed her under their own steam. Ahead of the cruiser, small motor craft released a smoke-screen, to cover the approach to Zeebrugge. Aboard the British vessels, men stared into the black at a great onshore searchlight scanning the hazy, overcast night. The harbour itself was completely dark.

Then the wind changed. The smoke-screen was swept away from HMS *Vindictive* and Zeebrugge harbour exploded into light. Star shells raced skywards, casting an eerie, shadowy glow over the raiding party. The searchlight swung around to face the oncoming British fleet and every gun on the mole opened up. Shells erupted from coastal artillery batteries – the guns spewed flame and then the shells hit the sea, sending geysers of water blasting across *Vindictive*'s decks. German machine guns peppered her hull, but she kept advancing. *Vindictive* brought herself up alongside the mole and dropped anchor. *Daffodil* raced to her stern to push *Vindictive* fully up alongside the jetty. Meanwhile, *Iris* steamed forward to offload its cargo of seventy Royal Marines onto the mole – one of which was David O'Sullivan.

Eighteen gangways aboard *Vindictive* dropped open and 200 marines charged down them. *Daffodil* was ordered to stay in place and keep *Vindictive* pressed up against the jetty. *Iris*, desperately exposed, chugged for the mole.

Marines prepared themselves with grappling hooks. David O'Sullivan got ready to charge up onto the jetty.

Suddenly, *Iris* suffered a direct hit from enemy artillery. The shell burst through the deck and detonated amongst the group of fifty-six Royal Marines who were waiting for orders to disembark. Forty-nine were killed outright; the other seven were badly wounded. Another shell burst in the sick bay killing a further thirty men. Many marines' bodies were blown out to sea.

Due to the failure to block the Zeebrugge canal, the daring mission was unsuccessful, and as *Daffodil* towed the battered HMS *Vindictive* back out to sea, the scene was one of speeding motor boats, searchlights, burning ships, machine-gun fire, smoking ruins of artillery emplacements, and general mayhem. The British suffered over 200 dead and a further 300 wounded. Among the corpses floating in the sea that night was David O'Sullivan from Cork. He had been one of the marines aboard *Iris*, blown out to sea while waiting to storm ashore. But while the story of David O'Sullivan's life is certainly tragic, the bizarre events surrounding him only started to happen after he had died ...

One month and a day after his body was blown out to sea, David O'Sullivan was washed up on the shores of neutral Holland after a massive storm the previous night. He was found by a local fisherman. His body had no legs, and was badly decomposed from the month at sea. O'Sullivan's bayonet was still in its scabbard, and on his belt was a grappling hook. By his side was a fellow comrade, and the two were buried together in a small ceremony the next day – a Sunday. They were buried in Cadzand Cemetery, and the Dutch ensured that they were laid to rest with full military honours.

But his story does not end there. David O'Sullivan was re-interred in 1919 in another cemetery, and then, due to the fact that several war veterans were buried in this cemetery, but that the cemetery was not always open for visiting relatives, his body was re-interred for a third time in 1992 in its present resting place – Flushing (Vlissingen) Northern Cemetery. He is one of only a few Allied casualties actually buried there. The layout of the older cemetery was copied, and the remains of David O'Sullivan and his comrades were placed side by side in the same order that they had lain for the previous eighty years.

That same year, 1992, David O'Sullivan's nephew, also named David

O'Sullivan, had decided to find out what happened to his uncle in the First World War. The younger David, with the help of a Dutch researcher, learned where his uncle was buried. So he travelled to Holland to pay his respects. However, he had no idea where exactly the graveyard was. He was travelling around Vlissingen trying to find it, when he came upon the graveyard quite by chance. There he met a Dutch caretaker who said that he knew where Private O'Sullivan's grave was. The younger David was expecting to find an untended grave. The slab of clean stone with his uncle's name and details, above a bed of fresh flowers and well-cut grass came as a complete surprise. The Dutch never knew his uncle; he did not even die fighting for the Dutch, but here was his perfectly tended resting place.

Other strange coincidences followed. The younger David returned home, and while visiting his sister he noticed a shell-casing in her garden that she was using as a flower pot. On the side of the shell was stamped 'FN April 1918'. FN stands for *Fabrique Nationale*, a Belgian weapon manufacturer. David O'Sullivan was killed in Belgium, and he was killed in April 1918.

On 23 April 1998, ninety years to the day that his uncle was killed, the younger David was faced with major surgery. While waiting to be brought to theatre, and to distract himself, David was reading a gardening article in the *Cork Examiner*. The article featured the iris flower. Private David O'Sullivan was killed aboard the Merseyside tugboat *Iris*.

On one of his pilgrimages to Holland, which David organised for 23 April – his uncle's anniversary – he found himself staying in the St George Hotel. This had not been the plan, but because of overbooking in the original hotel, he had been moved to this one. Then it dawned on him, 23 April is St George's Day.

He went to the grave on the evening of 22 April and found a candle there. It had been a year since he had last been here, and he had not left one behind. There was also no other family member who made the journey to Holland other than himself, so he was not quite sure how the candle had come to sit on his uncle's grave. Either way, it seemed fitting that he should light the candle, and after a few quiet minutes, David went back to the hotel. That night, there was a fierce wind blowing, and the next day when he returned to the graveside, the candle was still lit.

Before he left, David asked a Dutch person that he had befriended to tend the grave. He had just planted fresh flowers, and was hoping that someone would help them last, even just for a couple of weeks. A year later, he returned to find that they were still growing and well tended. The Dutch friend had been true to the local duty of honouring the fallen soldiers of the First World War.

To give an example of the obligation that some feel towards the men of 1914–1918, David once met a man who arrives every night at the Menin Gate Memorial in Ypres, Belgium, dedicated to those who fought around Ypres. He hops off his scooter and swaps his helmet for a cap before playing the Last Post on his bugle. This man has never missed a night in forty-eight years. He takes no holidays, even on Christmas he is there. And when he begins to play, David O'Sullivan insists that the sound of his bugle would bring a tear to anyone's eyes.

The younger David feels that he has to return to this place every year, that it is a pilgrimage of sorts, and he said to me when I interviewed him that 'I feel that if I don't go back, I'll be letting somebody down.'

JOHN CASCANI

One man who experienced the bizarre, and experienced it while still fighting the war, was John Cascani from Wexford. Cascani's father was an Italian sculptor, who had been commissioned to come to Ireland and produce a piece, only for this piece to topple when it was nearly completed and crack the sculptor's skull. Cascani senior did not die from the accident, however; a brain tumour ultimately took his life.

As for John Cascani, he made saddles and harnesses for a living, and was a pre-war regular who walked all the way from Bunclody to Carlow town to enlist. When the First World War broke out, Cascani – a gunner in 32nd Brigade, Royal Field Artillery – was sent to France as part of the original BEF. During his time in the war, Cascani received a head wound from shrapnel but did not die. His body was peppered with more shrapnel but he survived. On another occasion, he was riding along with a team of gunners when shellfire killed the outriders on either side of Cascani – he was unhurt in the middle. Then, finally, at the end of the war while in the vicinity of Mons, John Cascani witnessed something that he would swear to until his dying day. He looked up into the sky and saw a vision of the Last Supper in the air.

There, above the very town where the British had first met the Germans, and where some had sworn that they had seen an angel four years previously, John Cascani found himself looking at Christ breaking bread and drinking wine with the apostles. Cascani had only arrived in France on the day of the Battle of Mons back in 1914, and so he did not take part in the battle, but he had been in this area four years ago. Now, he was back where he had started and he could not explain or understand what he was seeing. But as peace was about to return to Europe, John Cascani would swear that he saw Christ preparing to absolve the sins of the world. To the Wexford man, he had just seen a miracle.

After the war, John Cascani worked in a Wexford harness shop before moving to Mullingar and working in Loftus' Shoes – leather being his trade. Aged ninety-five in 1982, he could still be seen cycling through Mullingar as spritely as a man half his age. And when he went to the pub, he always took an old policeman's baton with him in case anyone tried to cause trouble.

John Cascani – the former artilleryman who had seen Christ and his disciples in the sky over Mons in 1918 – lived for another seventy years after seeing his holy vision. He died in 1988 with shrapnel still in his head and limbs, aged 101.

EDWARD KING

Lastly comes the final chapter in the story of Captain Edward King – the 6th Royal Inniskilling Fusiliers officer from Cavan who had kept a diary through Gallipoli and won the Military Cross in Palestine. After the war, Edward King worked as personal assistant to Sir Fabian Ware, vice-chairman of the Imperial War Graves Commission. In the early post-war years, some relatives of deceased soldiers did not want to wait until the Commission erected memorials to their fallen loved ones, and so decided to purchase plots and build personal monuments out of their own pocket. This line of work led Edward King to hear some heart-breaking stories, but also one that is truly amazing. As Edward King recalled:

> One such case concerned a young soldier from Australia. He had fallen during an attack and in the maze of shell-holes, ruined trenches, barbed wire and mud his body was not recovered. None of his surviving comrades had any recollection of how or where he had fallen.

His father and mother made the long sea-journey to Europe. Enquiries among the records of his son's battalion had revealed no more than that his body might lie anywhere within an area of almost a square mile of devastated ground.

The father bought from the French government a tiny plot of land, just large enough for the base of a stone cross, at a spot which he selected after praying to God for guidance.

When the workmen dug down to lay the foundation for the cross, they uncovered a body. It was that of his son.

***

And so, wars can be full of astounding feats of survival, fateful coincidences and downright mysterious events. However, it must be remembered that for every medal that was won, a thousand other brave deeds went unrecognised. For every chance happening that ended well, fate ignored a thousand other men in need. And for every soldier who had a spiritual experience or found salvation in the trenches, there was a thousand men who lost their faith and found only blood, muck and Hell in the war.

A group photograph of Connaught Rangers attending a mass service. On the back of this photo, 'Xmas 1918' is written, which suggests that these men are soldiers of the 1ˢᵗ Battalion then stationed in Palestine, celebrating their first Christmas after the end of the war.

CHAPTER 9

THE WAR TO END ALL WARS

'Some lay as if they were sleeping quietly, others had died in agony or had had the life crushed out of them by mortal fear, while the whole ground, every foot, was littered with heads or limbs, or pieces of torn human bodies. In the bottom of one hole lay a British and a German soldier, locked in a deadly embrace, neither had any weapon but they had fought on to the bitter end.'

Father Willie Doyle, 8th Royal Dublin Fusiliers, August 1916

By 1918, the First World War had become so all-encompassing that it could not simply be ended; there was too much invested in it. So the war continued until one side – Germany – was reduced to ruin.

By that time, the world knew that the ideal of glorious warfare was no more. The German gas attack of April 1915 is often cited as the historical moment when modern warfare began. However, the First Battle of Ypres the previous year also went a long way towards introducing soldiers to the age of mechanised, industrial slaughter. The BEF lost 58,000 men and was nearly wiped out in the space of two months. Compare this to British casualties in the Crimean War and Boer War – 21,000 in each war, both over three-year periods, with seventy-five percent and sixty percent (respectively) of those being casualties from disease. In October and November 1914, in just two months, the British lost more men than in their previous two major wars combined.

The First World War was unlike any other war before it, simply because, with new technology, so many men could be killed or wounded in such a short space of time. One of the most poignant things about the war was that it was fought by millions – not thousands. Entire populations were dragged into the fighting. All in all, the First World War killed 20 million people (with a roughly fifty/fifty ratio of soldiers to civilians), and wounded 21 million more. Thirty-five to fifty thousand Irishmen lost their lives.

THE TRUE HORROR OF THE WAR

MICHAEL CURLEY

In November 1901, Athlone-man Michael Curley enlisted in the British Army. He claimed to be eighteen years old, but he was still two months away from his seventeenth birthday. Curley was only 5'3" and weighed only eight stone. For his young age, Curley had already done a lot in life. He was a reserve soldier, a member of the 6th Rifle Brigade, had previously worked as a labourer and as a printer and compositor, and had even done jail time for stealing two sacks of coal as a boy. Now he was a soldier in the 2nd Connaught Rangers.

He soon had a few run-ins with the military authorities, and following several bouts of rheumatism in 1902, Curley was transferred into the 1st Connaught Rangers and sent to Malta in March 1907. In April, however, he contracted syphilis (an 'occupational hazard' in those days, for which Curley was pre-scribed a treatment of mercury since there was still no cure for syphilis in 1907), and a medical board suggested that he change climate in order to help with the disease. So well before his overseas service was due to end, Michael Curley was sent back to Ireland in October 1907, arriving just before he devel-oped an ulcer on the cornea of his eye.

The following month, Curley married Agnes Gavin in St Mary's Church in Athlone and, in August 1908, the couple's first child was born. By now, Curley had also developed a strong friendship with fellow Athlone-man and

Connaught Ranger, Private 'Jack' West (his real Christian name is unknown). West was a 'character', and the pair were often involved in various antics. They were both fond of the drink and on one occasion while drinking in an Athlone pub, West – who was a champion boxer – was harassed by four Scottish soldiers of the Black Watch Regiment, which was stationed in Athlone at the time. They insulted West, Athlone, and the Connaught Rangers, which resulted in the four Scottish soldiers ending up in the barracks infirmary. However, Jack escaped being charged when his officers learned why West had raised his fists. The officers apparently muttered something about the 'damn Jocks insulting our honour' and congratulated Jack on being such a fine boxer!

Another time, after both Curley and West had been stationed away from Athlone for a while and had received no recent period of leave to go home, West suddenly went illegally absent from barracks. Curley was summoned by an officer – apparently there was a dispute between the Irish and English officers in the regiment and this Irish officer wanted the matter settled quietly, as the English officers would use West's disappearance as an excuse to criticise the Irish officers' handling of discipline – and so Curley was instructed to go back to Athlone and retrieve the missing West. If he was successful, Jack would not be charged and no one need speak about the event again.

As it turned out, Curley – annoyed at having had no leave for some time –

Above: Connaught Rangers' cap badge: One of the most famous Irish regiments, the Connaught Rangers was raised in 1793 as the 88th Foot by the Earl of Clanrickarde in response to the war with France. After fighting in Egypt, South America and Holland, they served throughout the Peninsular War under the command of Major-General Thomas Picton. He despised the Rangers, calling them 'Irish robbers and common foot-pads', and drove the men to prove him wrong. They forged a name for themselves in several major battles – soldiers of the Connaught Rangers were first through the breach at Ciudad Rodrigo – and by the end of the war they were one of the best regiments, if not the best, in Wellington's army. By then, they had acquired the nicknamed 'The Devil's Own' for their fierce reputation in battle. In 1881 the old 94th Foot joined the regiment and by the time of the First World War, the Connaught Rangers recruited from Galway, Sligo, Mayo, Roscommon and Leitrim, with the regimental depot in Galway. Their unit motto was Quis Separabit – 'who shall separate us'.

Members of the Midlands Volunteer Force council. Michael Curley is seated first from the left, and the document in his hand calls for 'every young Irishman who loves his country and is prepared to serve her as called upon [to] at once join the Volunteer Force'.

had handed Jack West ten pounds that he had saved up and told Jack to vanish. West, always one for devilment, took the money and started a drinking session as soon as he reached Athlone. Curley soon followed, and together the two men enjoyed over a week of 'rest and recreation' before Curley finally returned to barracks with the 'missing' Private West.

However, in April 1909 – now a corporal – Michael Curley was discharged from the regular army. His contract of service was up, and Curley chose not to renew it. Perhaps this had something to do with repeated bronchial infections that Curley suffered in 1908 and 1909, but either way, while he would still be kept on the army's books as a member of the active reserve, he was now free to return to civilian life. He soon began work in the local Athlone woollen mills, where most of the Curley family were already employed.

Following the Home Rule crisis and the formation of the UVF in Ulster,

Curley was instrumental in forming the Midlands Volunteer Force (MVF) – a nationalist organisation dedicated to the defence of Home Rule. As Sean O'Mullany wrote, in an article entitled 'Athlone started the Volunteer Movement' (*The Athlone Annual*, 1963):

> In September, 1913, a body of workers in Athlone formed a body of volunteers with the object of opposing the 'Covenanters' – as the militant supporters of [unionist leader] Carson were called – if need be by arms. They drilled openly, elected a committee, called themselves the Midland Volunteers and very soon had marches or processions in the town and vicinity with about fifteen hundred men.

The MVF – the council of which was comprised of predominately ex-British Army men who worked in the Athlone woollen mills – pre-dated the formation of the Irish Volunteers. When Liam Mellows – founding member of the Irish Volunteers – visited Athlone on 6 November 1913, the nationwide movement was still several weeks away from coming into existence. Also in November 1913, Roger Casement – another founder of the Irish Volunteers – wrote that 'I have in mind a great scheme of Volunteers for all Ireland. To begin in Athlone – they have begun there already ...'

It is a little known fact, but when the Irish Volunteers were formed on 25 November 1913 in Dublin's Rotunda Hospital, a similar organisation in Athlone had already existed for several months. However, the MVF soon decided to join the larger, national movement instead of remaining independent, and as recruitment and training began nationally, a report in the Irish Volunteers' journal of 10 October 1914 mentioned Michael Curley by name:

> Excellent progress is being made in Athlone and instructors P. Croghan and M. Curley express themselves pleased with the way the men under their command are conducting themselves and the wonderful progress made in drill.

Also in November 1913, Curley renewed his membership of the British Army active reserve for a further four years, which meant that, when war broke out in August 1914, Curley was summoned back to active service. Although he now had a wife and young daughter, he returned to the army. So, too, did the five fellow ex-British Army soldiers on the committee of the MVF (a council which only totalled nine members). When they were recalled to active service, not one of them protested.

Now twenty-nine years old, Curley was summoned to Galway on 5 August 1914 and was posted to his old unit, the 2nd Connaught Rangers, then stationed in Barrosa Barracks, Aldershot. Curley was promoted to sergeant two days later and sent to join his battalion. Everything was moving quickly and, a few days later, on 13 August – Curley and 2nd Connaught Rangers sailed for Boulogne and the war. It was while marching through the streets of Boulogne that the 2nd Connaught Rangers forged the link between the song, 'It's a Long Way to Tipperary', and the First World War. They sang it as an unofficial marching song – as reported by George Churnock in the *Daily Mail* – and the catchy tune aroused the interest of other groups of soldiers. Soon enough, the rest of the British Army were singing it, and by then, Athlone tenor Count John McCormack had recorded it, which spread the popularity of the song throughout France and America.

Michael Curley went on to fight in the Battle of Mons. During the subsequent retreat from Mons, 300 men of the 2nd Connaught Rangers – approximately one third of the battalion – were captured by the Germans on 26 August. Luckily for Curley, he was not one of them. He then fought at Villers-Cotterêts, the Battle of the Marne, the Battle of the Aisne, and each time he saw his fair share of the fighting. However, in October 1914, Sergeant Michael Curley was redirected to Ypres. To the east, beyond the devastated Belgian city, were desolate ridges occupied by Germans. Desperate to break through before the enemy had too much time to dig in, the British went on the offensive.

What happened was a disaster. The British were outnumbered five to one and were severely outmatched in terms of artillery. While the Germans had no shortage of firepower, the British guns were poorly supplied – most batteries only had shrapnel shells to fire, not heavy explosives. Ypres was flattened by German counter-fire, and to the east, men like Sergeant Michael Curley frantically dug shallow pits and trenches in woods, villages, beside roads and crossroads – anywhere that they could mount resistance – and fought back wave after wave of attacking German troops. The enemy also wanted to dislodge the

The Midlands Volunteer Force on parade on the fairgreen behind St Mary's Church, Athlone, 1913.

British before they had time to consolidate at Ypres, and so they threw everything that they had at the BEF.

Every day the shelling worsened and the Germans just kept coming. At Langemarck, Gheluvelt and Nonne Bosschen, at Zandvoorde, Zonnebeke and Hooge, the soldiers of both sides were massacred, and as British battalion after British battalion was decimated, the veteran professionals of the BEF disappeared into the muck.

The situation became desperate on several occasions, when it looked as though the Germans might break through and rout the British back to Ypres. England drew on the resources of its empire and an Indian division was summoned to Ypres. British Territorials entered the battle – the 1/14th London Regiment (London Scottish) was the first to arrive and suffered sixty percent casualties in their first engagement. But the line held, mainly due to the fact that the Germans were attacking predominantly veteran British troops – expertly trained and well entrenched. The Germans sustained terrific losses, especially in their poorly trained reserve battalions of student volunteers, so much so that they called the First Battle of Ypres *Kindermord* – the Massacre of the Innocents.

Sergeant Curley, who appears to have been in C Company, 2nd Connaught Rangers, attacked the Germans near St Julien on 21 October, but the attack was held up and the whole line had to entrench themselves. Two days later, as the war diary records, 'C Coy heavily shelled in trenches – 9 killed 20 wounded in C & D Coys – mostly in C.' The following day – 23 October – having just been relieved, Curley and his comrades were ordered to march east from Ypres up the Menin Road to a crossroads, to plug a dangerous gap in the British lines. Two of their party were killed and five wounded before being relieved that night. The 2nd Connaught Rangers assaulted enemy positions again on 29 October and two days later – with the fighting still ongoing and veteran soldiers being driven to the limits of desperation – C Company was still in the trenches. On that day – 31 October 1914 – Sergeant Michael Curley allegedly committed a crime known as 'fragging'. He supposedly killed one of his own officers.

Curley's descendents tell the story of how, while fighting the Germans early in the war, east of a shattered town and while positioned in trenches along a tree line at the base of a ridge, an officer led a party of 2nd Connaught Rangers forward. The attack was suicidal and resulted in terrible casualties. During the attack – when it was becoming obvious that it was doomed to failure – Michael Curley insisted to this officer that they should withdraw. The officer is said to have ignored Curley, and demanded that the assault be progressed against far superior enemy numbers. Positioned in a house of some sort, Curley realised that many of his comrades were either dead or wounded on the battlefield, and that if he did not do something, the rest would soon become casualties. So he exited the shack, took the pin out of a grenade, and tossed it back inside, fatally wounding the officer. It was then that a runner came charging up from rear headquarters – ironically the runner was Private Jack West – with a message ordering the officer to make an immediate withdrawal. If Curley had waited only a few moments, the officer would have been forced to obey and order the withdrawal anyway.

While the story cannot be officially confirmed, the particulars of the story do seem to tally with the death of a 2nd Connaught Rangers officer on 31 October

1914, as well as the account of the battle which led to his death. In consultation with Oliver Fallon – researcher with the Connaught Rangers Association based in King House, Boyle, County Roscommon – who is an expert on Connaught Rangers' history, we have uncovered a possible candidate for Curley's victim. As the war diary for 31 October 1914 states:

> In trenches – 1½ platoons C Coy under Lieut Saker attacked German trenches in support of a Coy of Berkshires who advanced along the Beceleare Road – Lieut Saker wounded & captured – 6 NCO & men killed – 30 wounded – 30 missing of whom many were taken prisoner.

The conditions of this action, which took place near the foot of the ridges east of Ypres near the edge of Polygon Wood, certainly might have resulted in Curley's alleged breakdown, and the argument that the Curley family story might be true is made stronger by the fact that there was considerable confusion surrounding what happened to Lieutenant Frank Harrison Saker on 31 October. Although the war diary does state that he was taken prisoner by the enemy on 31 October, it was later concluded that Saker had been killed, yet even then the accounts of his death are conflicting. Oliver Fallon has discovered in his research – which covers witness statements from soldiers, officers, and even Connaught Rangers POWs in German internment camps – that there is no one definitive account of how Saker died. Some men are confused about the day it happened on, while others cast doubt on the exact circumstances. However, one eye-witness, Captain White of the Connaught Rangers, states that 'Saker was the C Company subaltern. Our guns were shelling the enemy's trenches heavily. The Captain of C Company, therefore, tried to make an advance. Saker was told to take half the company and to advance up a line with my trench, and to dig himself in there … [but] Saker went beyond the dotted lines towards the concealed German lines'. It was here that the attacking troops jumped into what looked like an empty trench and Saker went into *an empty house* [author's italics]. White then states that he saw C Company 'standing about with their hands up' and surrendering to the Germans about thirty minutes to an hour later, after which some Germans went into the house where

Saker was and brought him out. 'I could distinctly see it was Saker through my glasses. It was about 250 yards [away].' Captain White goes on to state that 'I can't say where he [Saker] was hit', which clarifies that the lieutenant was indeed wounded at this point.

Either way, the Curley family have a story of how Sergeant Michael Curley killed an officer who persisted in pushing forward a suicidal attack around the time of the First Battle of Ypres (In a journal entry covering the period 30 October to 7 November 1914, Sergeant John McIlwain of the Connaught Rangers wrote: 'It is reported that one young officer named Saker, who brought up the last of the reserves from home, gets up on a raid on his own one night. He is wounded and, with all those left alive, taken prisoner' – which, when taken into consideration in light of Captain White's earlier statement that Saker purposely advanced beyond his designated objective, shows that the men certainly believed the attack had been reckless). However, according to Captain White, C Company surrendered, but Michael Curley was never taken prisoner by the enemy. On 27 November 1914 – just under a month after the action in which Saker died – Sergeant Michael Curley was evacuated back to Ireland. He was suffering from shrapnel wounds to his left shoulder, arm and side, and although these wounds could have been received in late October (with Curley spending the interim period in a French hospital until he was stable enough to be returned home), ultimately this means that the story remains impossible to prove, but either way, it serves to illustrate the confusion and desperation suffered by the British Army at Ypres in 1914. They were barely hanging on.

The First Battle of Ypres introduced the world to the destruction of total war. When the battle finally ended on 22 November 1914, Britain had suffered 58,000 casualties and the destruction of its regular army. Among the Irish dead was another of Michael Curley's comrades in 2nd Connaught Rangers – Private John Holian from Henry Street, Roscommon town. Holian was involved in an attack on 2 November when his friend was shot beside him. Holian grabbed his fallen comrade and started dragging him through the viscous muck, but the Roscommon man was now a slow-moving target and a German bullet found its mark. John Holian was killed age twenty-eight, leaving a widow behind him in Roscommon. Today he is buried in Poperinghe Old Military Cemetery.

After the First Battle of Ypres, only very few experienced men remained, and many of these had been badly wounded. As the war diary records, 2nd Connaught Rangers alone had suffered eighty-one men killed, 260 wounded and thirty missing in October and November 1914, one of which was Athlone-man Sergeant Michael Curley. However, unlike so many of his comrades, he was still alive.

After his return to Ireland, Curley recovered in hospital in Renmore, Galway, and later joined the 3rd (Reserve) Connaught Rangers in Kinsale on 2 February 1915. Here, he would have trained the men until he was once again called upon to enter the war. However, Michael Curley was not sent back to Belgium or France, nor was he detailed to fight in Gallipoli or Salonika. In fact, Michael Curley was sent to a warzone familiar to the modern soldiers of today. He was sent to Mesopotamia, a country which we know as Iraq.

In late 1914, the British captured the area around the southern port of Basra from the Turks. They had been after the southern oil wells – oil now becoming the staple fuel of army vehicles as well as naval vessels – and so with their supply secure, and inspired by the quick and easy victory that they had won over the Turks at Basra, the British sent an expedition north in early 1915. They planned to bring the fight to the enemy, instead of just remaining on the defensive.

Marching through blistering heat under a glaring sun, the British soldiers captured town after town while the Turks continually fell back. The British hugged the vital rivers and their life-giving waters, with riverboats sailing from Basra with supplies, and gunships steaming along in support of the advancing infantry. They pressed on to Baghdad, but, now far from Basra, the British supply lines were critically over-extended. There was not enough food, water, ammunition or medical supplies reaching the soldiers. And as the long caravan of British horses, camels, mules, donkeys, carts, cows, trucks, artillery pieces and columns of soldiers trudged north, the situation quickly deteriorated. Coupled with the flies and the thirst, the troops in Mesopotamia were struck with dysentery, cholera, plague, typhus, fever, malaria and heatstroke. Contaminated water poisoned the men, disease was everywhere, and so were the rats, lice and mosquitoes. The daytime temperature averaged 50°C. So, when the British soldiers neared Baghdad in November 1915, they were blistered, exhausted and sick.

After losing 4,600 of their 11,000-strong attacking force in a battle against the Turks – sixteen miles south of Baghdad in the desert plains around the ruins of the ancient palace of Ctesiphon – the British were forced to retreat and their army fell back towards the town of Kut-al-Amara. They managed to entrench themselves inside the town just before the counter-attacking Turks laid siege to it in early December 1915. The Turks breached the city's defences in several places, and waves of Turkish soldiers poured into the town, but the British held out, fighting bitterly to hold their ground. It was like a medieval siege, something that would not have been out of place in the crusades. Back in Basra, 380 miles south, the British hastily put together a rescue mission.

One of the men detailed to go on it was Sergeant Michael Curley, now of the 1st Connaught Rangers. In January 1916, while preparations were being made on the Western Front for the upcoming Battle of the Somme, Sergeant Curley and the 1st Connaught Rangers marched north from Basra along with the rest of the relief force. These men had different weather conditions to endure – the rain and humidity of the day, and the bitter cold of night – a Middle Eastern winter.

From the start, the relief force encountered problems. It had not enough artillery shells to bombard Turkish positions before an attack; foolish tactics were employed in assaulting some Turkish positions; and by April, it was raining as though the biblical flood had returned. Disease, hunger, thirst and heat soon claimed more and more casualties. Morale in the relief force started to plummet. Officers tried to keep the men going by reminding them that their comrades in Kut-al-Amara never had any rest, never had any reprieve and would starve to death or be slaughtered by the enemy if they were not reached in time. But there was a limit to how far the men of the relief force could be pushed.

On 17 April 1916, with time running out for the besieged in Kut-al-Amara, the relief force made one last attempt to break through by attacking the Turks at Bait Aisa. At 6.45am, the artillery opened fire. Five minutes after the barrage had commenced, the infantry went in behind the shellfire. Michael Curley and the 1st Connaught Rangers stormed the enemy trenches and raced around the traverses, hurling bombs ahead of them as they ran and consolidating themselves in some water channels. By the end of the day they had suffered 100 killed and wounded. Through the night the Turks mounted a counter attack and encircled the 1ˢᵗ Connaught Rangers and the 89ᵗʰ [Punjabis – a British Indian regiment]. The battalion fought back and succeeded in inflicting heavy losses on the enemy. However, the following day, on 18 April, the battalion had fallen back to shallow trenches and 'many men were killed by accurate rifle fire'.

In all, 17 and 18 April 1916 resulted in the 1ˢᵗ Connaught Rangers suffering 187 men killed and wounded. But the struggle to reach Kut-al-Amara was not over yet, and on Good Friday – 21 April 1916 – the 1ˢᵗ Connaught Rangers were ordered to get ready to move. However, after a separate attack failed on 22 April in the face of intense flooding and determined enemy counter-attacks, the Connaught Rangers' assault was called off. The British tried one last time to reach Kut-al-Amara by riverboat when the steamer *Julnar* attempted to sail up the Tigris with supplies on 24 April. It never made it, and on that day – the same day that the Easter Rising broke out on the streets of Dublin – the garrison in Kut-al-Amara knew that all was lost. Five days later, having survived on daily rations of a few ounces of bread and some horseflesh, the men in Kut-al-Amara surrendered to the Turks. Thirteen-thousand soldiers became POWs, and due to disease, thirst, starvation and violent treatment at the hands of their Turkish captors, 8,000 of these men never survived to be released.

For all their tireless fighting, Sergeant Michael Curley and his comrades in the 1ˢᵗ Connaught Rangers had not managed to break through in time. There would be no more battles in Mesopotamia in 1916, no more attempts to press north. And as the summer heat returned, so did the incredible thirst and hunger, the diseases and plagues. Thousands of men succumbed to the harsh conditions, and more soldiers were evacuated due to sickness than battle injury from this theatre. On 23 May 1916, Michael Curley became one of them. He was evacuated home, finally leaving behind the deserts of the Middle East – having served, like many modern soldiers, in the land between Baghdad and Basra.

He served once more for a period in the Connaught Rangers' depot in Galway, and then in the 3ʳᵈ (Reserve) Connaught Rangers in Kinsale, before returning to the war in April 1917, although this time to France. A month after he returned to the fight, in May 1917, his second daughter was born. Michael

Curley was now in the 6th Connaught Rangers, and after taking part in the Battle of Messines Ridge, he was in reserve when the Third Battle of Ypres was launched on 31 July. However, three days later, Michael Curley's luck ran out. Having served for eleven years altogether, having survived the horrors of the First Battle of Ypres, and having returned from the deserts of Mesopotamia, Curley was fatally wounded in the abdomen – most likely by a shell fragment or piece of shrapnel. He lingered on in great pain for a short while before dying in the 32nd Casualty Clearing Station at Brandhoek later that day – 3 August 1917 – thirteen days before his eldest daughter's ninth birthday. The war diary states that on 3 August:

> Shelling was considerable throughout the day and it was impossible to do much work on the lines which were in a terrible condition, nearly all portions of trench which had been dug being under water. Casualties were heavy ...

Curley was thirty-two years old, one of the founders of the first nationalist Volunteer movement in Ireland, and he died without ever seeing his second daughter. Back home in Athlone, the *Westmeath Independent* of 4 August 1917 soon carried the following article:

> The news was heard with much regret in Athlone of the death of Sergt. Michael Curley, 6th Batt. Connaught Rangers, which took place on August 3rd at a casualty clearing station in France. Late on Thursday night Mrs Curley received a telegram from the Record Office, Cork, stating her husband had died from gunshot wounds. The deceased Sergeant, who was well known in Athlone prior to the outbreak of the war, had been an instructor to the original Corps of the National Volunteers, and had seen much service in France. He was one of the original Expeditionary Force, was in the retreat from Mons, was severely wounded in the chest at Ypres, and went through several battles unscathed. Recently he was the recipient of a Vellum Certificate for gallant conduct and devotion to duty in the field. Much sympathy is extended to the widow and family in their bereavement.

In the years that followed, his family mistakenly came to believe that he had died on the last day of the war – 11 November 1918 – and that he had been 'blown to pieces' by a shell. The truth was that Curley died on 3 August 1917 and, today, his remains lie in Brandhoek New Military Cemetery No. 3.

THE RIGHT TO STAY ALIVE

ROBERT MORROW

At the opposite end of the political spectrum from Michael Curley was Private Robert Morrow of the 1ˢᵗ Royal Irish Fusiliers, born in Newmills, Dungannon, County Tyrone. Morrow was a Presbyterian and twenty-three years old in 1914. His father had died when he was just four, leaving Robert's mother and his eldest brother to support the family of nine. Two of his older sisters had helped to bring in some money by working as fertilizer spreaders – spreading manure on fields – and on this meagre income, the family had had to make do. Then in 1911, Robert Morrow enlisted in the army in Armagh, aged nineteen. In 1912, he signed the Ulster Covenant, in order to, as the Covenant states, 'defeat the present conspiracy to set up a Home Rule Parliament in Ireland'.

Private Robert Morrow from Newmills, Dungannon, County Tyrone. In the regimental history of the 1ˢᵗ Royal Irish Fusiliers, he was described as a 'simple, unassuming lad … not conspicuous as a soldier'.

Robert Morrow and the 1st Royal Irish Fusiliers were not present at the Battle of Mons in August 1914, but they joined the retreating BEF very soon after – just in time for the rearguard Battle of Le Cateau. The battalion later fought at the Marne, when the Germans were finally pushed back after their steamroller advance on Paris; at the Aisne, where British troops tried unsuccessfully to break through the German defence lines; and then during the First Battle of Ypres, although his battalion was not involved in any major fighting.

After the end of the battle came Christmas, and Christmas Day 1914 saw the famous truce between the British and Germans. Prior to Christmas, both sides

Private Robert Morrow's signature on the Ulster Covenant.

had been subjected to the same appalling conditions – waterlogged trenches, cold, rain, rats, bad food – and with British and German positions in some places only a few dozen yards apart, conversations across no-man's-land were sometimes struck up. Some degree of disillusionment towards the war was also setting in, and it made men more open to being friendly with the enemy. That and of course Christmas was approaching, the time of good will to all men when soldiers started longing for home, for comfort, for peace. In the days leading up to 25 December, several local truces had been reported along the British line, although in each instance they were short-lived and often ended with one side or the other opening fire.

During the evening on Christmas Eve, a day of rock-hard frost, Robert Morrow and the 1st Royal Irish Fusiliers were positioned in their trenches near Ploegsteert Wood (known as 'Plugstreet' to the men). This was the location where the Germans started lugging Christmas trees and lanterns onto their parapet. Both sides started singing hymns and, in some places, the famous truce began with both sides exiting their trenches and making agreements to allow each other to bury their dead. The equally infamous British *v* German football match in no-man's-land has never been confirmed, with many units saying that it happened to their neighbouring regiment. When these neighbouring regiments were asked about it, they in turn said that it happened to a battalion on their flank. There appears to be some truth to the match, however, since the score is nearly always the same, 3–2, to the Germans.

It was not long before Private Robert Morrow started to make a name for himself. One day, during the winter, water was badly needed in the trenches so Robert Morrow took an empty two-gallon, stone rum-jar and ran for a nearby farmhouse about 600 yards away. German snipers in front of the Royal Irish Fusiliers' trenches opened up with rifle fire. Somehow Morrow managed to get past the hail of bullets and fill up the jar. He made his way back to the trenches, struggling with the now-50lb awkward weight. Just as he was about to dive over the parapet to safety, a bullet shattered the rum-jar. Frustrated but determined, Morrow gathered water bottles and sped back to the farmhouse, bullets biting into the earth around him. He filled the bottles up and bolted for safety, managing to make it back in one piece.

Spring 1915 soon arrived and on 14 March, Robert Morrow and the 1st

Royal Irish Fusiliers were relieved from their position, having manned the same stretch of trench for four months. They returned to billets, where they soon had a chance to unwind by way of an inter-platoon football competition final. With St Patrick's Day approaching, the men received best wishes from their commanding officer, and, illustrating that sectarian strife had a way of disappearing on the battlefields of Europe, the battalion – who were predominantly northern Irish Protestants – were deeply upset when Father Ryan, a popular character with all of the men, left them to take up duty at GHQ.

On 16 March the battalion marched into Armentières with colours flying and regimental drums playing. When they arrived, they were treated to dinner followed by a concert. Their hosts were the soldiers of the 28th London Regiment (Artist's Rifles), who actually waited on them during dinner – some of whom had marched seven miles to give their service. It was all down to a double celebration: St Patrick's Day on the following day, and the recent anniversary of the Battle of Barrosa. The Battle of Barrosa is famous in Royal Irish Fusiliers' history. The battle was fought on 5 March 1811 near Cadiz in Spain, and it was on this day that the first French Imperial Eagle – the standard used by Napoleonic French regiments – was captured by the British. And it was the Royal Irish Fusiliers (then known as the 87th Foot) who had captured it; Ensign Edward Keogh died taking the Eagle, with Sergeant Patrick Masterson finally securing it.

On St Patrick's Day the 1st Royal Irish Fusiliers re-entered the trenches. The days that followed were quiet but full of snow. March

Royal Irish Fusiliers' cap badge: This regiment was formed in 1881 by the amalgamation of two units – the 87th (Prince of Wales' Irish) Foot and the 89th (The Princess Victoria's) Foot, both raised in 1793 for the fight against France. The 87th was the more famous of the two, and was the first British regiment to capture an Imperial French Eagle – the standard used by Napoleonic regiments – at the Battle of Barossa during the Peninsular War. It recruited from Armagh, Monaghan and Cavan, with the regimental depot at Armagh town.

went and April came, and on 9 April – now back in camp – a match was held between B and D Companies to see who would get the honour of representing the battalion for the Brigade Cup. Robert Morrow was in D Company, but, unfortunately for him, B Company won. That night, there was a fierce thunderstorm that raged on for hours. In the darkness, the sounds of thunderclaps intermingled with the devastating eruptions of high explosive shells all along the line – British and German – that flashed eerily, giving the front a constantly rippling dim illumination.

Then on 12 April 1915, with the 1st Royal Irish Fusiliers scheduled to be relieved, later that day, from their trenches below Messines Ridge along the Douvre River, the Germans opened fire on the battalion. Howitzers and heavy guns tore up the sodden earth, laying waste to the British-held Dead Cow Farm, before turning their attention on the section of trench manned by Robert Morrow and D Company. It was badly hit. Men were killed by shell-bursts, while others were buried alive. Duckboards, lintels, planks and posts were splintered into deadly missiles.

Robert Morrow and his surviving comrades fled from their position into the support trenches to the rear. But Private Morrow was very aware that there were wounded left behind – men that were covered in soil and debris, too weak, or too badly injured, to dig themselves out. So he raced back into the front line, shells churning up the ground all around him, and frantically dug out the first wounded comrade that he found. He dragged the man as fast as he could back to the support trenches. This was hardly out of harm's way but it was certainly safer than the firing trench, which had been almost totally destroyed.

Then Robert Morrow went back. In the chaos of an artillery bombardment – reportedly more intense than anything the battalion had yet encountered – Morrow returned to rescue another comrade. He carried this man back to the support trenches, then immediately ran back out into the storm of shellfire. Again and again, he dragged back wounded soldier after wounded soldier, continually charging back into the front line each time.

When the 1st Royal Irish Fusiliers were relieved that night they marched into camp at Bailleul, narrowly missing a German zeppelin bombing by about two hours. Robert Morrow was congratulated on a job well done – he had saved six comrades in total – his only reward being a battalion bath on 14 April.

17 April saw B Company beat the Royal Dublin Fusiliers in a football match of the Brigade Cup. The score was 4–1. The victory was short-lived, as on 22 April they were hammered 7–1 in the final. The following day, an ominous warning circulated through the battalion: 'Be ready to move at short notice.' This was the Second Battle of Ypres.

Two days after the Germans introduced the Western Front to poison gas on 22 April, Robert Morrow and the 1st Royal Irish Fusiliers were instructed to move into position for attack, the men being issued with grenades and sandbags along the way. On the morning of the 25 April, after a wet night, Private Morrow and his comrades looked to the south to see Ypres in flames. The first phase of this battle – the Battle of Gravenstafel – was over, and now it was time to start the second phase – the Battle of St Julien. The 1st Royal Irish Fusiliers were ordered to advance from their current position on the Wielje-Fortuin Road and plug a gap between the town of St Julien itself and the Suffolk Regiment. There could be no weak points in the British line if the attack was to succeed.

The attack was launched at 3.45am with Robert Morrow and D Company at the head of the assault. The troops initially advanced without much opposition, but then the Germans opened up with machine gun and rifle fire, causing heavy casualties amongst the Irishmen. Unable to locate the Suffolk Regiment, the 1st Royal Irish Fusiliers fought their way to a ridgeline, only to find it impossible to press on any further. The 2nd Royal Dublin Fusiliers on their left met with stiff resistance and were forced to retreat, leaving the left flank badly exposed. German troops suddenly appeared, attempting to exploit this weak point in the British line and counter-attack. Robert Morrow and his comrades plastered the enemy with fire and the Germans were driven back. But the 1st Royal Irish Fusiliers' position was untenable. The Germans counter-attacked again and the Irishmen started to withdraw. The enemy guns began to pound the British lines with shells and the British artillery returned fire – only to hit their own retreating infantry by mistake. These British troops were forced to fall back further than was necessary.

It was chaos, and in amongst the explosions and the detonations of shellfire, men of the 1st Royal Irish Fusiliers were wounded and buried by the hail of earth and metal. Once again, Robert Morrow raced back through the erupting no-man's-land and towards the oncoming enemy. Repeating his previous heroic feat, he started dragging his fallen comrades towards safety. However, this time he was not so lucky.

At the end of the day, Robert Morrow was lying on a stretcher in a barn loft beside a crossroads that was being used as a dressing station. During his brave attempt to rescue more wounded comrades out from under enemy shellfire, he had been badly wounded himself. His battalion had managed to secure a new line, but were finding it impossible to advance. German resistance was just too fierce. Once again, the war had lead to stalemate.

The following day, 26 April 1915, Private Robert Morrow died of his wounds, age twenty-three.

Robert Morrow's Company Commander, Colonel GVW Hill, had this to say about the private's actions on 12 April:

It was due to his [Morrow's] work and astounding bravery that the company's casualties were not trebled. Morrow was a small unostentatious man, almost boy, whom one would never imagine as doing outstanding things, yet under fire he was one of those who did not know what fear was. His bravery was the talk of the

Medals of Private Robert Morrow (from left: Victoria Cross, 1914 Star, War Medal, Victory Medal, Russian Cross of St George third class). The Victoria Cross was established on 29 January 1856 to reward acts of heroism performed during the Crimean War (the first ever recipient of the medal was Charles Davis Lucas from Scarva, County Armagh) and to this day remains the highest award for valour in the face of the enemy that Britain can bestow. All VCs, even to this day, are made from melted down cannons captured from the Russians during the Siege of Sevastopol. Soldiers of all ranks were eligible to earn this award.

Company, but unfortunately he never knew he had won the Victoria Cross, for he was wounded near St Julien on 25th April 1915 and died shortly after. It was early in May that we heard he had been awarded the VC.

Private Morrow was also described by a comrade as 'an Irishman who literally did not know the meaning of fear'.

The Tsar of Russia had even awarded him the Russian Cross of St George, Third Class. Morrow's citation for the VC appeared in the *London Gazette* of 22 May 1915 and read:

> For the most conspicuous bravery near Messines on 12th April, 1915, when he rescued and carried successively to places of comparative safety, several men who had been buried in the debris of trenches wrecked by shellfire. Private Morrow carried out this gallant work on his own initiative, and under very heavy fire from the enemy.

The following year in October 1916, Robert Morrow's mother received a letter stating: 'It is a matter of sincere regret to me that the death of Private Robert Morrow deprived me of the pride of personally conferring upon him the Victoria Cross, the greatest of all distinctions.' The letter was signed 'George R.I.' – King George V. It had become standard practice for the king himself to pin the Victoria Cross on a recipient's tunic, but with Private Morrow dead, his mother was invited to Buckingham Palace to receive it in her son's place. She did so, and took his medal from the king on 26 November 1916. But she decided not to keep it.

Even though Margaret Morrow was still struggling to make ends meet, and even though a Victoria Cross with such providence would get a decent price, she offered it to the regimental museum. When the officers of Robert Morrow's unit learned of his mother's plans, they collected a fund for her – feeling that they could not accept such a prized possession for nothing. And so at a parade in the Armagh depot in August 1919, Margaret Morrow handed over her son's Victoria Cross to his regiment, and the regiment, in return, handed her the deeds to some much-needed land adjoining her farm.

Back home in Dungannon, a memorial fund was put together by a local committee to erect a monument to Private Morrow in Newmills, and also to care for his bereaved mother. Donations were made to the treasurer of the committee, and the monument was soon erected. And just to prove that Robert Morrow's heroism has never been forgotten by the people of his home, the local pub is still named the VC Inn, and when, years later, Morrow's monument was destroyed in a car accident, it was immediately replaced so that the brave soldier's deeds would always be remembered. Today, Robert Morrow's name is as significant in Royal Irish Fusiliers' history as that of Ensign Keogh and Sergeant Masterson – he was the first Royal Irish Fusilier (and Tyrone-man) to earn a Victoria Cross. His body now lies in White House Cemetery, St Jean-les-Ypres.

UNSUNG HEROES – STRETCHER-BEARERS

MARTIN FITZGERALD

The fighting could also change men in personal ways that would only ever be known to the men themselves. Thousands of Irishmen went to war and seemingly returned the same, but, deep down, every man was altered by the fighting.

One such man was Martin Fitzgerald from near Ballybrittas, County Laois. Unlike the majority of his countrymen, Fitzgerald was not a soldier. He was a Red Cross man, and they had the unenviable job of being stretcher-bearers. Stretcher-bearers were not armed and had to go out into no-man's-land to retrieve the wounded, often while under direct enemy fire.

One day, somewhere on the Western Front, Fitzgerald and a comrade were carrying a wounded soldier across no-man's-land after a battle when they came across a badly wounded German. This man was the enemy, and they already had a wounded British soldier on their hands.

Forced by their consciences to do the humane thing, Martin Fitzgerald and his fellow stretcher-bearer put down the stretcher and started patching up the wounded German. Neither of them knew a word of German, and the enemy soldier did not know a word of English, so the two Red Cross men used hand

Stretcher-bearers struggle in mud to carry a wounded man to safety near Boesinghe, during the Battle of Pilckem Ridge, 1 August 1917. The man third from the left has been possibly identified as Jimmy Coates of the 36ᵗʰ (Ulster) Division. Often, so-called 'conscientious objectors' – men who refused to kill or bear arms against their fellow man, but who were willing to do their duty for their country – were allowed to enlist as stretcher-bearers, where they would only help, not harm, other men. Initially, many saw them as cowards, but the bravery and compassion displayed by the stretcher-bearers soon earned them a proud reputation. Martin Fitzgerald may or may not have been a conscientious objector, but he almost certainly served with men who were.

gestures to let the German know what they were doing and to try and keep him calm.

When they had dressed his wounds as best they could, they stood up and tried to explain to the German that they would be back to get him once they had got the other wounded man to safety. So Fitzgerald and his friend picked up the stretcher, turned, and started on their way. It was then that a shot rang out and Martin Fitzgerald's friend, and fellow stretcher-bearer, dropped to the ground 'as dead as a maggot', as a man who knew Fitzgerald would later put it. Fitzgerald dropped the stretcher and the wounded British soldier hit the ground and moaned terribly. Looking over the body of his friend, Fitzgerald saw the wounded German holding a rifle. He had let the British stretcher-bearers tend to his wounds and then fired at them as they walked away.

The German had either no more strength or no more ammunition, but somehow Martin Fitzgerald managed to get away, dragging the wounded British soldier on the stretcher to a dressing station. Then he made a decision and, right there and then, the war changed Martin Fitzgerald forever. He walked back to the front-line trenches and picked up a rifle. He climbed up over the parapet and found his way back to the enemy soldier. Then, with the butt of the rifle, Martin Fitzgerald beat the wounded German to death.

UNSUNG HEROES – MEN OF GOD

DONAL O'SULLIVAN

The war did not discriminate against young or old, soldier or stretcher-bearer, rich or poor – and it certainly did not discriminate against men of the cloth. The Irish priests of the First World War earned their reputation the hard way.

On 5 July 1916 – four days after the start of the Battle of the Somme – Father Donal O'Sullivan from High Street, Killarney, County Kerry, found himself in a rear area when he suddenly learned that his soldiers, men of the Royal Munster Fusiliers, were pressing forward in an attack as the British tried to renew their

PADRE'S FATE.

The Rev. D. O'Sullivan, of Killarney, killed at the front, where he was serving as Army chaplain.

Father Donal O'Sullivan from Killarney, County Kerry.

efforts on the Somme. Word had reached Father O'Sullivan that many of his men were wounded and dying in the trenches – Catholic soldiers in need of the last rites.

Father O'Sullivan rushed up to his commanding officer and, like hundreds of other priests in the First World War, he demonstrated the reckless courage and devotion to his flock that Irish Catholic chaplains in particular had become famous for. He pleaded to be granted permission to go to the front, and after winning the argument with his commanding officer, Father O'Sullivan rushed towards the shell bursts. A witness would later state that in the chaos of the battle, Father O'Sullivan went about his holy duties – anointing the wounded and the dying – until he was killed himself by enemy fire. He was only twenty-six years old, and today is buried in Bouzincourt Communal Cemetery.

WILLIE DOYLE

Probably the most famous Irish priest of the war was Father Willie Doyle from Dalkey, County Dublin. Ordained as a Jesuit in 1907, he volunteered to serve as a military chaplain in 1914 and joined the 8th Royal Irish Fusiliers on the Western front in November 1915 (he would later serve with the Royal Inniskilling Fusiliers, the Royal Dublin Fusiliers, and the Royal Irish Rifles). During Easter Week 1916 – the infamous gas attack on the 16th (Irish) Division at Hulluch – Father Doyle gave last rights to his men, exactly like Father Donal O'Sullivan soon would, in amongst the bullets and shellfire, with absolutely no regard for his own safety.

Then, only a month later (as recounted in *Father William Doyle SJ* by Alfred O'Rahilly, 1922, which quotes extensively from Father Doyle's diary):

> I was standing in a trench, quite a long distance from the firing line, a spot almost as safe as Dalkey itself, talking to some of my men when we heard in the distance the scream of a shell ... none of us had calculated that this gentleman [the shell] had made up his mind to drop into the trench itself, a couple of paces from where I stood. What really took place in the next ten seconds I cannot say. I was conscious of a terrific explosion and the thud of falling stones and debris. I thought the drums

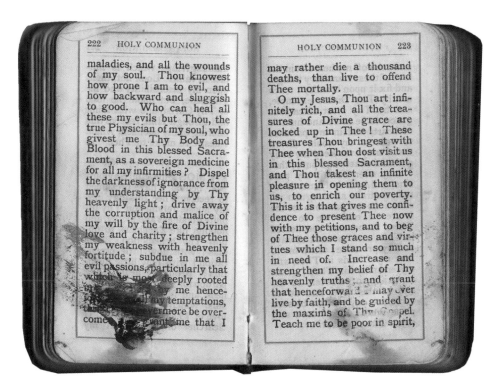

222 HOLY COMMUNION

maladies, and all the wounds of my soul. Thou knowest how prone I am to evil, and how backward and sluggish to good. Who can heal all these my evils but Thou, the true Physician of my soul, who givest me Thy Body and Blood in this blessed Sacrament, as a sovereign medicine for all my infirmities? Dispel the darkness of ignorance from my understanding by Thy heavenly light; drive away the corruption and malice of my will by the fire of Divine love and charity; strengthen my weakness with heavenly fortitude; subdue in me all evil passions, particularly that which is most deeply rooted in ... me hence... my temptations, ... ermore be over-come ... me that I

HOLY COMMUNION 223

may rather die a thousand deaths, than live to offend Thee mortally.

O my Jesus, Thou art infinitely rich, and all the treasures of Divine grace are locked up in Thee! These treasures Thou bringest with Thee when Thou dost visit us in this blessed Sacrament, and Thou takest an infinite pleasure in opening them to us, to enrich our poverty. This it is that gives me confidence to present Thee now with my petitions, and to beg of Thee those graces and virtues which I stand so much in need of. Increase and strengthen my belief of Thy heavenly truths; and grant that henceforward I may ever live by faith, and be guided by the maxims of Thy Gospel. Teach me to be poor in spirit,

Above: *Prayer was very important to many soldiers in the trenches, and millions of little prayer books like this one were distributed to soldiers, often by nuns. This one was owned by Joseph Kelly – a Church of Ireland soldier from Clara, County Offaly. On the Somme, he used to drive a truck back and forth to the front. It was full of ammunition on the way up, and full of dead bodies on the return journey. Kelly's bloodstained thumbprints – evidently bloodstained from having to lift these corpses out of his truck – can still be seen on this page.*

of my ears were split by the crash, and I believe I was knocked down by the concussion, but when I jumped to my feet I found that the two men who had been standing at my left hand, the side the shell fell, were stretched on the ground dead, though I think I had time to give them absolution and anoint them. The poor fellow on my right was lying badly wounded in the head; but I myself, though a bit stunned and dazed by the suddenness of the whole thing, was absolutely untouched, though covered with dirt and blood.

Later on the Somme, Father Doyle was involved in the battles of Ginchy and Guillemont in August 1916. This was what he saw at Leuze Wood:

> The first part of our journey lay through a narrow trench, the floor of which consisted of deep thick mud, and the bodies of dead men trodden under foot. It was horrible beyond description, but there was no help for it, and on the half-rotten corpses of our own brave men we marched in silence, everyone busy with his own thoughts ... Half an hour of this brought us out on the open into the middle of the battlefield of some days previous. The wounded, at least I hope so, had all been removed, but the dead lay there stiff and stark with open staring eyes, just as they had fallen. Good God, such a sight! I had tried to prepare myself for this, but all I had read or pictured gave me little idea of the reality. Some lay as if they were sleeping quietly, others had died in agony or had had the life crushed out of them by mortal fear, while the whole ground, every foot, was littered with heads or limbs, or pieces of torn human bodies. In the bottom of one hole lay a British and a German soldier, locked in a deadly embrace, neither had any weapon but they had fought on to the bitter end. Another couple seemed to have realised that the horrible struggle was none of their making, and that they were both children of the same God; they had died hand-in-hand. A third face caught my eye, a tall, strikingly handsome young German, not more, I should say, than eighteen. He lay there calm and peaceful, with a smile of happiness on his face, as if he had had a glimpse of Heaven before he died. Ah, if only his poor mother could have seen her boy it would have soothed the pain of her broken heart.

In December 1916, Father Willie Doyle found himself in a world of ice and snow. Of course, Christmas brought no reprieve from the misery of the war.

> I found the dying lad – he was not much more – so tightly jammed into a corner of the trench that it was almost impossible to get him out. Both legs were smashed, one in two or three places, so his chances of life were small, and there were other injuries as well. What a harrowing picture that scene would have made. A splendid

young soldier, married only a month they told me, lying there, pale and motionless in the mud and water with the life crushed out of him by a cruel shell. The stretcher-bearers hard at work binding up as well as they may, his broken limbs; round about a group of silent Tommies looking on and wondering when will their turn come. Peace for a moment seems to have taken possession of the battlefield, not a sound save the deep boom of some far-off gun and the stifled moans of the dying boy, while as if anxious to hide the scene, nature drops her soft mantle of snow on the living and dead alike.

On another occasion, he was administering to another badly wounded soldier:

The Rites of the Church were quickly administered, though it was hard to find a sound spot on that poor smashed face for the Holy Oils, and my hands were covered with his blood. The moaning stopped. I pressed the crucifix to his lips and he murmured after me: 'My Jesus, mercy,' and then, as I gave him the Last Blessing, his head fell back and the loving arms of Jesus were pressing to his Sacred Heart the soul of another of His friends.

But for all that he did for his men – for all the times he bravely went out under fire to anoint the dying – and for all the horrific battles he fought in, the war did not spare Father Willie Doyle. After receiving a Military Cross for bravery in January 1917 for his part in the earlier Battle of Ginchy, and having served in the Battle of Messines Ridge on 7 June 1917, Father Doyle was killed by a shell on 16 August 1917 during the horrific action on Frezenberg Ridge in the Ypres sector. He was supposedly recommended for both the Distinguished Service Order and the Victoria Cross but received neither. He was forty-four years old and, with no known grave, today his name is commemorated on the Tyne Cot Memorial.

General William Hickie – from Terryglass, County Tipperary; the commanding officer of the 16th (Irish) Division and later a member of the Free State Seanad (Senate) – referred to Father Doyle as 'one of the bravest men who fought or served out here'. Not long after his death, the *Morning Post* had this to say about the brave priest from Dalkey:

> His familiar figure was seen and welcomed by hundreds of Irishmen who lay in that bloody place, walking with death with a smile on his face, watched by his men with reverence and a kind of awe until a shell burst near him and he was killed.

Perhaps the most amazing tribute to Father Doyle was paid by a Belfast Orangeman – an unlikely source of praise for a Catholic Irish priest – in the *Weekly News* of 1 September 1917:

> God never made a nobler soul. Fr. Doyle was a good deal among us. We could not possibly agree with his religious opinions, but we simply worshipped him for other things. He didn't know the meaning of fear and he did not know what bigotry was. He was as ready to risk his life and take a drop of water to a wounded Ulsterman as to assist men of his own faith and regiment. If he risked his life looking after Ulster Protestant Soldiers once, he did it a hundred times in the last few days. The Ulstermen felt his loss more keenly than anybody, and none were readier to show their marks of respect to the dead hero priest than were our Ulster Presbyterians.

Like the Home Rule-figure Major Willie Redmond before him on Messines Ridge, Father Willie Doyle was mourned by diehard unionists.

BITTER BEGINNINGS

MICHAEL MORAN

Sapper Michael Moran of the Royal Engineers was from Emo near Portlaoise. In early 1914 he found himself living with his sister in England. She was married to a British Army officer named Frederick Underhill and, according to Moran's great-nephew, Terry Moran, Frederick convinced Michael to join the army. He enlisted in the Royal Engineers and when the First World War broke out he was

Sapper Michael Moran from Emo, County Laois. As a young man, Moran had tried to join the IRB, but had been turned down because he was considered too young. Bitterly disappointed, Moran left for England in search of work. He was a blacksmith by trade.

sent to the trenches, joining the war on 20 November 1914 – two days before the First Battle of Ypres officially ended.

The European winter had set in and conditions were bitter, but over Christmas, as Michael Moran waited in his freezing trench for the spring to come, he made a card for his mother. On the card he wrote a short verse, then he glued a pressed flower – a forget-me-not – onto the page and wrote the words 'Forget Me Not' above it. On a chilly winter's day, Michael Moran dropped the card into the mailbag and turned to get on with the war. Two months later, his mother in Ireland received a telegram, stating that Sapper Michael Moran of 23rd Field Company, Royal Engineers, had been killed by shellfire on 3 February 1915. Today, Michael Moran's remains lie in Cambrin Military Cemetery.

The 'Forget-Me-Not' Christmas card sent by Michael Moran to his mother during the winter of 1914-15. As if to destroy the nerves of a grieving mother, it arrived after the telegram informing her of his death. Her son had intended the card to be a sentimental Christmas greeting; it was now a poignant and deeply moving memento of the last days of his life.

MICHAEL McGRATH

After the end of the Battle of the Somme in late 1916, Sergeant Michael McGrath joined the war for the first time. However, Sergeant McGrath was a man with an already long and colourful military career.

Born in Fourmilewater, County Waterford, he was a plumber by trade and only eighteen years old when he enlisted in the army in Dublin on 30 January 1901. A young soldier of considerable promise, eight months after joining the Connaught Rangers he was promoted to lance-corporal in the 1st Connaught Rangers.

Between 1902 and 1913 McGrath served in South Africa, Malta and, for six years, in India. During his early military career, Michael McGrath was severely reprimanded on several occasions: for being drunk, for neglect of duty, for disobedience of orders, using 'improper language,' and for creating a disturbance in a Maltese brothel and resisting arrest by the Military Police.

He also suffered a number of illnesses, including influenza and necrosis of his nose. Necrosis was a rotting of tissue, caused by an infected injury and if left untreated became extremely serious. Necrosis in the foot, for example, could lead to a gangrenous leg and amputation of the limb. To cure Michael McGrath surgeons removed skin and bone from his nose and halted the infection.

By the time war broke out in Europe, Michael McGrath was considered a 'very good NCO, hardworking and willing'. His earlier misdemeanours had obviously been forgiven and forgotten. Having completed courses, such as one

on instruction of musketry and another on grenades, he was now serving as a permanent staff instructor with the 3rd (Reserve) Connaught Rangers.

Michael McGrath remained with the battalion as an instructor, being promoted to acting company sergeant-major in August 1915,

Sergeant Michael McGrath from Fourmilewater, County Waterford.

getting married in early 1916 and having a child later that year, before reverting back to sergeant in October 1916 due to a reduction of the unit establishment. The war was two years old at this stage and McGrath had yet to enter a war-zone, but on 22 November 1916, it was finally decided that he should serve overseas. He was posted to the 6th Connaught Rangers in France, part of 16th (Irish) Division, and sailed from Folkestone to Boulogne on 24 November. He initially went to the Infantry Base Depot in Étaples, nicknamed 'Eat Apples' by the men, to receive training prior to actually entering the trenches.

It was standard procedure in Étaples to put every soldier – be they a raw recruit or a seasoned veteran – through a rigorous course of preliminary train-ing. This course was an insult to those who had already experienced the horrors of the war. Some of these men had been wounded several times and were on their way back to the front.

On 5 December 1916, Michael McGrath finally joined the 6th Connaught Rangers in the trenches. Then, early on the following morning, Sergeant McGrath and his comrades were subjected to one of the rarer weapons of the First World War. As the war diary records:

> At 6.55am this morning the enemy fired on sunken road with aerial darts and at 11.30am they fired eight aerial darts.

Aerial darts, or flechettes (from the French word *fléchette*, meaning a 'little arrow' or 'dart'), were four-inch long steel missiles with a pointed nose and a vaned tail for stable flight. Dropped from an airplane, they gathered speed as they fell, and were capable of punching through a shrapnel helmet and lodging in the victim's skull. It is actually extremely rare to hear of their use in primary sources from the First World War.

Throughout the rest of 6 December, both sides returned to using more tradi-tional weapons – namely artillery, trench mortars, and howitzers. The defences on both sides were damaged, and repairs carried out. A German patrolling party were taken prisoner.

Later on 7 December, German trench mortars were fired at the brigade on the Connaught Rangers' right, British artillery returned fire, and the Connaught Rangers launched rifle grenades into the enemy lines. With winter setting in, infantry assaults were not feasible, so each side was focusing on bombardment. At stand-to that evening – a time for manning the fire-step in case of an attack – the Connaught Rangers spotted more German working parties out attempting to repair barbed wire. Irish sentries and snipers opened fire.

More trading of artillery fire took place on 8 December, and then on 9 December there was, according to the war diary:

> [the] usual machine gun and rifle fire. About 5pm, Sally [codename for an enemy position] was active, one of our [fire] bays was blown in and we had six casualties. Retaliation was asked for and received. Sally was silenced.

However, when men of the 6th Connaught Rangers went to retrieve the six dead, one of the bodies they found was that of Sergeant Michael McGrath.

Michael McGrath had only been at the front for four days, having served in the army for the previous fifteen years, and his death serves to illustrate that in this new modern war, skill and experience mattered little in the face of machine guns and shells.

Sergeant Michael McGrath was thirty-four years old when he died – his daughter turned three months the same day – and today his body lies in Pond Farm Cemetery. After his death, his wife soon received a small package from the army, containing his few personal possessions: some letters, a prayer book, rosary beads, and a scapular.

MUCK, ICE AND SNOW

TIMOTHY CULHANE

No book on the First World War is complete without the mud, muck and slop of the trenches. Or the misery that arrived with the bitter snows of winter. On 20 December 1916, twenty-two year old Private Timothy Culhane from Rathkeale, County Limerick joined the 2nd Irish Guards on the Somme. Tim was a shopkeeper from a fairly well-off family; they ran a pub and owned a good amount of farmland.

Although he had landed in France in October 1916, he had been serving for the past few months with an entrenching battalion, but now it was time to join an infantry unit. When Tim joined the 2nd Irish Guards in the trenches, he joined a battalion of weary, mud-soaked, mentally exhausted men. With the snow had come the muck. One day the air would turn icy sharp and everything would freeze, the next day there would be a thaw and parapets, fire-steps, trench walls, and everything else would dissolve. Handling the frozen spools of barbed wire was painful and carrying supplies and equipment was almost impossible. Men became furious at the mud holding them stuck. Their bodies hurt everywhere and their exhausted minds reeled.

Above: Winter could be defined during the war by two distinct periods. First came the freeze – the cold, ice, and snow – followed by, as this picture shows, the thaw, when temperatures rose and the whole world was turned to slop. These periods could alternate several times during a winter. Here, the commanding officer of 12th Royal Irish Rifles is making an inspection down a collapsed communication trench.

On 25 December itself, Private Tim Culhane found himself in the front-line trenches. While back home in Ireland, his family got together before blazing fires, and ate and drank whatever they could afford, the young Irish Guardsman manned a frozen trench in a desolate corner of France, standing knee-deep in muck. Tim was under constant threat of enemy shells, and he only had terrible rations to fuel his tired body.

Mercifully, he was relieved that night, but when he returned to the front on 29 December he might as well have boarded a sinking ship. The trenches were filling with water and everything was collapsing in on itself. The men bailed for all they were worth but the water kept coming. The soldiers' hands were either red raw from being soaked in ice cold water or cramped from trying to shovel and push sloppy clay back onto the parapet. Enemy shelling tore up the duck-boards and so carrying parties had to trudge through deep swamps of mud to reach the front.

Even when Private Tim Culhane left these trenches in early 1917, he and his battalion were still detailed for working parties, and so they spent weeks at various locations building, digging, hauling, and carrying in sub-zero temperatures and under intermittent shellfire. No one ever knew when the next salvoes would come crashing down, so the soldiers tried not to think about it. Their only experience of indoors was when they slept in the corrugated iron Nissen huts, packed in to try and keep warm. The Somme was now a surreal sight, glazed over with snow and ice, splintered trees and mangled limbs protruding from the ground.

Over the following months of early 1917, Private Tim Culhane and the 2nd Irish Guards took part in pursuing the Germans when the enemy began retreating on the Somme. They were then transported to Belgium where they began a period of extensive training in preparation for the Third Battle of Ypres. It was during this time that Tim Culhane trained to become a Lewis machine-gunner.

Then at 3.30am on 31 July, every artillery gun on the British Army front at Ypres opened up on the Germans. The day was overcast and misty and the world turned into a nightmare cacophony of deafening explosions. Near the 2nd Irish Guards, oil-drums were used to incinerate whole sections of the enemy line. A searing heat washed over Tim Culhane's face as horrible bursts of orange flame raced through the German trenches, blackening the soil and roasting

Lewis Automatic Machine Gun M1914: This weapon, made by the Birmingham Small Arms Company, became the British Army's main infantry support weapon after the outbreak of the war (while the Vickers machine gun was used by the specialist Machine Gun Corps). Portable and versatile, the Lewis gun was also fitted on fighter planes and (briefly) on tanks. Although it was a rather complex weapon to maintain, it was deemed by many to be the most successful light machine-gun design used during the First World War.

men alive. This was the start of the Battle of Pilckem Ridge.

Private Tim Culhane and the 2nd Irish Guards, along with the 1st Scots Guards, led the attack of 2nd Guards Brigade against the Germans. Their objective was to assault Pilckem Ridge, capture enemy positions beyond it, and then progress to the Steenbeek River. However, it was only after Private Culhane and the Guards had charged up through the German trench network and reached Hey Wood that they encountered serious opposition in the form of enemy machine guns.

Machine guns in a pillbox in Artillery Wood also had to be outflanked to be captured, and at one point, the British creeping barrage inflicted casualties on friendly infantry. German artillery then opened fire on the attackers, and after firing on the first 600 yards of their old front line – which was now in British hands, and through which follow-up waves of British troops were advancing – the enemy switched to using high explosive and gas shells all across the battlefield.

By 9.50am, six hours into the battle, water was being called for. It was

Wounded Irish Guardsmen in a trench on Pilckem Ridge, 31 July 1917.
Private Tim Culhane from Rathkeale, County Limerick never got this far.

another two hours before it reached the troops, and around this time – 12.30pm – the advance was over. The 2nd Irish Guards began to consolidate themselves in their new positions. That night, they were relieved from their forward positions and were sent to Roussel. For their trouble, they were given a tot of rum to calm them down.

31 July 1917 cost the 2nd Irish Guards roughly 300 casualties, and among the dead was Private Timothy Culhane from Rathkeale, County Limerick. Having been ordered to bring his machine gun forward, to cover advancing infantry and prevent the Germans from enfilading British positions, he found himself cut off from his comrades. The Germans tried relentlessly to push him and his Lewis gun crew back, in order to assault the British flank, but Tim held on as long as he could. His father would soon write to the army, wanting to know whether his son would be awarded a posthumous Military Medal for bravery. As it turned out, he was not. Tim was killed age twenty-three and his body was never recovered. Today, his name is commemorated on the Menin Gate Memorial in Ypres.

Regimental Headquarters,Irish Guards
Buckingham Gate,London,S.W.1.
6th.October 1919.

Sir.

In reply to your letter dated 2/10/19,I have to inform you that,your son the late No.10532 Gdsn.T.Culhane,was not awarded the Military Medal.He would however have been entitled to receive the British War Medal,and Victory Medal,but these Medals are not yet available for issue.

Your letter has been forwarded to the Sec.Imperial Institute,South Kensington,who will deal with the question of any monies to which you may be entitled.

Captain
Regimental Adjutant,Irish Guards
for Officer i/c Records.

Mr.Michael Culhane
The Square
Rathkeale,Co.Limerick.

THOMAS NEWMAN

Other surreal experiences of war in winter were had by Thomas Newman, a driver in the Army Services Corps from Ballymahon, County Longford. Newman was the son of a six-foot tall Dublin Metropolitan Policeman. He had tried to follow in his father's footsteps in 1906 but had been rejected by the police for being too short. With no other work available, he had enlisted in the army, and before 1914 arrived, Thomas Newman had already completed the terms of his enlistment and had been discharged. When war broke out, although he was now working on his father's farm back in Ballymahon, he was still liable to be recalled, and so in 1914, Thomas Newman put back on the khaki uniform.

The work of a driver in the Army Service Corps was not as dangerous as an infantryman – you would never be ordered to charge across no-man's-land into a wall of enemy bullets – but it was still perilous enough. Some historians refer to them as the unsung heroes of the First World War, as they risked life and limb, to provide the infantry with everything they needed, but received none of the recognition. Drivers in the Army Service Corps had to bring their carts up roads that were more often than not pre-targeted by enemy artillery. When the Germans saw a horse and cart full of supplies clicking up a road, they took no chances. The supplies could be artillery shells, rifle ammunition, rations for British troops, or other pieces of equipment that would aid the British in their fight against them. Often, these roads were also terribly exposed and visible for miles around, and when supply carts were spotted, German gunners would waste no time in opening fire.

On one occasion during a harsh unrelenting winter, Newman found that night was approaching and he had no shelter. The temperature was freezing so he stopped his horse and planned to flip his empty wagon upside down to use it as a makeshift hut. But first he would need to scoop out some snow off the ground, in order to create a hollow that he could get into beneath the upturned cart. With his entrenching tool, he started to dig, when suddenly he hit something buried beneath the white surface of the snow. He dug around it and the mystery object groaned. Thomas Newman unearthed a sleeping British soldier. He was not wounded or sick, just sleeping – totally buried beneath a snowdrift.

On another occasion, Newman was sitting on the parapet of a trench. The area was quiet, and it was safe to do so. Near enough to Newman was a sentry, who was standing up – dead still – keeping watch. Another soldier came shuffling down the trench and walked up to the sentry. The newcomer looked up at Newman. 'I think we should have an Irish wake for this lad,' he said. Newman frowned. 'Why?' he asked, confused. The newcomer tugged the sentry back from where he was standing. The sentry was ghostly pale and rigid. 'Because he's stone dead,' said the newcomer. The sentry had been shot much earlier and had been left where he died. Because of the extreme cold, he had frozen stiff where he stood. Thomas Newman had been sitting beside a corpse. That was what the festive season brought to the trenches of the First World War.

NO RESPECT FOR RANK

WILLIAM O'KEEFE

With junior infantry officers expected to lead from the front, the average life expectancy of a young subaltern could often be measured in minutes or hours. The phrase 'lions led by donkeys' is often used to describe how the brave ordinary

Lieutenant William O'Keefe from Wexford, aged twenty.

infantryman was led by foolish officers, but the truth is, both officer and enlisted man often displayed as much courage and determination as the other. And even in the rear, neither rank nor status could protect an officer from danger.

In the lead up to the Battle of Arras in April 1917, Second-Lieutenant William O'Keefe from Wexford, an officer in the Royal Field Artillery, found himself pounding the enemy lines with his guns. O'Keefe was twenty years old and had a passion for modern machines – he was able to drive a motor car and a motor bike. However, this was not O'Keefe's first tour of the war. Commissioned in February 1915, on 5 August that year, he had received word that he was soon to enter the war and had written a letter to his sister Daisy in Rathgar, Dublin, telling her that 'of course we do not know what Brigade or what part of the front we are likely to be sent to', and that he promised to 'send home a German trophy of some sort'. O'Keefe then sailed from Southampton to Le Havre, landing in France on 24 November 1915.

O'Keefe's first tour of the war had been relatively uneventful for him. Posted to the 18th Divisional Ammunition Column, attached to 18th Division, and then briefly to 83rd Brigade Royal Field Artillery, he took part in the stockpiling of shells in the days before the Battle of the Somme. On 9 June 1916, O'Keefe arrived in Southampton on leave, before travelling on home to Ireland. The leave was initially supposed to last only one week, which would have seen O'Keefe back in France in time for the opening of the Somme, but when he developed lumbago and accompanying insomnia, due to 'active service conditions' in the field, the leave was extended until 2 July. The guns of William O'Keefe's detachment had in the meantime been involved in the week-long shelling of enemy positions.

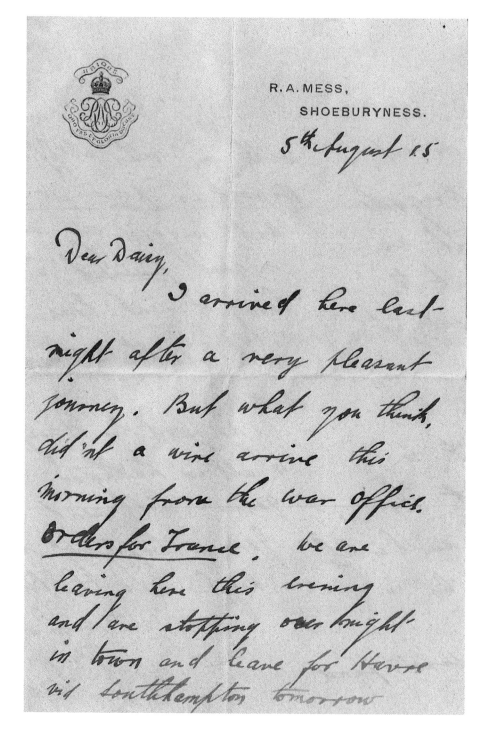

R.A.MESS,

SHOEBURYNESS.

5th August 15

Dear Daisy,

I arrived here last-night after a very pleasant journey. But what you think, did'nt a wire arrive this morning from the war office. Orders for France. We are leaving here this evening and are stopping over tonight in town and leave for Havre via Southhampton tomorrow

Letter written by Lieutenant William O'Keefe to his sister Daisy in Rathgar, Dublin, 5 August 1915.

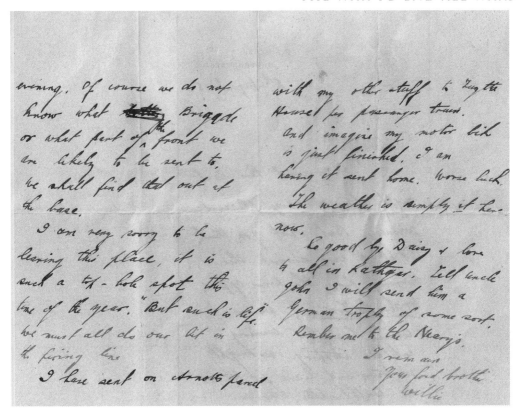

It was not until 15 July 1916 that Second-Lieutenant William O'Keefe was declared fit for duty, having been examined by a medical board in King George V Military Hospital in Dublin (now St Bricin's Military Hospital). However, he was not sent back to France but was posted to the 5A Reserve Brigade Royal Field Artillery, joining them on 20 July in Athlone barracks.

William O'Keefe might have been sick and on leave when the bloodiest day in British military history had occurred, but the Somme was still being fought when he was finally ordered back to the war in October 1916. By April 1917, O'Keefe was serving with the 23rd Battery, 40th Brigade, attached to 3rd Division, and there was a new battle to be fought – the Battle of Arras.

Arras was a British attempt to break through the new German defences of the Hindenburg Line in support of a major French offensive further south. In preparation for the infantry assault, just under 2.7 million shells were fired into the German lines. The troops were due to go over the top on 9 April 1917, and so along with every other gun in the region, O'Keefe's guns opened fire five days in advance, on 4 April. Unlike the Somme, the British artillery pounded the enemy positions with masses of high explosive shells. This time, while the German soldiers were still secure in their deep dugouts, the trenches outside were reduced to shallow ditches. Barbed wire was blown apart and as the clock ticked down towards zero hour, the British loaded gas shells into their guns and entombed the German lines in clouds of poisonous fumes.

Just before the attack, which was due to be launched at 5.30am on 9 April, scouts were sent into no-man's-land, to report on the success of the shelling. They returned with stories of first- and second-line German trenches that had been completely destroyed, and of tiny bits of iron on the ground that was all that was left of barbed-wire coils. The five-day barrage had been a resounding success. The attack was given the go-ahead, and at 5.25am, with only five minutes to go, O'Keefe and his fellow artillery officers ordered their gunners to lay down a frenzy of shells. The British guns whipped up a terrific bombardment to flatten any enemy positions left standing and to blast away what little morale remained in the opposing German infantry. Five minutes later, the British soldiers exited their trenches.

Initial progress far exceeded expectation, but, over the days that followed, attempts to press further east became more and more difficult with each yard of ground. On 7 May 1917, William O'Keefe of the Royal Field Artillery – now a lieutenant – wrote a letter to his mother, saying:

I do wonder what you think of me for not writing for such a long time. But you really must forgive me as you can quite imagine what sort of a life we are having just now. Really we never get a moment's rest. Last night was the first night's sleep I have had for a week. I really did enjoy it. Well I must say I have been extraordinary lucky since this show started and I thank God for it all. We had the sad luck to lose an officer about ten days ago. Poor fellow he was killed in our last position. I miss him horribly as he was a most amusing fellow and one of the best of pals. He had just been recommended for the M.C. for great bravery before this show started.

I had a long letter from Gladys yesterday evening. It was very cheery and bucked me up immensely. I wrote to her last night. Our R.C. padre called in to see me this afternoon. He is a most charming chap and as brave as a lion ... How goes life at home? I hope you are all in the best of health. The papers arrive very regularly, many thanks for sending them. Well cheereo [sic] & the best of love to you all. Write soon.

Your affectionate son. Willie.

Four days later, on 11 May, William O'Keefe was wounded when a piece of shrapnel sliced his chin. The wound was only very minor and, on 16 May, he wrote another letter to his mother saying:

> I am back with the battery and feeling as fit as ever ... Fritz did succeed in drawing blood at last; not bad after two years! We had the worst time yet the day I was hit ... We expect to get four day's rest on the 19th. We really do need it. Have written to Cyril to try get him come and see me. Says he has a car handy. I shall say goodbye & love to all. Write soon.

Your affectionate son. Willie.

Three days later, on 19 May 1917 – the day his unit was to be relieved for four day's rest – Lieutenant William O'Keefe from Wexford was killed. As the war dairy records:

> Capt Perkins, Lt O'Keefe, Lt Harker and 2nd Lt Lloyd, all killed by a 5.9 [inch shell] which burst in the doorway of the Officers' Mess.

He was still alive for a few seconds after the blast, then he was gone. O'Keefe was only two months away from his twenty-first birthday.

The following day, in the presence of fifty or so officers and the men of his battery, the Catholic chaplain interred William O'Keefe's body, in what would become Faubourg D'Amiens Cemetery, Arras. The priest, Father Bellanti, then wrote a letter to O'Keefe's mother in an attempt to console her, telling her that her son was 'the life and soul of the place, ready to bump into the conversation with chaff and reminiscences and a happy smile'. The grieving Mrs O'Keefe also soon received a letter from her son's batman – Gunner J Fraser – who wrote:

Copy of the Chaplains letter

France, May 27th 1917.

Dear Mrs. O'Keefe,

I am taking the liberty of sending you a few lines in addition to what you will have received from Major Laird & Lieut. Love; the only surviving officers of your boy's Battery - because I had come to know and love your boy and still find it difficult to believe he is taken away from us.

I see from my diary that I was lunching with the Officers of the 23rd Battery on the Thursday before the fatal shell landed. As usual I had been going my rounds, picking up my Catholic Gunners, for Confession and a little chat - to carry the Blessed Sacrament to the batteries is too dangerous I fear - and I drew up about 1 p.m. to lunch with the officers - as happy a family as ever I set eyes upon, - and your boy always "Pat" to them and was as usual the life and soul of the place, ready to bump into the conversation with chaff and reminiscences and a happy smile. I've only been 2 months with the 3rd Division R.F.A. (previously they had been without a Chaplain) and so cannot pretend to have a long acquaintance with your boy, he was one of the very few Catholic Officers in the Divisional Artillery, he naturally was more to me than the others, and we had several long chats together. Need I re-assure you that he was a splendid Catholic boy. and that I am morally certain he was not an unprovided, though necessarily a sudden & I believe painless death. - Only for a few seconds after the shell exploded among

them as the four sat at breakfast - Was he seemingly alive - precious moments, as I hope and believe to a good boy and a God-fearing Catholic Officer.

In the bravery and gallantry with which the Gunners continuously face day and night, asleep or awake, the possibility of a sudden death - they certainly yield to none. Your boy had chosen to serve in a body where casualties are heavy and where unlike the Infantry - the strain is rarely relieved. From his C.O. you will have heard what a reputation he has made for himself; - as a capable Artillery Officer - a splendid comrade and a well loved friend. I remember slightly he took the graze on his chin - a few weeks ago. It was a narrow escape, but it left him as simple and self-reliant as ever, without any trace of nerves or shock. I buried him in a specially blessed grave in the Cemetery of the City of -   with all the battery and at least 50 or 60 officers present, on Sunday evening, May 20th - May the dear gallant boy rest in peace.

Sections of a letter written by Father Bellanti to Lieutenant William O'Keefe's mother after his death, 27 May 1917.

Lieutenant William O'Keefe's original grave-marker in Faubourg D'Amiens Cemetery, Arras.

Dear Madame,

No doubt you have been informed of the death of Lieut. W.H. O'Keefe, killed in action with three other officers, all being killed instantaneous. It is a sore blow to me having to write this, and the task is nearly too much for me, for by his death it has robbed me of a good master, and not only is he mourned by me, but by the whole battery which have missed him so much, the majority of which followed his remains to the grave [side] under full military honours, the four being buried side by side. All arrangements have been made for the sending home of his kit which will most probably reach you soon.

Enclosed are a few photos etc which were in his pocket at the time of his death. And now I feel sure by writing more will be only hurting your feelings so [I] will conclude with sincerest sympathy from one who was honoured to be his servant.

I remain yours very respectfully, Gnr. J Fraser.

Among Lieutenant William O'Keefe's possessions, that the army soon returned to his mother, was a broken set of rosary beads.

Today, apart from the headstone above his grave in France, William O'Keefe is also commemorated in his native Wexford. The Church of the Assumption in Bride Street, Wexford was designed by Robert Pierce, a student of Augustus Welby Pugin, and in the church is a two-light stained-glass window, depicting Our Lady with St Patrick and St George. This window was made in 1920 by the famous Harry Clarke, and it is dedicated to the memory of Lieutenant William O'Keefe.

THE WAR AT HOME

JOHN SINNOTT

It should not be forgotten that danger and the risk of death during the First World War was not something that existed solely on the battlefields. The zeppelin raids on London, although nothing like the Luftwaffe raids of the Blitz during the Second World War, had brought death and destruction to people miles away from the fighting, but the real cause of non-battlefield death from 1914 to 1918 was sea travel. With German U-Boats sinking everything that did not fly the German flag, thousands of innocent civilians and non-combatants were killed by torpedo blasts or drowned as their ships sank. In fact, the worst loss of life ever recorded in the Irish Sea – a sad record that still stands to this day – was on a ship sunk during the First World War. It was an event witnessed by an Irish sailor named John Sinnott.

On 10 October 1918, the war was drawing to a close. On that day, on the Western Front, the Hindenburg Line had finally collapsed. Back in Ireland, heading for the port of Kingstown (now Dún Laoghaire) in Dublin, sailor John Sinnott – a thatcher by trade from Wexford – found himself serving aboard RMS *Munster* as it steamed west towards harbour. Just east of Dublin Bay, *Munster* was about to pass by RMS *Leinster* which was travelling the other way. *Leinster* was the Kingstown to Holyhead mailboat and she had just left Dublin with 771 people – crew and passengers – onboard, 500 of which were soldiers and nurses. The two ships were east of the Kish bank, and John Sinnott was staring at the passing *Leinster* when suddenly he spotted something in the water. Something was heading towards *Leinster*, drawing a white trail in its wake beneath the surface – a torpedo.

Sinnott raced to the nearest officer and blurted out what he had seen. The officer walked to the rail, looked out to sea, and saw nothing, just RMS *Leinster* steaming safely past. Sinnott insisted that he had seen something in the water, but the officer dismissed him. Then there was an explosion.

Lurking near Dublin Bay was the German submarine *UB-123*. She had fired a torpedo at *Leinster* – the one that John Sinnott had seen – missed, and then fired again. This time, she hit the target. *Leinster* was torpedoed on the port side and the captain immediately turned the ship in a desperate attempt to make it back to Kingstown before they sank. Then, with a massive explosion, a third torpedo slammed into *Leinster*. Lifeboats were launched and passengers and crew leapt overboard and clung to life-rafts. But *Leinster* went down fast in a flurry, taking 529 people with her. It was the greatest single loss of life ever to occur in the Irish Sea or aboard an Irish ship.

As for *UB-123*, she slipped away into the Irish Sea and sailed off for Germany. But nine days after sinking *Leinster*, she passed through a North Sea minefield and was never heard of again. All of her thirty-six crew were drowned.

THE LAST TO FALL

PATRICK MURRAY

When the Germans were at last defeated and forced to the peace table, they accepted the terms of an armistice and signed it at 5am on 11 November 1918. Six hours later, the impossible would happen – impossible as far as so many veterans were concerned. On the 11/11 at 11, Germany would unconditionally surrender to the Allies. A ceasefire would be in effect, and there would be peace in Europe.

The time set for the cessation of hostilities was just two hours too late for Private Patrick Murray from Lugmore,

Above: 5th *Royal Irish Lancers' cap badge: Formed in 1689 as Owen Wynne's Dragoons, the regiment fought at the Boyne under the command of King William of Orange and later at the Battle of Aughrim. Having served in Ireland during the 1798 rebellion, the unit was disbanded in 1799, following (apparently false) claims that its ranks had been infiltrated by rebels. For a further fifty years, no regiment of dragoons was permitted to be numbered the 5th. This gap in the numbering system was to stand 'as a memorial of [the regiment's] disgrace'. In 1858, they were reformed, and after fighting in Egypt and during the Boer War, they were sent to France as part of the original BEF in 1914. In fact, Private George Ellison of the 5th Royal Irish Lancers is believed to be the last British soldier to die in the First World War.*

Doocastle, County Mayo. The family had emigrated to Chicago in 1912, where the young Patrick had got a job with Sears, Roebuck and Co – the famous mail-order catalogue company – but while serving in A Company, 124th Machinegun Battalion, US 33rd Division around 9am, on 11 November 1918, Private Murray was hit in the head by a lump of German shrapnel. He died on his way to the first aid station – only twenty-two years old – and today his body lies in Saint-Mihiel American Cemetery, near Thiaucourt, Verdun.

Two hours after he died, the guns fell silent along the Western Front, with some units fighting right up to the final minute.

HENRY McBRYDE

When the armistice was declared, British and Allied POWs in German camps could finally look forward to going home. One of these POWs, Sergeant Henry 'Harry' McBryde from Portarlington, County Laois, had joined up at the outbreak of war and had served in the South Irish Horse, until the unit was disbanded in 1917 and reformed into the 7th Royal Irish Regiment. It was with this unit that Harry – having taken on the role of an infantryman and entered the trenches – was captured by the Germans during their tremendous assaults of 1918. He spent the last few months of the war interred in Langensalza Camp, Germany.

After celebrating the armistice on 11 November 1918, Harry believed he would soon be free. But old wounds began to flare up and he started to feel ill. He was admitted to hospital on 4 December with influenza, but this quickly developed into pneumonia. Harry McBryde's

Above: *South Irish Horse cap badge: The South Irish Horse was not a regular unit of the British Army but rather a Special Reserve Yeomanry unit comprised of part-time soldiers. However, unlike other non-regular units, elements of the South Irish Horse actually departed with the original BEF for France upon the outbreak of the war. Formed in 1902, the unit had squadrons based in Limerick, Dublin and Cork, and in 1917, when the difficulty of utilising cavalry in modern warfare was finally being acknowledged, the unit was dismounted and turned into infantry – becoming the 7th Battalion of the Royal Irish Regiment.*

Sergeant Henry McBryde from Portarlington, County Laois, May 1916.

condition rapidly worsened and, on 8 December 1918, nearly a month after the armistice, he died in hospital. Today, his remains lie in Niederzwehern Cemetery in Germany. Harry's father would later receive a letter – dated 2 January 1919 – from a very close friend of Harry's, who wrote:

> I feel I must write you a few lines of sympathy on the death of your son Harry. I have just returned from Langensalza, where I was a prisoner with your son. We were comrades in misfortune ... He passed away peacefully on Sunday evening at 8pm, 8th December. I spoke to him on the morning of the 8th and told him I would write you, but we hoped then that he would recover. He was buried with military honours; the Union Jack covering his coffin, and also two large wreaths, one from the Irish boys and the other from ... where he worked. We all missed his presence from amongst us. He was a good pal & very popular in the barrack room. Corporal Egan promised to call in with you & give you his few possessions. He can tell you everything. You have my deepest sympathy with you in your sorrow & I personally feel I have lost a true friend. With kindest regards.

> Yours sincerely,
> Thomas Morrow

Henry 'Harry' McBryde had survived the war and had been so close to coming home.

Sergeant Henry McBryde and his troop of the South Irish Horse.

DESPERATE MEASURES

THOMAS HOPE

On 17 August 1914, the 2nd Leinster Regiment sailed from their station in Ireland to Holyhead. From there, they entrained for Cambridge, arriving on the following day. With them was a man named Private Thomas Hope from Mill Road, Mullingar, County Westmeath, and on this day he simply disappeared. Hope absented himself from duty illegally. On 8 September, the battalion sailed from Southampton to St Nazaire in France. When they disembarked and started the march to war, Thomas Hope rejoined his unit at Dhuizel. But before long, he absented himself again. When he was finally found for the second time, he was tried by court-martial, found guilty of absenting himself on two occasions, and given an incredible fifty-six days of the torturous Field Punishment No. 1.

Field Punishment No. 1 was a particularly harsh form of discipline. It involved the convicted offender being forced to do hard manual labour, while restrained in handcuffs or fetters or both. Diet was restricted, and sometimes, the soldier might even be tied to a post or a gun-wheel and forced to work. There was a limit to how much time per day he was allowed to be tied to a heavy object, but even so, the punishment was effectively torture.

Thomas Hope served out his fifty-six days of Field Punishment No. 1, but then soon after earned himself a further three months of the same punishment by absenting himself again. What was beginning to emerge, as far as Hope's superiors saw it, was a man who was a bad example to others, a curse on morale and discipline, and who could not be trusted to face the enemy. There is no record of *why* Thomas Hope absented himself so frequently.

When he finally entered the fighting with the 2nd Leinster Regiment, Hope was involved in the attacks on the Aisne and the assault on the Armentières-Wytschaete line in mid-October 1914. Hope survived the First Battle of Ypres and, with Christmas approaching, he was detailed to leave the front-line trenches on 23 December as part of a ration party. All Thomas Hope had to do was travel 800 yards to the rear, collect rations along with some other men for the various platoons in his battalion, and then return to the trenches to distribute them. At 6.30pm, Sergeant Stephen Barnwell – the man who had detailed the ration party – saw Hope leave the trenches. About an hour later, between 7.30pm–8pm, Acting Quartermaster Sergeant Christopher Saunderson saw Private Hope and the rest of the ration party come down to draw rations for each platoon. They drew their supplies and headed off, but when Sergeant Saunderson returned to the trenches later on, he was informed that Private Thomas Hope was missing. Once again, the Mullingar man had absented himself illegally – using his time out of the front line to disappear into thin air. It was two months before he was seen again.

On 9 February 1915, Captain Milthorpe of the 1st Rifle Brigade was serving at Armentières when 'he went round the company billets, and found a drunk soldier of 2nd Leinster Regiment outside the door.' This drunken soldier was a private named Donoghue, and beside him was a lance-corporal wearing a great-coat and a police badge. Captain Milthorpe asked the lance-corporal why he had not arrested the drunken Private Donoghue, only to find out that the lance-corporal was drunk too. Obviously disgusted at the situation, Captain Milthorpe asked the lance-corporal for his name. 'Lance-Corporal Stout', was the reply. Captain Milthorpe then placed the lance-corporal under arrest.

In fact, Lance-Corporal Stout was really Private Thomas Hope from Mullingar. Later that day, about 4.45pm, he was brought to Company Quartermaster Sergeant William H West of the Rifle Brigade. When asked his name, Hope once again claimed that he was a lance-corporal named Stout. Hope then 'asked permission to fall out to get a relief, as he would be placed in arrest if he did not report at 6pm'. On 14 February 1915, Thomas Hope was tried by Field General Court Martial. The charges were desertion, drunkenness, and Section 40 – conduct prejudicial to good order and military discipline. Hope pleaded not guilty to all charges.

During the trial, Hope had no 'accused's friend' – usually an officer who would fight the case of a man on trial – and he declined to call any witnesses in his defence. The prosecution called four witnesses, and the story that emerged was of an untrustworthy soldier who had repeatedly gone illegally absent from duty and who then went missing for two months before turning up drunk using a false name and claiming to be a lance-corporal.

In his defence, Hope claimed that:

> On the night of December 23rd 1914, I was very much upset owing to the death of my two brothers of which I had just heard. I had no intention of going absent when I left the trenches. It was a sudden impulse. (Then I wandered about until I got into the French trench after [crossed out on original document]). The first night I was away I went by mistake into the German trenches. The enemy kept me 3 days, and took me to their headquarters at Lille. I escaped from the Germans during an attack and got into the French trenches and I stayed there two days. Then I met some British troops and stayed there some 3 or 4 days. I have been walking round since, and tried to find my own regiment.

Thomas Hope claimed that his two recently deceased brothers were Private 9701, P Hope, 1st Royal Munster Fusiliers, and Driver 24610, J Hope, Royal Field Artillery. Hope could not provide any evidence to support the story that they had been killed, and when the army attempted to verify Hope's claim, they could not. The army could find no evidence that these two men even existed.

A photograph purporting to show a British Army firing squad about to execute a blindfolded prisoner wearing a greatcoat, possibly in the summer of 1915. The authenticity of this photograph has never been established, but it gives a sense of Private Thomas Hope's last moments.

Apparently, Hope had made them up. As for the story of entering the German lines, only to escape to French territory – there is no mention of whether or not this tale was deemed to be true or false. The commanding officer of the 2nd Leinster Regiment stated that Thomas Hope 'has made up his mind not to serve creditably, and to avoid all military duty'. Thomas Hope was sentenced to death.

Although Hope was a troublesome soldier, the real reason behind his death penalty might be clarified by two comments – one by Hope's commanding officer, another by General Horace Smith-Dorrien commanding Second Army, of which 2nd Leinster Regiment was a part. Concerning Hope's case, the CO of 2nd Leinster Regiment wrote that 'I consider him [Hope] a bad example to other soldiers.'

Meanwhile, General Smith-Dorrien wrote:

> The Brigade discipline is 2nd worst & the Battn. discipline [2nd Leinster Regiment] also the 2nd worst in the army. The case is a very bad one indeed & I recommend that the extreme penalty be carried out.

Thomas Hope was sentenced to death for two reasons. Firstly, because he continually absented himself illegally from duty, and secondly – and perhaps more significantly – because he was in a badly disciplined unit and his comrades needed to see what happened to undisciplined soldiers.

At 7.05am on 2 March 1915, Thomas Hope was executed by firing squad. Lieutenant Wright of the Royal Army Medical Corps wrote soon after that:

> I hereby certify that 9689 Pte T. Hope – 2 Leinsters – having been condemned by Field General Court Martial, was shot at 7.[0]5 A.M. on 2nd March 1915, and died instantaneously.

Hope was one month away from his twenty-first birthday, and today, with no known grave, his name is commemorated on the Ploegsteert Memorial.

However, that was not the final chapter in Thomas Hope's story. In 2006, ninety-one years after being executed by firing squad for absenting himself from the line, Thomas Hope was pardoned under Section 359 of the Armed Forces Act 2006, 'as recognition that he was one of many victims of the First World War and that execution was not a fate he deserved.'

This document records that

Pte T Hope of the
2nd Battalion, Leinster Regiment

who was executed for desertion on
2 March 1915 is pardoned under Section 359
of the Armed Forces Act 2006.

The pardon stands as recognition that he was
one of many victims of the First World War
and that execution was not a fate he deserved.

Secretary of State for Defence

Private Thomas Hope's official pardon, signed by the then-British secretary of state for defence, Des Browne, 2006.

THE 'JOINT CALVARY' OF NORTH AND SOUTH

JOHN 'JACK' HUNT

After the Battle of Messines Ridge in June 1917, the British opened the Third Battle of Ypres on 31 July with an attack on Pilckem Ridge, but by August, the area around Ypres had become a true nightmare. After the Battle of Pilckem Ridge it had started raining. The incessant shellfire of the past three years had destroyed all drainage channels, and as the torrential rain had nowhere to go, water flowed into shell craters, trenches and dugouts.

Still, the war had to be fought. The weather continued to worsen – the rain never ceased – and so attacks went on across a landscape of black slush. Shells burst in the sodden muck and showered soldiers in cement-like mud. Men were filthy and exhausted from struggling through, at times, waist-high sludge. The water in the shell craters turned green and putrid; bodies and limbs and severed heads were washed into these holes in the earth. Tanks could not move across this terrain. The entire battlefield became a swampy wasteland and moving a few miles could take days.

The new mustard gas blinded men and the poison seeped into clothes – if they went into confined spaces, even days after they had been gassed, they were still liable to poison everyone in the room. Columns of troops were seen walking single file across the battlefield, eyes wrapped in bandages, one hand on the shoulder of the man in front. Gas masks proved useless; fumes got in through your skin and made your body blister and your throat close and burn.

But still the Allies attacked the Germans and the Germans counter-attacked. Trenches ceased to exist; men lived in narrow waterlogged slits in the ground. Duckboards and planks were laid across the battlefield to try and speed up the movement of troops, but they were narrow, and men lost their footing. Those that did vanished into the mud. Their comrades attempted to pull their friends out, but often it was no use. Wounded men could literally drown in the mud.

Those that survived went beyond hoping for a 'blighty one' – a non-fatal injury that would allow them to go home. It kept raining, and as the shells from 10,000 artillery guns, the gas, the bullets and the endless waves of muck washed over them, filling their mouths and nostrils and ears, many soldiers were forced to fight hand to hand – with bayonet or fist – because guns were so clogged with mud.

The Third Battle of Ypres, also known as the Battle of Passchendaele (a town east of Ypres, or as the men bitterly called it: 'Passion Dale'), saw some of the worst fighting of late 1917. It fell to the Canadians on 6 November and, four days later, the Third Battle of Ypres came to an end. The British suffered

250,000 killed and wounded; the French and the other forces of the British Empire incurred a further 250,000 between them, while the Germans suffered an estimated 400,000 casualties. In total, that brings the combined number of killed and wounded on all sides to nearly 1 million men in a period of just over three months.

Sadly, the Irish also have their own tale of the Third Battle of Ypres. In early August 1917, the 16th (Irish) Division found themselves manning the sodden Frezenberg Ridge. Then, on 16 August – only a little over two weeks after the Battle of Pilckem Ridge, a time since which the men had been continually lugging heavy equipment through the mud while subjected to heavy shellfire, mustard and phosgene gas, and aeroplane attack – the exhausted British Fifth Army were ordered to attack the Germans opposite their position. Alongside the 16th (Irish) Division and also in Fifth Army was the 36th (Ulster) Division, and so once again, Irishmen from north and south would be symbolically advancing side by side.

In the 48th Brigade of 16th (Irish) Division were several battalions of the Royal Dublin Fusiliers. They were all under strength and, due to casualties, were missing many officers. However, they would still be required to participate in the attack.

Leading the 48th Brigade's assault were the 9th Royal Dublin Fusiliers and the 7th Royal Irish Rifles, and commanding the former was Lieutenant-Colonel John 'Jack' Hunt. By August 1917, Hunt was easily one of the most experienced soldiers in the British Army. A Dubliner, his soldiering days began when he joined the Royal Dublin Fusiliers on 22 December 1891 as a private, aged sixteen. By 1910 – having served in the Boer War, been mentioned in dispatches and wounded in action – he had risen to the rank of colour-sergeant and was an instructor to the Officer Training Corps unit at Dublin University. Five years later in October 1915, Hunt – by then a sergeant-major – received a commission and became a second-lieutenant. At the time, and still to this day, such a move was not always viewed as positive. A sergeant-major commanded great respect among his troops, and even a commission to become a second-lieutenant could still be seen as a far fall in standing. Some preferred to hold the highest of the enlisted ranks, rather than the lowest of the commissioned ones. Regardless, Hunt did not remain as a junior subaltern for long, and by August

1917, he had risen to the rank of lieutenant-colonel and was now commanding a battalion of the Royal Dublin Fusiliers – a far cry from his early days when he had been a private soldier serving in the ranks.

On the night of 15 August, Hunt's 9th Royal Dublin Fusiliers and the 7th Royal Irish Rifles moved forward under cover of darkness to assembly areas ahead of the British front-line trenches – a task made difficult by the fact that 'the R.E. [Royal Engineers] officer detailed to lay out tapes on Assembly Position was wounded and his party scattered'. A creeping barrage was to be used to provide supposed protection, and behind this, the first waves would advance. By 11.30pm, the first wave troops were in place, but, as the 9th Royal Dublin Fusiliers war diary records:

> During the whole night the enemy maintained an intermittent bombardment ... this was intensified ... and became a barrage about Zero hour [4.45am], which made it extremely difficult to [advance].

The British rear was also shelled, and in the 8th Royal Dublin Fusiliers – the reserve battalion who were sheltering in gun pits – 'enemy fire was attracted by the establishment of a dressing station'.

The men in the forward areas waited in darkness until the assault was launched, and then, all along the line, British troops began to struggle forward through the muck. It was not long before a tragedy started to unfold in the 9th Royal Dublin Fusiliers at the head of the attack.

> At 7.30 a.m. a message was received from 2/Lieut Hickey (B Coy) saying Battalion held up about 100 yards from strong point and most of assaulting waves killed or wounded.

However, Lieutenant-Colonel Hunt had no idea where Hickey was. It was assumed, given the time on the message and the fact that signal flares had been sent up, that he was in front of the German-held Bremen Redoubt. However, Hunt needed to be sure, and to find out what was going on:

2/Lieut Martin and 2 O.R. to-gether with the runner who brought the message from 2/Lieut Hickey were sent out to ascertain the situation. The runners became casualties soon after leaving Headquarters but 2/Lieut Martin apparently managed to get in touch with the Battalion and was returning to Headquarters about 2 hours later but when within 20 yards of Battn Headquarters was shot through the head by a sniper and killed instantly. Any information this Officer may have gained was probably verbal as no written messages were found on his body.

German machine guns were inflicting heavy casualties, runners were unable to deliver messages back and forth between units and higher command, and word was filtering through of a number of German counter-attacks and that fresh German troops were being brought up from the rear. It was chaos on Frezenberg Ridge, with British artillery falling short and causing casualties amongst the attacking troops.

Another officer – Second-Lieutenant Jamson – was ordered forward in a renewed effort to find out exactly where Hickey and the 9th Royal Dublin Fusiliers were. He returned later to Hunt at HQ to report that they were a hundred yards from their objective, but that they were now cut off by the enemy. As the war diary ominously states: 'He only saw wounded men.' From Hunt's perspective, his battalion was being annihilated.

Meanwhile, in the second wave, A and B Companies of 2nd Royal Dublin Fusiliers advanced in support behind the 9th Royal Dublin Fusiliers and 7th Royal Irish Rifles respectively. The war diary records the fate of these companies:

[B Company] was wiped out before reaching its objectives by enemy Machine Gun and Artillery Fire, only Two Officers and 3 Other Ranks surviving. A Company ... moved forward in rear of 7th R.I.R. ... and succeeded in reaching the Support Company of 7th R.I.R. who were held up ... they dug in. By this time all the Officers with A Coy had become casualties ... the remainder of the Company [consisted] of a N.C.O. and 6 Other Ranks ... [they] were compelled to fall back ...

A and B Companies of 2nd Royal Dublin Fusiliers soon tried to advance again, as did the third, reserve wave – C Company, 2nd Royal Dublin Fusiliers and an attached company from 8th Royal Dublin Fusiliers – but regarding their progress, the war diary is full of lines such as '... suffered severe casualties ... could make no further progress on account of heavy Machine Gun Fire ...'

The war diary of 8th Royal Dublin Fusiliers actually covers the advance of the attached company (which only comprised six officers and eight-five men) more thoroughly. Coming under fire as they advanced, the commanding officer spotted:

> ... what appeared to be a firing line in shell holes and gullies. By glasses I could see the 9th and 2nd Battalion's 'flash' on the shoulders of some. The next rush brought us nearer and I could see that they were all either dead or wounded being particularly thick along road ... The ground near us was dotted with numerous dead.

However, after linking up with the survivors of C Company, 2nd Royal Dublin Fusiliers – which was only two officers and twelve men – the diarist goes on to state that 'I could see none but wounded and dead to my North and none of our men at all to the South.' It was then that Lieutenant-Colonel Hunt stepped in and sent a message to the officer commanding 8th Royal Dublin Fusiliers, informing him that the Germans commanded the British flanks and that he must withdraw – that his men were currently in danger of being over-run. So the Dubliners retreated back the way they had come, but unable to take up positions in holes and ditches along the way because they were so water-logged, the men were forced to return all the way to their starting trenches. Night soon fell, all captured ground had to be abandoned, but Lieutenant-Colonel Hunt's men of the 9th Royal Dublin Fusiliers continued to suffer casualties when a dug-out received a direct hit from enemy artillery and 'intermittent sniping and shelling' continued throughout the night and the next day.

At the start of 16 August 1917, Lieutenant-Colonel John 'Jack' Hunt had commanded sixteen other officers and 353 men in 9th Royal Dublin Fusiliers. By the end of the day, eleven of his officers had been killed and six wounded, along with thirty-five men killed, 158 wounded, and thirty-four missing. These

The infamous mud of Passchendaele. Australian troops walk along duckboards through the remains of Chateau Wood during the Third Battle of Ypres, 29 October 1917.

figures represented a sixty-six percent casualty rate. The 2nd Royal Dublin Fusiliers went into the battle with fourteen officers and 293 other ranks. By the end of the day, seven officers and 125 men had become casualties (fifty percent of those engaged). B Company only had sixty-four able-bodied men remaining. As for the composite company of 8th Royal Dublin Fusiliers, not including officers they lost five men killed, twenty-nine wounded, and twelve missing. Similarly, in 7th Royal Irish Rifles – the other battalion in 48th Brigade, 16th (Irish) Division which had been in the first wave – out of twenty-one officers and 423 other ranks, they lost seventeen officers and 269 men (sixty-four percent of the attacking force).

The assault on Frezenberg Ridge (part of the larger Battle of Langemarck – phase two of the Third Battle of Ypres) was a disaster with no gains made, and Irish journalist Kevin Myers believes that this is the First World War 'joint Calvary' of northern and southern Ireland, a battlefield more worthy of national remembrance than Messines Ridge. On a divisional level, the 16th (Irish) Division suffered 4,231 killed and wounded while the 36th (Ulster) Division suffered 3,585 casualties. In these already under-strength divisions, such losses were devastating, and given this fact, coupled with the esteem in which Irish soldiers were held by higher command, General Sir Douglas Haig – Commander-in-Chief of the BEF – severely criticised the commanding officer of Fifth Army, General Hubert Gough, for 'playing the Irish card' and wasting the lives of so many dependable troops in such an unsuccessful venture. It was actually the losses suffered on Frezenberg Ridge that paved the way for the final destruction of the Irish divisions during the German 'Spring Offensive' of March 1918.

Out of all the descendants of First World War veterans who contacted me, not one had a story to tell about a relative at the Third Battle of Ypres. The simple explanation for this is that, at Ypres in 1917, men were far more likely to die than survive, and those that did were often so terribly weakened that they never lived long enough to impart their stories.

As for Lieutenant-Colonel Hunt, he ultimately survived the war before receiving a commission in the Irish Army. He became a full colonel and was at one point the Chief Instructor of the Irish Army School of Instruction. He died on 24 April 1938 at his home in Dundrum, County Dublin.

One year and a day after the end of the Third Battle of Ypres, the war finally ended. But the wounds that would never heal and the scars of vicious battles remained. The darkness of the war would linger for generations to come.

A Christmas postcard from 1917, commemorating recent battles in which the 16th (Irish) Division took part. The most recent battle listed, the Battle of Langemarck (Frezenberg Ridge) on 16 August 1917, had nearly annihilated the division.

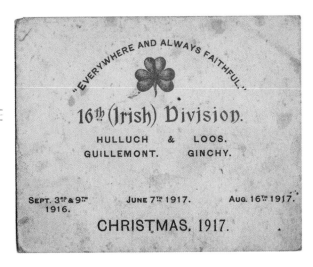

CHAPTER 10

HOMECOMING

'Keep the Home Fires Burning,

While your hearts are yearning

Though your lads are far away, They dream of home

There's a silver lining, Through the dark clouds shining

Turn the dark cloud inside out, 'Til the boys come home.'

Chorus from the popular 1914 song, 'Keep the Home Fires Burning', by Lena Guilbert Ford

When the armistice was declared, all across Europe, towns and villages, even whole cities, had been reduced to ruins. In some cases, there was simply nothing left to indicate that a town had once been there, just blasted earth for miles around. France and Germany were separated by over 400 miles of barren wasteland. This was the outcome of imperial rivalry – of the fight over colonies, territories, navies and trade agreements.

Twenty million people had died and a further 21 million had been wounded. Germany was forced to take full responsibility for the war with the signing of the Treaty of Versailles, which stripped her of territories, limited the size of her army, and ordered her to pay £11.3 billion pounds, taken at 1919 value, in reparations for damages. The country was made bankrupt, and the civil unrest that followed paved the way for a previously unknown First World War corporal and Iron Cross recipient named Adolf Hitler to rise to power and restore Germany's military might.

Armistice celebrations on La Place de République, Paris, France.

As for Ireland, 200,000 Irishmen had gone to war, and between 35,000 and 50,000 were never coming back. Survivors were faced with an uncertain future. Having been cheered off to war in 1914 by Home Rule supporters, they were now returning to face the suspicion and anger of republicans. They were also returning to a world in recession, where jobs were scarce. Soldiers became desperate to be the first to be demobilised. Everyone thought that those who got home first would be the ones to get the jobs. Finally, there were those men who were coming home without arms or legs, or suffering from shellshock, whose futures would now be forever dictated by their war wounds. All of these men

Men of the Irish Guards celebrate as one of their officers reads out the armistice.

had a struggle before them – be it against political opinion, poverty, physical disablement, psychological trauma, or against the influenza pandemic that broke out in 1918, killing 50 million people. Even those who went on to take up the republican cause, or those who came from educated or secure financial backgrounds, still had challenges to overcome.

However, what shines through most clearly from the stories of veterans' post-war lives is the determination to face new challenges. These men may have become hardened and scarred by the war, but most Irish First World War veterans came from a generation that knew hardship, disease and poverty. This had bestowed upon them the ability to persevere against all odds.

A FROSTY WELCOME

MICHAEL AHERN

From Tralee, County Kerry, Michael Ahern enlisted in the Royal Engineers on 4 January 1912 – aged twenty. He was a cooper by trade. On 18 August 1914, he deployed to France, serving at Mons, Le Cateau, the Marne, the Aisne, La Bassée and during the First Battle of Ypres. Then, after a period of home service, he was sent back to France, where he was gassed on 26 September 1915 during the Battle of Loos. Following this, he was posted to India as a lance-corporal with a training company, where he remained until the end of the war. In later life, Michael Ahern committed a few words to paper about his early days and his life as a cooper. His short autobiography tells the story of an Ireland that has long since disappeared:

> I was 2 years old when Parnell died. I used to hear my parents talking about him, the O'Brienites and the Parnellites during an election. Those days were firey [sic] as regards faction fighting and at every meeting during the election period the R.I.C. were there in large numbers after an election when the results were known. Woe to the opposite if he met an opponent whom he knew was on either side. Tis then the shelalies would be wielded. It was a short stout stick with a knob, tied to the wrist

Sapper Michael Ahern from Tralee, County Kerry.

with a cord. I was about 5 years old when I remember how the ladies wore fashion; mutton chop sleeves and the bustle was disappearing.

I was living in Dingle then. My father and mother took all the family out of Tralee by train to Dingle. It was a triving [sic] town. There was to my estimation 10 curing sheds and 4 cooperages making fish barrels and were kept going ...

We lived in a small cottage as you go the road to Milltown. They were owned by a Mr O'Sullivan – flour and meal merchant. All we had to do was run across the road and swim in the sea ... Near at hand I saw the ruins of the first curing shed built in Dingle. The owner was Mr Ireland. It was situated just outside our cottage, built on the strand not very far from the row of new houses built on the left as you go to Milltown.

My father worked for Mr P Devane. He was the biggest buyer of fish and at times the people cleaning the fish worked till the small hours of the morning and often the wages would be round about £4 per week, which was big money those days when the cost of living was small – a glass of whiskey, 3 pence ½.

I went to the Christian Brothers School until I was aged 12 yrs. The father put me at coopering. He worked then for Mr Houlihan – merchant, Dykegate Street – where he had a curing shed and saw mill. I used to hear the old people say that the mackerel was so numerous that the fish swam up to the beach in thousands all around the coast – Milltown, and even Ventry and Ballydavid. The farmers scooped them up as manure for their land. They were so plentiful. I don't know how the situation now is but there seems to be no barrels made there now ...

My father worked for Mr P Houlihan until his death, 1909. I worked on for a year or so until for some reason the ... small boats ... failed to catch any more mackerel ... Work got slack ... I decided to try my luck so I left Dingle about 1911 and crossed Connor Hill down to Castlegregory and worked for Anthony Fitzgerald. I left Castlegregory, December 1911, and tried Tralee but I did not succeed in finding any work so I saw no hopes and decided to join the army, January 4th 1912, and passed a test for the engineers. Our pay weekly was £1.5.6 which was good money those day [sic] ...

I was stationed at the Curragh and when the 1914 war broke out we were shipped to France and we were taken by rail to a town in Belgium called Mons and that was where we came face to face with the German army and had to retire from the Germans as we were outnumbered. The retirement lasted 10 days and nights [sic]. All we had to eat was dog-biscuits and tins of bully beef. In fact, we were walking in our sleep until we met the French army on the Aisne River [sic], 12 kilometres from Paris. From there we were sent in lories [sic] by road & rail until we came to the end of our journey and arrived in a place called Ypres. And the fiercest of battles was fought there. As for shell-fire, I think they were firing them from all quarters until the city was on fire. There was a nuns' convent and it was in a blazing mass. The Connaught Rangers and also the Munster Fusiliers carried the nuns out of the building in their arms ..

I had to report sick with a fever and also hernia, so I was not sorry to leave behind destruction and death. So after an operation I had to report back to the barracks at Chatham and from there I was sent to India where I remained until the truce was signed. [Strangely, he doesn't include his 1915 tour of France, the Battle of Loos, or being gassed in his account]. I enjoyed my time in India, most especially the bazaars. You see the shoe maker and the smith at work, and various other trades and the fashion as regards foot wear and clothes was the women wore trinkletts on ears and nose and arms and twas very amusing to see them working in the fields and a child strapped to their backs. In fact, they did manual work, even loading coal into the big liners.

After a day or so, we left Bombay and arrived in a place which was called Bangalore and was stationed there until the truce was signed, Nov 1918. I was asked to sign on but I had enough of army life and so returned home to Tralee town.

By 1918, when Michael Ahern finally came home, old Ireland was gone. He could find no work in Tralee – not because of a lack of jobs but mainly because no one would employ him. Employers with nationalist leanings would not hire ex-British Army men, while neutral employers refused to employ former trench soldiers because they did not want to upset the republicans on their staff. So Ahern turned to an unlikely saviour – his brother-in-law – the local IRA commandant. This man got Michael Ahern work, making butter kegs for Slattery's bacon factory, solely because of the family connection. Other than this, Michael Ahern never got another permanent job in Tralee.

In 1923, he married Eileen Hogan – who was, again ironically, a Cumann na mBan woman. Then, in 1942, with the economy in Ireland performing poorly and still with no work available, Michael Ahern emigrated to Britain, returning in 1950 after the end of the Second World War. However, he always felt that he would have been better off if he had just left Ireland for good, but with a wife who loved her native Tralee, and with several young children, he decided to stay put. Of course, the army pension of twelve shillings a week helped, along with the four shillings and six pence that he received from the dole. Michael Ahern died in 1978, aged eighty-eight.

JAMES BLACKWOOD AND MICHAEL McLOUGHLIN

Most veterans only spoke to other veterans about their experiences which is another reason why so many personal histories have been lost to time. But a fear of Irish nationalists is not solely to blame here; they spoke only to other veterans because no one else could understand what they had been through. The

Left: Another man who only talked about the war to old comrades in pub corners was Private Thomas Whelehan from Athlone, a medic with the Royal Army Medical Corps. After enlisting in Ballymore while cycling back from a dance in Mullingar, he served in Gallipoli and on the Western Front where he always knew that gas was coming because the trenches would fill with rats heading the other way. Gassed himself, he returned home to Athlone after the war and worked for CIE on the trains and later as the secretary of the local Labour Party. He would often meet with old comrades privately and reminisce, but no one else would be allowed to sit in on these chats. Whelehan suffered from terrible chest problems until the day he died in 1955. He was only in his sixties.

average person on the street had no conception of war. It is because of this that we only have scraps of surviving information on men like James Blackwood – from Drogheda, County Louth – and Michael McLoughlin – a former medic from Nenagh, County Tipperary.

Blackwood was born in 1881 and served in the Boer War before fighting in the First World War. He was a Protestant but married a Catholic girl. Together, they had two daughters, only for Blackwood's wife to die young. Blackwood then emigrated to Scotland for many years, before returning to Drogheda. Even as an old man, he could still put up a fight in a pub if the situation called for it. He died in 1951, age seventy-nine, but no one knows anything about the conversations he had in pub corners with former comrades. All that survives is a nickname – 'Nugger Black' – and a tantalising reference to Blackwood's reputation as a soldier. His former comrades used to say, 'We always tried to get behind him. He couldn't be beaten'.

As for Michael McLoughlin from Nenagh, he grew up in John's Lane in Nenagh. He enlisted – along with an entire family of boxing champions named

Maher – simply to escape from John's Lane, and after two years as a medic with the Royal Army Medical Corps, McLoughlin was discharged due to illness on 14 November 1917. Then, aged thirty-one, he returned to a Nenagh, where there was little or no work, and was forced to keep his head down because of his previous life as a soldier. He managed to acquire casual labouring jobs every now and then, and occasionally went shooting for rabbits. Like many other ex-soldiers he was forced to pawn his medals for some extra money. A local ex-serviceman's club, named 'The Hut', gave him a place to meet with men like him, and McLoughlin was always involved in the veterans' marches on Remembrance Sunday, even if the locals were never pleased. One of his lasting memories was of the fact that, in Nenagh, many of the families of men who went to the trenches – regardless of whether these men survived the war or were killed in action – never spoke about their sons ever again. They just erased them from history.

THOMAS HOLLIGAN

Before the war, Thomas Holligan had had a few jobs. From Kilkee, near Castledermot, County Kildare, he worked for a while as a farm labourer on a large estate in Wexford. Then he got a job as a chauffeur for a doctor in Carlow. He had a love of horses, and so when he got married in early 1914 and could find no work, he set off for Castledermot Barracks to join the cavalry. He enlisted in the South Irish Horse – a Special Reserve cavalry unit – and after his initial training, he was assigned to B Squadron and started work as a farrier.

Unfortunately for Holligan, this was only a few months before the outbreak of war, and so in August 1914, he departed Royal Barracks in Dublin (now Collins Barracks Museum) for France, B Squadron of the South Irish Horse being one of the very few non-regular units that actually comprised the original BEF.

It had always been hoped that the infantry would create a gap in enemy lines that the cavalry could exploit, but this was never to be. So in 1917, when there was no more use for the South Irish Horse as cavalry, the unit was officially dis-mounted (most cavalry units had been performing dismounted tours of the front for some time by this point), turned into infantry, and re-designated the

7th Royal Irish Regiment. However, Thomas Holligan – now a sergeant – did not follow the rest of his comrades into the infantry. He was assigned to the Labour Corps and given the job of guarding prisoners of war.

When he was finally demobilised and sent by boat back to Dublin, Holligan was met by a hostile crowd, booing the disembarking soldiers, throwing rocks at them, and trying to mob them. Anti-British sentiment was high in Ireland, and Thomas Holligan was brought under protective guard back to Royal Barracks – the very place where his war with the South Irish Horse had begun five years earlier. He had to wait here for two weeks before it was actually safe to leave.

It was then that Holligan came to understand what the war had done to the men in the trenches. After he returned to Kildare, tramps regularly visited his home. Every three or four months, the same faces would turn up, passing by on their routes around the county. Thomas Holligan's wife would give them a bowl of soup or some bread and they would sit quietly on the porch and eat what they were given. This went on for years and years, until Thomas Holligan's children became old enough to understand what had happened to these men. They were First World War veterans, men suffering from shellshock, incapable of returning to society. Ireland had not welcomed them home, and their families and friends had ignored their pain, in some cases throwing them out of their homes. So they wandered aimlessly around the country, poor vagrants calling to the houses of men like Thomas Holligan who would show them sympathy. These men had left their futures behind on the battlefields of Europe.

Thomas Holligan never turned away one of his former comrades and he lived on long after the war ended. He had four sons and two daughters, and died aged seventy-eight.

JAMES NEVIN

However, it was not only militant republicans that returning First World War veterans had to be wary of. When the War of Independence began, many trench veterans took up arms for the nationalist cause. The Black and Tans subsequently developed a suspicion towards many former soldiers, seeing the

The new challenge faced by many returning veterans: Disabled soldiers learn to walk again, using their newly fitted artificial legs, at the workshops of JE Hanger at Roehampton, Surrey.

veterans as well-trained, potential IRA recruits. Ironically, at the same time, the British government were attempting to retain the loyalty, or at least the neutrality, of veterans by offering them benefits for their families.

One man who was on the receiving end of such contrasting treatment was James Nevin from Portumna, County Galway. Not long before the war, Nevin was living in Jersey City, New Jersey, USA, but he returned to his native Portumna after his father died so that he could look after his mother. When the war broke out, Nevin enlisted at the local recruiting station. There had always been a strong military tradition amongst many rural Galway families. This was, after all, the home ground of the 'Devil's Own', the Connaught Rangers.

James Nevin became a private with the 5th Connaught Rangers. In 1915, he was sent to Gallipoli, where on one occasion he came across a dead German officer in amongst the scrub of the dusty hillsides – one of the Kaiser's military advisors to the Turkish Army. This was a rare enough sight in Gallipoli, and Private Nevin took a few rounds of the German officer's pistol ammunition as a souvenir.

He survived the war and returned to Portumna, where he got work as the local postman. He would frequently drink with other ex-Rangers, although they did not speak of the war. However, when the War of Independence was at its most tense, the Tans burst into his house one night to search the place. Nevin insisted that he was not an IRA sympathiser, and that the Tans would find nothing illicit in his home. But then one of them found the pistol ammunition taken from the dead German officer in Gallipoli. Refusing to believe James Nevin's claims that the ammunition was just a war souvenir, he was hauled into Renmore Barracks in Galway, to appear before a military court. Luckily for the former Private Nevin, the officer in charge of the proceedings in Renmore was actually his old CO from Gallipoli. This officer was well aware of how this ammunition had come into James Nevin's possession, and after the two had a laugh about it, Nevin was dismissed and allowed to return to his postal duties in Portumna.

When Nevin finally married and had children, his children were always proud that their father had been in the British Army – and this was mainly because every year, without fail, new Clarke's shoes would arrive all the way from Dublin, compliments of the British Army. James Nevin never returned to America and lived out the rest of his life in his hometown of Portumna. He died in 1957.

STRUGGLING ON

PETER TOAL

In 1912, Peter Toal – a Catholic from Armagh town – joined the British Army. After serving in India, he fought at Ypres in 1914 and 1915 and then at the Somme in 1916 with the Royal Irish Fusiliers. Toal and his comrades were often so starved of rations that they used to catch and roast the huge rats that infested the trenches. It was during the Battle of the Somme that he was wounded. Shot in both legs, Toal lay on the scorched earth in amongst hundreds of other dead and wounded. Toal remembered being found and carted away by either army personnel or French civilians. The wounded were just lifted up and piled like corpses in the carts, to make their agonising way back to the clearing station.

Peter Toal survived the war and every 12/13 July, he would proudly wear his medals and his navy blue suit – the only suit he had – during the British Legion parade. He always enjoyed these days, would always take 'a brave sup of drink' (as his son recently put it), but would never forget to bring some leftover buns back home for his children. They could always tell when he was nearly home as he would come up the road singing 'Kevin Barry' – it was the only rebel song he knew.

After the war, work was hard to find. Worse still, Peter Toal was suffering from callipers on his legs – the result of his war wounds – and so he was not fit to work for some time. The family of six boys and four girls had to survive on his army pension of twelve shillings. However, when Toal was finally well enough, he travelled to England where he worked as a hud carrier. But since the money he sent home was not always adequate to provide for the family, his navy blue suit and his war medals often saw the inside of the local pawn shop. The half crown that his family would get for these items would be enough to survive on until money arrived from England. The family would then buy back the suit and the medals. Of course, the pawnbroker made three shillings and six pence profit each time. Unfortunately, on the last occasion when they were pawned, Peter Toal's medals were mixed up with those of someone else and the Toal family only recently realised the mistake. These medals were to two other Irishmen: Private John Lennox of the Royal Irish Regiment and Private Michael Maguire of the Royal Dublin Fusiliers.

After the period in England, Peter Toal returned home to work on an extension to the Royal School in Armagh. His son used to bring him his lunch every day – it was only ever a bit of bread and jam, no butter, and that was all Toal had to eat on the building site from 8am when he started work until 6pm when he came home.

When he died in 1957, his widow applied to the British Legion for a funeral grant. Although he lived in Banbrook Hill, a staunchly Catholic area of

Armagh town, and was a Catholic himself, Peter Toal had always enjoyed a great relationship with local Protestants – many of whom had been his former comrades during the war, and many of whom attended his funeral. However, his family did not wish his coffin to be draped in the Union Jack, and because of this, the British Legion turned down the grant application for burial costs. So Peter Toal's widow was forced to pay the considerable funeral expenses of £39 – a huge amount of money in 1957, especially for a recently widowed woman.

MARTIN GAFFEY

Martin Gaffey was born in Athlone, but was orphaned as a young boy. Martin was raised – according to his daughter, Eileen Kavanagh – by a tyrannical aunt named Kate Kilroy, who took every penny that Martin earned from his work as a labourer. In October 1915, twenty-two-year-old Martin enlisted in the army. Posted as a private to the 1st Irish Guards, he arrived on the Somme on 27 September 1916 and served all through the winter and on into the following year. After the start of the Third Battle of Ypres, he was shot in the neck, left arm and left knee on 3 August 1917 while the 1st Irish Guards were being relieved. He survived and spent fourteen months in English hospitals before finally being discharged in October 1918, just before the end of the war, and being allowed to return to Ireland. During his recuperation period, the army had taught him how to weave, the policy at the time being to teach disabled veterans a new skill. However, the policy was a joke, since a man with no legs, for example, was hardly going to be able to support his family by making straw baskets, and weaving was not going to support Martin Gaffey when he returned to Athlone.

Martin got into the building trade and over the following years helped to build the vast majority of houses on the Dublin Road in Athlone. In February 1919, he married Ellen Gilligan, a girl he had lived next door to, after moving away from Kate Kilroy. With Ellen, he started a family and, in 1921, Martin applied for an ex-serviceman's house in Athlone. Providing such houses was just one of the ways in which the British government were attempting to keep Irish war veterans out of the arms of the IRA.

Although Martin Gaffey had applied for a house before a Mullingar-based

*Martin Gaffey from Athlone,
County Westmeath in later life.*

review committee in 1921, and had been approved for a house in 1923, he was still living in a one-room flat by 1931, only now he and his wife had seven children. Ellen wrote on Martin's behalf (Martin could barely sign his own name) to his former regiment, the Irish Guards, saying that a new batch of ex-servicemen's houses were now under construction, and asked them if there was anything that they could do to help. They agreed to review his case.

Even though Martin was soon awarded a much better house, the outbreak of the Second World War attracted him to England. The pay a munitions worker received was much better than anything Martin could earn in Ireland, and with so many children, ten at this stage, he had to bring in as much money as he could. So he emigrated with his family to Birmingham. It was here that Martin Gaffey received word from the British Army about his son, Martin Gaffey Jnr. The younger Martin had followed in his father's footsteps and had joined the British Army, only to be sent to the Pacific Theatre and captured by the Japanese in the early years of the war. Horrendously treated and terribly starved, Martin Gaffey Jnr. was one of the thousands of Allied POWs that the Japanese used as slave labour to build the famous 'Railway of Death' and the bridge over the River Kwai. Martin Jnr. ultimately survived his ordeal and the war, but his experiences never left him.

Back in Birmingham, Martin Gaffey Snr. had firsthand experience of Luftwaffe bombings. Air-raid sirens might go off at any time and he would have to flee into shelters. On one occasion, every building on the street where his wife Ellen ran a sweet shop was badly hit and reduced to crumbling piles of rubble – every building, that is, except the sweet shop.

After the war, Martin and his family moved back to Athlone and Martin

8, 1, 31

Martin Gaffey
Late of I G No 9956
Upper Irishtown
Athlone

Dear Sir

I am writing these few lines in regards of an ex Soldier house as I put in a claim to this Office in 1920 I was brought up before a Committee in Mullingar in 1921 they told me my case for a house and plot was Sancioned in 1923 the houses was built

2

in Cloghanboy and Kilmaco and I dod not get one and I filled in Several Forms to the land Trust Sence and now there is after been a new lot built and 2 years and 5 months ago I filled in a form and was promised one and no later then 12 months ago I filled another Form I would be thankfull if you would

3

look into my case as I have a wife and 4 Children and living in one room and kitchen the Houses is built now and I am made to believe they are set and as I said before there is people with good houses getting them I would be more than thankful if you could do some thing for me I reman Your Obedent Servant M Gaffey

Letter written by Ellen Gaffey, on behalf of her husband Martin, to the Irish Guards, requesting assistance with the acquisition of an ex-serviceman's house in Athlone, 8 January 1931.

Letter written by Ellen Gaffey, on behalf of her husband Martin, to the Irish Guards, requesting advice and assistance with regards to finding work in Britain, 29 December 1939.

picked up where he left off in the building trade. He distrusted banks completely and asked his foreman – a very close friend – to hang on to his wages for him. What money Martin did take home, he kept stuffed in his bedposts.

Then in 1951, his wife Ellen fell sick with TB. Her doctor insisted that she go to a clinic for treatment, but Ellen refused to leave her home. As a result, local shops gave her free milk, eggs, and butter, to try and build her up, but unfortunately it did not work and she died in July that year, aged only fifty-seven.

Martin's children were terribly worried about how they were going to pay for the funeral, so Martin made a trip to his foreman, returning with fistfuls of banknotes. The funeral and the wake were held, and then Martin Gaffey disappeared. For a week, no one could find him, until he turned up in a bad state in Tullamore, completely devastated at the loss of his wife.

He lived out the rest of his life in his native Athlone, and used to change the subject or go completely silent when anyone ever asked him about the war. Then, while living on Griffith Street, Martin Gaffey died in May 1976, aged eighty-two. Known for his enormously bushy black eyebrows and the large scar on the left side of his neck, he was sadly missed by his family and friends. However, unlike so many other Athlone men who fought in the First World War, he, at least, was buried in his hometown.

The story of Martin Gaffey's son in the Second World War is sadly not a tale unique to the Gaffey family. The sons of many First World War veterans followed in their father's footsteps and joined the British Army, but in many cases, while their fathers had survived, the sons did not. Already mentioned in this book is the story of Kildare sniper Lar Molloy – killed on 21 March 1918 during the German Spring Offensive. He left behind a widow and son in

Monasterevan, and this son went on to be killed in action while serving in the RAF during the Second World War.

In another Athlone family, there was also a similar tragedy. Former Sergeant Jack Kelly survived the trenches and had nine children, only for his son Thomas to enlist as a private with the 2nd South Lancashire Regiment and die on 6 May 1942, aged twenty-five, during Operation Ironclad – a successful attempt to capture the Diego Suarez naval base and harbour from Vichy French forces on the island of Madagascar. Today, his body lies in the Diego Suarez War Cemetery.

Sergeant Jack Kelly and his family from Athlone, County Westmeath c1917. Thomas Kelly, the son who died during the Second World War, is the baby seated on his mother's knee in the photograph.

THE LEGACY OF WAR

Even today, there are parts of France and Belgium still dotted with craters and criss-crossed with trench networks, left over from the First World War. At Vimy Ridge, there are areas of land that tourists cannot walk on, due to unexploded shells just beneath the surface of the soil. Similar to the way in which the landscape is still scarred from the war, so too were men scarred physically for the rest of their lives, by wounds, trauma, or gas poisoning.

PATRICK CALLINAN

It was difficult for wives and children to understand what their husbands and fathers had been through during the war. Patrick Callinan from Graigue Cullen, County Carlow, had fifteen children, and while they were growing up, they used to get irritated by the fact that their father's breathing difficulties stopped him from working. They were annoyed at the way he would often go quiet or retreat into himself. But years later when they learned why their father acted like this, their anger turned to guilt.

Patrick Callinan had lost two brothers in the war: Private Peter Callinan, 1st Royal Dublin Fusiliers, who was killed, aged nineteen, in Gallipoli on 12 July 1915, who has no known grave and is today commemorated on the Helles Memorial, and Sergeant Matthew Callinan, 1st Leinster Regiment, who was killed in Belgium on 6 September 1915. Today he is buried in Houplines Communal Cemetery Extension. Furthermore, Patrick Callinan had been standing beside one of these brothers when the brother was blown to pieces by a shell, and the breathing difficulties that his children were so familiar with in later life were the result of gas poisoning. For years, Patrick Callinan's family simply did not understand his pain. The same could be said in thousands of other cases.

PATRICK O'DONNELL

As for Patrick O'Donnell, he similarly suffered ill-health that affected the rest of his life. When he was eighteen years old, O'Donnell – from Four-Mile-

House, County Roscommon – emigrated to America. He wanted to become a priest, but when America declared war on Germany in 1917 he was conscripted into the US Army.

Sent to France towards the end of the war, poor conditions and lack of food (O'Donnell and his comrades were forced to eat mostly turnips and roots) caused Patrick to fall violently ill with dysentery, malaria and ague. He was admitted to hospital and he was still there when the armistice was declared. Patrick O'Donnell never fired a shot.

Initially sent back to America as an invalid, he decided to return home to Roscommon where he was nursed by his family, although at first, they did not believe that O'Donnell would survive. He recovered sufficiently to be able to lend a hand again on the family farm. However, he was frequently plagued by bouts of sickness. He would often be found lying in bed suffering from terrible fevers, a thin sheet draped over him and steam rising up into the air. On other occasions, he would begin to shiver uncontrollably and complain that he was freezing.

Religion always remained extremely important to Patrick O'Donnell. As one family member put it, 'If rain was threatening and a field of hay ready to be saved, he would get on his bicycle and go to church to confess his sins first.'

He never married, but did make one half-hearted attempt, as a family member recently recalled:

> A certain lady who was over forty years of age and who was also very religious took his fancy. One Sunday when he knew she would be at second Mass, he took courage and called to her father's house and asked her father for her hand in marriage. Her father, a sensible man said, 'Well I'm afraid you will have to ask herself.' Patrick came home and informed his people of what he had done. His sister stamped her foot and said, 'There are enough old people in this house without bringing in another. If you want to get married, at least get a young one.' I'm afraid that put a damper on his romantic notions.

O'Donnell's family passed away one by one, until only Patrick himself was left. So he gave the family farm to a nephew and went to live in the Nazareth Home in Sligo. The Catholic cathedral in Sligo was just across the lawn from the home and frequently O'Donnell used to go missing. Every time, the nuns would find him in the cathedral.

Patrick O'Donnell died in the early 1970s – his brief time in France during the First World War having cursed him with a lifetime of sickness. He was eighty years old.

JOHN RIVERS

The sad thing is that war could also destroy the lives of a soldier's children, as it did in the case of John Rivers. Rivers was from just outside Tullamore in County Offaly and was born in 1885. He enlisted in the regular army in March 1904, aged eighteen, having previously served with the reserves. Posted to the 2nd Leinster Regiment, he served in South Africa and Mauritius before the First World War. By 1914, he was married and had become a sergeant and a specialist instructor in signalling and bombing (throwing grenades). He was also an experienced recruiting sergeant and, in 1915, he became an instructor in how to protect against gas. Rivers had an excellent service record at a time when most men had at least *some* infraction on their conduct sheet – he had absolutely no breaches of discipline to his name.

In 1917, John Rivers learned of the death of his brother in the trenches. Sergeant Michael Rivers of the 2nd Leinster Regiment was killed in action on 7 June 1917, during the Battle of Messines Ridge. With no known grave, today his name is commemorated on the Menin Gate Memorial in Ypres.

Then, in June 1918, John Rivers finally entered the war; he was sent to France and joined the 2nd Leinster Regiment in the field. The war was nearly over and when it ended in November 1918, John was still alive and well. However, he had to stay on in France as part of the post-war army of occupation, only returning home in May 1919. As a career soldier, he stayed in the army after the war, but sadly lost his wife due to heart failure in 1920 – she was only twenty-seven years old. Then, after another year at home, he was sent to Silesia in Poland in July 1921. He served there until February 1922 when he was suddenly evacuated to hospital in Woolwich due to an illness. John Rivers had contracted TB, and he never recovered from it. He died in May 1922. Back home in Birr, County Offaly – where John Rivers' three children were living with family – the news was devastating. The Rivers children had lost their mother in 1920, and now their father was gone too.

In 1924, two years after John Rivers' death, his daughter was found wandering the streets of Birr. Apparently she and her two brothers were in the care of grandparents, but as a court order soon stated, they 'do not exercise parental guardianship', and so the children were placed in care. Rivers' daughter was sent to the local convent, where she remembers being well treated by the nuns. She also remembers that a soldier would regularly visit her in the convent. He would ask to see her schoolwork; she would sometimes do some Irish dancing for him, and she distinctly recalled unwrapping his puttees – the 'bandages' that soldiers of the time had wrapped around their legs – on one occasion. Then, when she was about sixteen, the soldier stopped coming. It is very likely that this mystery soldier was an old comrade of John Rivers, a man who had promised to keep an eye on his children if anything ever happened to him.

However, John Rivers' two sons were unfortunately sent to Letterfrack Industrial School in County Galway. As an official report (Ryan Report) showed in 2009, the treatment of boys in Letterfrack by priests was appalling, and John Rivers' sons were abused. Years later, as old men, even the mention of the place would make them go deathly silent. Regrettably, even though they had lost their mother and their father, Ireland failed to take care of the Rivers' children.

JOSEPH BERTRAND 'BERTIE' McAREVEY

On 23 November 1917, the 36th (Ulster) Division were back in action at Cambrai, having achieved the impossible on the first day of the Somme but having suffered severe losses in the process. Now, they had been refitted, and serving in its battalions were a lot of new faces, one of which was Captain Joseph Bertrand 'Bertie' McArevey. Twenty-one years old from Newry, County Down, Bertie had been educated in Clongowes Wood and was studying medicine in University College Dublin when war broke out. In March 1915, having previously been a cadet of the Officer Training Corps attached to the Royal College of Surgeons, he applied for a commission with the 3rd (Reserve) Royal Irish Rifles. The president of UCD wrote him an official letter of recommendation. Bertie's application was ultimately successful and he was commissioned as a second-lieutenant.

By 23 November 1917, Bertie – now a captain – had already proved himself to be a brave and daring officer (he was the recipient of the Military Cross). However, on that day, in an attack against the Hindenburg Line at Cambrai, he was hit in the left arm and also sustained a severe head wound. Bertie was evacuated immediately and rushed back to England, arriving on 28 November. The following month he was still alive, and in the running for a full commission in the regular army (to replace his temporary commission which would be void once the war ended). His commanding officer praised him for distinguishing himself on all occasions, and for the

NOTABLE DISTINCTION FOR BRILLIANT NEWRY SURGEON.

DR. J. BERTRAND M'AREVEY.

We are pleased to observe that the National University of Ireland have conferred the Degree of M.Ch. (Master of Surgery-Ophthalmology), the highest degree in surgery it is in their power to confer, upon Dr. J. Bertrand M'Arevey, youngest son of Mr. J. J. M'Arevey, the well-known Newry merchant.

Dr. M'Arevey, who was educated at St. Colman's Diocesan Seminary, Newry, Clongowes College, and the National University, Dublin, in which centres he achieved most distinguished records, proceeded to specialise in diseases of the eye, and studied ophthalmology in Dublin and Vienna.

He has since made quite a name for himself in the Free State Metropolis, and is now in private practice as Surgeon Oculist at Bagot Street, Dublin, and holds the very responsible positions of Ophthalmic Surgeon to the Royal Victoria Eye and Ear Hospital, Dublin; St. Brecin's Military Hospital, Dublin; St. Vincent's Hospital, Dublin; and the Children's Hospital, Temple Street, Dublin.

Dr. M'Arevey served in the Great War as a Captain in the Royal Irish Rifles, and was awarded the Military Cross for bravery on the field.

We congratulate our brilliant young ʼsman ɔ his latest triumph, and wish ʼ in the profession he

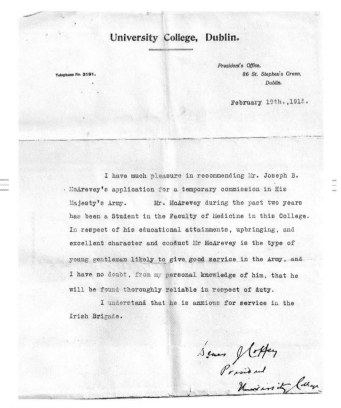

University College, Dublin.

Telephone No. 3191.

President's Office,
86 St. Stephen's Green,
Dublin.

February 19th., 1918.

I have much pleasure in recommending Mr. Joseph B. McArevey's application for a temporary commission in His Majesty's Army. Mr. McArevey during the past two years has been a Student in the Faculty of Medicine in this College. In respect of his educational attainments, upbringing, and excellent character and conduct Mr McArevey is the type of young gentleman likely to give good service in the Army, and I have no doubt, from my personal knowledge of him, that he will be found thoroughly reliable in respect of duty.

I understand that he is anxious for service in the Irish Brigade.

Denis J Coffey
President
University College

Above: Captain Joseph Bertrand 'Bertie' McArevey from Newry, County Down.

Left: Letter from the President of UCD, recommending Bertie McArevey for a commission in the army.

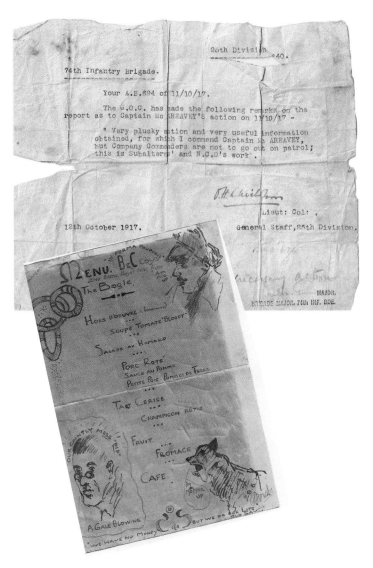

MR. J. B. McAREVEY, DUBLIN.

We regret to announce the death of Mr. Joseph Bertrand McArevey, 3, St. James's Terrace, Clonskeagh, Dublin, which occurred on Saturday of last week. Aged 54, the deceased gentleman was husband of Mrs. Eva McArevey, formerly Miss O'Keefe, late of Faythe House, Wexford. An old boy of Clongowes Wood College, Mr. McArevey was senior oculist to St. Vincent's Hospital, Dublin, and had a distinguished career as an eye specialist. He came to Dublin to study medicine, but his studies were interrupted by the 1914-1918 war. He joined the Royal Irish Rifles and attained the rank of captain before leaving the army. He fought in France and was awarded the Military Cross. Resuming his studies at the National University, he obtained the B.Sc. degree in 1920 and the M.B. a year later. He then went to Vienna to study eye diseases. Returning to Dublin, he was appointed oculist to Temple Street Children's Hospital, and this was followed by similar appointments in the Royal Victoria Eye and Ear Hospital, Adelaide Road, and St. Vincent's Hospital. He became a Master of Surgery in 1928. Mr. McArevey was the youngest son of the late Mr. J. J. McArevey, of Courtney Hill House, Newry, and his brother was the late Mr. John J. McArevey, a prominent Dublin solicitor. Deep sympathy is felt for his widow and four children. The deceased was brother-in-law of the Misses Mollie, Eileen and Maeve O'Keefe of The Bungalow, Rosslare Strand, and of Mr. Raymond P. O'Keefe, Landscape, and Faythe Maltings, Wexford. He was an uncle of Mrs. J. R. Colfer, New Ross. A member of the Rosslare Golf Club, he was a constant visitor to it each summer. There he made many friends who sincerely regret his passing. The funeral (which was private) took place after Requiem Mass in St. Vincent's Hospital, Dublin, to Dean's Grange Cemetery on Monday. The celebrant of the Requiem Mass was Rev. H. King, S.J. The chief mourners were: Mrs. Eva McArevey (widow); the Misses Eleanor, Ann and Mary Rose (daughters); Mr. Harry McArevey (brother); Mrs. McArevey (sister-in-law); Mrs. R. Flood (sister) and Dr. R. Flood (brother-in-law); Colonel J. MacCaffrey (brother-in-law); Mrs. MacCaffrey (sister-in-law); Miss Valerie McArevey and Mrs. Aveen Colfer (nieces); Dr. Derek Flood, Mr. Ian McArevey, Mr. Roddy MacCaffrey, Mr. Jack MacNally and Mr. Aiden MacNally (nephews); Mrs. Jack MacNally, Mrs. Aiden MacNally, Miss Daisy O'Keefe, Miss Molly O'Keefe, Mr. Raymond P. O'Keefe, Mr. Cyril Keefe and Mr. Colfer (relatives).—R.I.P.

AN APPRECIATION.

The following appreciation by "R. McK." appeared in the "Irish Times" las Monday:—

Joseph Bertrand McArevey—known to many as Bertie McArevey—has left us. These simple words will cause a pang of deep regret in many a heart from Fair Head in Antrim to Mizzen Head in Cork and from Slyne Head in Galway to Howth Head in Dublin. A great gentleman of marked courage and independence of character—a gifted ophthalmological surgeon beloved by the poor, one born, not made—has been snatched from us at the height of his power, when his healing gifts will be missed most by those who could profit from his unequalled knowledge, his incomparable sense of judgment and his unrivalled technique in ophthalmic surgery. His loss will be keenly felt, not onxy by his patients, who, literally speaking, loved him, but also by the nursing and domestic staffs with whom he worked, and by his colleagues, to whom at all times the benefit of his wide experience and vast knowledge was always freely available.

Top left: *While serving in 2ⁿᵈ Royal Irish Rifles during the Third Battle of Ypres in 1917, Bertie was promoted to lieutenant and served as acting captain, was awarded the Military Cross for his part in an action at Westhoek, and then led a patrol out into no-man's-land on 11 October 1917, for which his commanding officer wrote this report.*

Middle: *A sample humorous mess menu – 28 June 1917 – from the 2ⁿᵈ Royal Irish Rifles officers' mess, kept as a souvenir by Bertie McArevey.*

Right: *Bertie McArevey's obituary.*

highly efficient running of his company. This was followed by a recommendation from no less than the Field Marshal Commander-in-Chief of British
Armies in France, stating that Captain McArevey should be granted a full commission. As a result, this was soon made official, and Bertie was appointed a
captain in the Royal Irish Rifles.

However, the war had left a permanent scar on Bertie McArevey's health. By
March 1918, the full extent of his head wound was starting to become apparent. He had previously had perfect vision, but now, the world was starting to
blur. His eyesight had been badly affected by the injury, and for the rest of his
life, he would have to wear glasses. Seeing this as an impediment to continuing
on in the army, Bertie wrote the following to the adjutant of the 3rd Royal Irish
Rifles:

> Sir, I have the honour to request that you will place before the Commanding
> Officer for his consideration, approval, and recommendation, this my application
> to be permitted to resume my Medical Studies at the Medical School, Cecilia
> Street, Dublin …

After reviewing Bertie's case, taking into account his wound and deteriorat-
ing vision and his professional studies, the army granted Bertie's request and
discharged him on 25 June 1918. He returned to university and continued his
medical studies, receiving a B.Sc. in 1920 and his M.B. in 1921. Doctor
McAevery specialised in ophthalmic surgery, and became ophthalmic surgeon
to the Royal Victoria Eye and Ear Hospital, Dublin; St Bricin's Military Hospital; St Vincent's Hospital; and Temple Street Children's Hospital. In 1928,
Bertie became a Master of Surgery (M.Ch.) in ophthalmology.

In 1944, he delivered a paper entitled 'The Social and Medical Problems of
Phlyctenular Disease in Dublin', concerned with the low-standard of living
endured by Dublin's poorest citizens. This paper was for the Montgomery Lec-
ture, which he had been asked to give by invitation of the Council of the Royal
College of Surgeons, Ireland. Doctor McArevey also had a private practice on
Baggot Street and was a member of the Prevention of Blindness Committee of
the National Council for the Blind in Ireland.

Then, on 24 February 1951, while living at St James's Terrace in Clon-skeagh, Dublin, Bertie McArevey passed away. A very young man for all of his substantial achievements, he was only fifty-four years old. Typical of most doctors in the First World War, he never actually claimed the campaign medals that he was entitled to. However, his family still have his Military Cross, commemorating his act of bravery in those far off days long ago. His story proves that although the war affected every veteran's future, in at least one case, the outcome was ultimately positive.

LEAVING HOME AGAIN

Sometimes, men – for one reason or another, be it ill-health or economic necessity – were ultimately forced to leave Ireland again, having made it home safely, while in other cases, men emigrated to make a fresh start.

THOMAS KERR

Thomas Kerr was a native of Timahoe, County Laois. Aged eighteen, he had fought at the Somme and Ypres with the Royal Inniskilling Fusiliers and had suffered terrible gas poisoning. He managed to survive the war, but was inflicted with chest problems for years after. Advised by a doctor to emigrate to a warmer climate, Thomas Kerr – the owner of Timahoe's first car – packed up and boarded the boat for New Zealand in 1927. He started a new life on the far side of the world, his health improved, and he left the war behind him. But then the war caught up with him.

In 1991, seventy-four years after fighting on Belgian soil (at Ypres in 1917), Thomas Kerr was tracked down and awarded an extremely late Belgian King Albert Medal for veterans, in recognition of the fact that he had fought in defence of Belgium during the First World War. This makes Thomas Kerr one of the last ever recipients of the medal (if not the last), and in a ceremony in New Zealand, covered by the local media, Thomas Kerr had the medal pinned on his chest. He died the following year, aged ninety-six.

THOMAS KELLY

One day, after the war, Thomas Kelly simply walked up to a farmer in Arklow, County Wicklow, and asked the man could he work for food. The farmer was not sure at first, but when Kelly produced three war medals and offered them up as collateral, that clinched the deal. Kelly worked in the fields, was fed by the farmer, and lived in the barn adjacent to the house. He never spoke about where he had come from or what he had been through in the war, and the farmer soon got the impression that Thomas Kelly simply had no family and nowhere else to go. Then, one day, as mysteriously as he had arrived, Kelly vanished, never to be seen or heard from again. But he did not attempt to retrieve his medals – he left them in the possession of the Wicklow farmer who had taken pity on an old war veteran.

From archival records, it has been possible to learn that Thomas Kelly was a pre-war regular who served with the Royal Irish Regiment, and that he landed in France for the first time on 19 December 1914. Also, Kelly's hometown can finally be revealed. He was from the townland of Newtown, near the village of Coolgreany in County Wexford, just south of the Wicklow-Wexford border.

BACK IN UNIFORM

While the majority of Irish First World War veterans were made to look back upon their days in khaki with guilt and shame, there were some men whose war days were accepted – even valued – by their fellow Irishmen. These were the veterans who 'put their skills to good use', as Irish nationalists saw it, and joined the IRA during the War of Independence or the anti-Treaty IRA or the National (Free State) Army during the Civil War.

PADDY HORKAN

In 1915, Paddy Horkan from Castlebar, County Mayo – a plumber by trade – set off for Coventry. He was only twenty-five when he arrived in England, and when he started work in the munition factories he was paid three pounds a

IRA Captain Paddy Horkan, training republican soldiers in the Mayo hills. The IRA wanted their soldiers to be trained in the use of small arms and guerrilla tactics; how to use defensive cover, learn the components of a rifle, and how to make bombs from lead piping.

week in gold and silver sovereigns. Men at the front used to grumble and complain about how much munitions' workers were paid, in comparison to their meagre wages.

In the heady days of 1915, Paddy Horkan witnessed the British war propaganda machine in full swing. Posters called for men to fight to free little Belgium. They reminded citizens that priests were being hanged and churches were being burned. Speakers from their podiums would shout about how nuns were being raped, children's hands were being sliced off and how the German race should be wiped from the face of the earth (later propaganda would include the fictitious stories of German 'corpse factories' where candles and grease were supposedly made from the body-fat from dead Allied soldiers). So Paddy and a friend, 'Old George', enlisted in Chester in late 1915, to fight for Catholic freedom. Not too long after, Horkan would laugh at the innocence of it all.

Paddy was planning to join the engineers but when his friend wanted to join the infantry, he begged Paddy to go with him. Old George wore glasses and he

IRA Captain Paddy Horkan in uniform.

could not see very well, so without Paddy, he knew he would be done for. The pair ended up in the Worcestershire Regiment and they were soon off to Salisbury Plain for training. There was not a house in sight, only army huts, and the men were woken at 7am each morning. In Horkan's own words, 'the instructors would bring you out in only your trousers and socks... [with your] shoes off for a run of three or four miles and back for your breakfast. It was a great life. They had a canteen with beer and stout.'

However, it cannot have been *that* great a life for Paddy. For, in April 1916, while on leave in Castlebar, the talk was all about how the war would soon be over. Horkan decided that there was no point in going to war if it would only be for a month or two and he made up his mind to desert. His father had other ideas. He refused to let his son choose the life of a fugitive.

So, having overstayed his leave, Paddy ended up returning to the army. When Paddy arrived back to his battalion, he was immediately arrested and court-martialled. The charge: desertion. Horkan was brought up before a judge and asked, 'What have you to say for yourself?' The Mayo man thought fast. News of the Easter Rising was just hot off the presses.

> Well, sir, under the circumstances, with the rebellion in Ireland, there was no trains running. I found it very hard to get to Dublin to embark ... I done the best I could. I couldn't be here any sooner with the troubles and from the very west of Ireland with no trains running.

Case dismissed.

This was not the only time that Paddy Horkan was court-martialled. Later in his army career, he was brought up on charges of not presenting himself for parade. A sergeant came to where he was housed and arrested him. Paddy's excuse: the parade was for a Protestant minister, he was Catholic and there was no Catholic chaplain in the battalion. To attend a Protestant service would be against his religion. Case dismissed.

When his training was over, Paddy Horkan was sent to France with the 14th (Severn Valley Pioneers) Worcestershire Regiment. They were attached to the Royal Naval Division, soon to be re-designated the 63rd Royal Naval Division, which had come into existence in 1914. With not enough ships to accommodate the large numbers of naval reserves, the surplus was formed into a division to fight as infantry. They had fought at Antwerp in October 1914 and Gallipoli in 1915, where they had suffered terribly, and when Paddy's unit joined the Royal Naval Division they were preparing for the coming Somme offensive. According to Paddy, the new navy recruits knew nothing about constructing barbed wire defences, or making dugouts, digging trenches, or building firing bays. That was why his battalion had been attached to them – to show the navy men how to work as army men.

Paddy Horkan landed at Le Havre on 21 June 1916, just over a week before the opening of the Somme, and marched into position behind the front. Here, the trench digging and the backbreaking work began, and Old George soon decided that he wanted out. When Paddy and he were alone, doing work out beyond the parapet, he would beg Paddy to break his arm, and every time Horkan would slam down with the shovel, Old George would pull his arm out of the way just in time. He just could not hold still. But somehow Paddy managed to get the job done, and with his arm in a sling, Old George then received an out-of-the-blue notice to say that he was wanted back in Coventry to work on gun sights in the ordnance factories. Begrudgingly, Paddy escorted his friend to Le Havre, and, promising that he would write and that he would send cigarettes, Old George boarded the ship for England. Paddy Horkan never heard from him again.

Having to console himself with the navy tot of rum, issued to all men attached to the 63rd Royal Naval Division, Paddy went on to serve as batman to a second-lieutenant and accompanied the young officer on inspections of the firing bays. After their rounds, the pair would retire to the officer's dugout, where the officer would produce a bottle of brandy and raise the subject of Irish nationalism and the recent Easter Rising – perhaps just to get a rise out of Paddy. On one occasion, Paddy turned around to the officer and said, 'Sure ye bastards know if Germany won the war and took six of your shires down south, would you not be looking for them back?' There is no record of the officer's reply.

Then, on 29 April 1917, the day after the capture of Gavrelle by the 63rd Royal Naval Division during the Battle of Arras, the war diary records:

> The men of the Coy to which Pte Horkan belongs whilst advancing over the open to a fresh position were caught in an enemy barrage. Several men were wounded and were consequently left on the top without cover. Pte Horkan who is a stretcher-bearer showed great courage and devotion to duty in getting to these men under enemy fire, tending their wounds, and eventually bringing them under cover. He himself was wounded but returned to duty after getting the men to the dressing station and having his own wound tended to.

The last man that Paddy Horkan brought in that day was a sergeant named Harrison. He had previously been helping Paddy with the wounded. For his efforts, Paddy Horkan was awarded the Military Medal for bravery. Both he and Sergeant Harrison were sent to hospital, and Harrison ended up in Manchester Royal Hospital where he heard one of the nurses being called Horkan. He asked the girl did she have a brother serving in the Worcestershires. 'I have,' she said. 'Patrick.' 'He saved my life,' the sergeant told her.

Meanwhile, Paddy was brought out on a stretcher to meet King George. The king was on a visit and Paddy had only recently won his Military Medal. He later recalled that the king was a little man, and it seems that Paddy felt sorry for him. The king asked Paddy where he won his decoration, and then reached out 'his little hand and he shook hands with me and hoped I would be alright'.

When Paddy had finally healed, instead of going back to his old unit – 14th Worcestershire Regiment in France – he specifically asked to be sent to a different battalion. So he was posted to 1/8th Worcestershire Regiment and travelled

Paddy Horkan, former First World War private and IRA captain, meets Dev during a visit to Mayo along with other War of Independence veterans.

to Italy to join them. Then, during the Battle of the Piave River in June 1918, Paddy was wounded and evacuated again – which made three times in all.

As the end of the war drew near, Horkan found himself in Portsmouth and 'under the influence of drink'. The German *Kaiserschlacht* had failed and the Allies were driving the Germans back. It looked as if the war would soon be over. But a drunken Paddy Horkan was trying to get back to France. He marched up to the embarkation officer and showed him his papers.

'What the hell are you doing?' was the reply. 'The war's nearly over, lad. If you get stuck over there when it's done, you could be facing two more years of duty.' The embarkation officer stuffed a ticket for the last rest train into Paddy's hand and told him to go back to Ireland. Like all men being discharged, Paddy Horkan was given a choice: thirty bob or a Martin Henry suit. Patrick took the thirty bob and headed home to Mayo.

In the early days of the War of Independence, Paddy was approached by local IRA command to train volunteers, certainly due to the fact that his family had strong links to the republican movement. Paddy agreed and became a captain in A Company, 1ˢᵗ Battalion, Castlebar IRA, West Mayo Brigade. His brother James Horkan became a republican magistrate and on one occasion was arrested by the Black and Tans. If it was not for the intervention of the prison governor, they would have beaten him to death. Paddy's other brother Peter was continuously on the run with his flying column, and received many a mention in IRA dispatches and RIC criminal reports.

After the War of Independence came the Treaty. While Paddy Horkan knew that the people would ratify it, because the country was desperate for peace, he sided with the anti-Treaty republicans. He believed he could not dishonour his oath to the Republic. In one day, his men robbed three banks in Castlebar. They gave receipts to the banks, leaving the Free State Government to foot the bill. Then, with £50,000, Paddy escorted his IRA colleague Mark Killea by train up to Dublin, to hand over the money to his comrades in the Four Courts, the anti-Treaty IRA having recently occupied the building. Having secured an IRA receipt for the money at the Four Courts, Paddy headed back to catch the train home to Mayo.

The next day, 28 June 1922, Michael Collins shelled the Four Courts and the Civil War began. Paddy Horkan had been lucky during the Battle of Arras, and his luck continued to hold when he missed being trapped in the Four Courts by just one day.

During the bitter Civil War that followed the shelling of the Four Courts, Paddy was involved in fighting around Clifden, Newport, and Castlebar. On one particular day, 29 October 1922, his column of thirty men raided three National Army barracks in Clifden. They secured the surrender of the first barracks by blowing up the gable end of the building with a mine doused in petrol, and used an armoured car made out of an old hotel boiler welded to a Crossley chassis – nicknamed the 'Queen of the West' – to assault the second one.

However, Paddy Horkan was always adamant that the National Army soldiers, once they had surrendered, should be properly treated. In the evening after attacking the three barracks, Paddy was having a pint in a pub when he learned that some of his men were conducting a court-martial of the day's prisoners. Furious, Paddy stormed out the door.

I put a bullet in the breach of my rifle and I said what are you doing to these?

For Bravery in the field
Gavrelle
April 1917

George V
Medal
1914 - 1918

The Great
War For
Civilisation
1914 - 1919

L. D. F.
1921 - 1971

Old I.R.A.

F.C.A.
1939 - 1946

Paddy Horkan's medals [top row from left (British): Military Medal for bravery, War Medal, Victory Medal; bottom row from left (Irish): War of Independence 1971 Survivor's Medal, War of Independence Medal with 'Comrac' bar for combat service, FCÁ Emergency Medal 1939–1946].

'We're court-martialling them.' I said I gave my word to them that they would not be harmed and I said, 'If you do anything I'll shoot you at the first opportunity. They gave up as prisoners of war and I told them that they would be alright. If you interfere with them I'll shoot you.'

Paddy was obviously concerned that the court-martial would end in execution. The prisoners were treated fairly after that, and they were placed out on an island to be interred. However, the National Army soldiers soon overpowered their sentries, stole a boat, and took off.

Not long after, Paddy Horkan was forced to go on the run, but was ultimately captured in March 1923 by the National Army and jailed, firstly in Claremorris Workhouse and then in Castlebar Prison. When he was imprisoned in Ballycastle, he was OC of 300 anti-Treaty IRA prisoners. He had a good relationship with his jailer, however, a National Army commandant named Andy Lohan, who would regularly chat to Paddy and have a smoke with him, listen to his complaints, and do his best to fix any problems.

When a ceasefire was declared on 30 April 1923, effectively ending the Civil War, the National Army did not immediately release IRA prisoners. By October 1923, they were still in Free State jails, and on account of this, the anti-Treaty IRA chose to go on hunger strike. Over a two-month period, 8,000 IRA men began to starve themselves, in protest, and Paddy Horkan's experience of this lasted for thirteen days. He was then released on Christmas Eve 1923, having been moved to the Curragh by this point, and given a ticket to Castlebar.

Paddy Horkan returned home to Mayo and, after initially planning to emigrate to America, he secured a maintenance job in the local mental hospital. When the IRA had to abandon arms, Paddy buried the decommissioned weapons in the hospital grounds. Along with his two First World War service medals and his Military Medal for bravery, he soon had a War of Independence medal with 'Comrac' bar (for men who had been engaged in combat) to add to his collection. This was followed by an FCÁ Emergency medal, which Paddy earned for army reserve service during the Second World War, and finally, in 1971, he received a War of Independence survivor's medal, in recognition of the fact that fifty years after the War of Independence had ended, he was still alive and kicking. Paddy Horkan died ten years later in 1981, aged ninety-two.

JAMES McLOUGHLIN

On the National (Free State) Army side during the Civil War was another trench veteran. James McLoughlin – the son of a shepherd from Enfield, County Meath – was only eighteen when the First World War broke out. He enlisted in the Royal Garrison Artillery, and by the end of the war he had risen to the rank of corporal, had served as part of the gun crew of two twelve-inch, rail-mounted howitzers (heavy battery) on the Somme, and had lost the index finger on his left hand and suffered a head wound which left a piece of shrapnel in his skull for the rest of his life. Furthermore, he had been commended on one occasion for rescuing his battery right out from under the noses of advancing Germans while being wounded in the process.

In 1922, with the Treaty ratified, James McLoughlin – by then a twenty-six-year-old sergeant – left the British Army and enlisted in the new National Army. Because of his years of experience, he was given a commission and placed in command of Innishannon outpost, before joining the 59th Battalion in Kinsale. One of the many ex-British servicemen that were forming the nucleus

Irish Army Captain (later Lieutenant-Colonel) James McLoughlin from Enfield, County Meath.

of the National Army, bringing all of their experience to the new recruits, James McLoughlin ended up in the Artillery Corps in Kildare in 1924. His superior was Commandant Patrick A Mulcahy, another First World War veteran. In 1930, McLoughlin became an instructor in the Military College on the Curragh under Mickey Joe Costello. The two of them were very good friends.

During the Second World War and the Emergency period in Ireland, James McLoughlin was appointed commander of 5th Brigade based at Kilkenny in April 1941. In January 1943, he was reassigned to command 3rd Brigade in Collins Barracks, Cork, itself a part of Costello's 2nd 'Spearhead' Division. By this stage, James McLoughlin was a lieutenant-colonel. When the Emergency ended, he was stationed in Athlone and then appointed as the Director of Artillery – a post he held from January 1949 to 7 November 1955.

When he retired, he decided to live out his remaining years in Whitehall, Dublin. In 1966, having served in the British Army, the National Army, and the Defence Forces of the Irish Republic, James McLoughlin died aged seventy-one. For hundreds of Irishmen like him, the First World War sowed the seeds for a career as a professional soldier – a career which ultimately led to respect and recognition from Irish society. This was, perhaps ironically, the one profession in which trench veterans could more or less 'clear their name'. Only by staying in uniform and continuing to fight could they find a place in modern Ireland, and it is surprising to note how many of Ireland's military leaders were former British soldiers.

James Emmet Dalton – born in America but raised in Dublin – served with the Royal Dublin Fusiliers, rose to the rank of Major, and won a Military Cross for his part in the Battle of Ginchy on the Somme. Later, during the War of Independence, he became involved in Michael Collins' 'Squad' and rose to the rank of major-general in the National Army during the Civil War. Dalton was actually beside Collins during the infamous ambush at *Béal na mBláth* where Collins was shot and killed. In 1958 he founded Ardmore Studios in Bray, and it was his film company who helped produce the famous First World War movie *The Blue Max*. He died in 1978, aged eighty.

Then there was Wexford-man William Murphy, who served as an officer with the South Staffordshire Regiment during the First World War and who fought at Loos, the Somme, Ypres, and in Italy. He ended the war as a lieutenant-colonel with a Military Cross and Distinguished Service Order to his name. He was the National Army commanding officer for County Kerry during the Civil War, and later helped form the special branch of An Garda Síochána, before organising two auxiliary forces at de Valera's request during the Emergency – the Local Defence Force (army) and the Local Security Force (police). He died in 1975, aged eighty-five, and is buried in Bray, County Wicklow.

In fact, at various times, all three branches of the Irish military (army, navy and air corps) have been commanded by trench veterans. Waterford-man Patrick A Mulcahy enlisted into the Royal Engineers as a sapper (private) during Easter Week 1916. Ironically he was the brother of Easter Rising participant and IRA chief-of-staff Richard Mulcahy. Patrick Mulcahy became Lieutenant-General Chief-of-Staff of the Irish Army from 1955–59, having served as commander of the Artillery Corps and later as Director of Artillery. Also a War of Independence veteran, he died in 1987, aged ninety.

Colonel AT 'Tony' Lawlor served with the Royal Flying Corps during the First World War, took part in the War of Independence and founded the Irish Naval Service. He was also a former officer commanding Curragh Command, and he died in Howth in 1987, aged eighty-nine.

Finally, Colonel Charles Russell – a Dubliner who served with the Royal Flying Corps during 1914–1918 – was the officer commanding the Irish Air Corps in 1924 (fellow trench veteran and Dubliner James Fitzmaurice, famous for co-piloting the first east-west transatlantic flight aboard the *Bremen* in 1928, was appointed second-in-command of the Air Corps the following year). Russell died in London in 1965, aged sixty-nine.

PATRICK GAFFEY

However, for those Irishmen that continued soldiering after the war, not all of them swapped over to an Irish uniform. In some cases, with no civilian jobs on offer, with the tense political climate in Ireland, and sometimes out of personal choice, many Irishmen remained in khaki and stayed in the British Army.

One such man was Patrick Gaffey from Athlone. He was a pre-war regular who had been serving with the 1ˢᵗ Leinster Regiment in India at the outbreak of war. His battalion had returned to Europe and entered the trenches in time for the winter of 1914, after which Patrick was evacuated due to illness. On 28 August 1915, his older brother Hubert – a corporal serving with the 5ᵗʰ Connaught Rangers in Gallipoli, also a pre-war regular – was killed, aged twenty-nine, during a fierce Turkish counter-attack on the Kaiajik Aghala hill-side, where the Turks had outnumbered the Irishmen by at least six to one. Hubert Gaffey has no known grave and is today commemorated on the Helles Memorial. Patrick then returned to the trenches in 1916 in time for the Somme, where he was wounded at the Battle of Delville Wood in August and evacuated again, after which he transferred into the Machine Gun Corps (ominously known as the 'suicide squad'), was promoted to corporal, returned to the war in late 1917 and served throughout the battles of 1918.

After the war, he married and moved to Exeter – and although he was soon discharged, initially choosing not to renew his contract with the army, he was soon back in uniform. On 14 April 1921, after a little over a year out of the army, Patrick Gaffey re-enlisted as a private for ninety days' 'emergency service' in the 5ᵗʰ Devon Regiment. With the Irish War of Independence now being fought, the British were concerned that it might soon get out of hand, and so they began recruiting men to form defence forces. Although Patrick enlisted specifically under the conditions that he would *not* have to serve in Ireland, if things in Ireland had deteriorated, then his battalion would have been used to free up another British unit to head across the Irish Sea.

Patrick Gaffey's ninety days of emergency service ended on 2 July 1921, and not long after he applied for an army compensation award. He was now suffering from pulmonary tuberculosis, and the prospect was not good. With a wife, he was hoping to get some kind of financial support from the army – whom he had served for sixteen years at this stage – but they rejected Patrick's claim in November 1922, stating that there were no grounds for the award. While men living in Ireland were given Christmas presents of clothes and shoes, and while others were granted houses, Patrick Gaffey in Exeter was told that he would not receive compensation for his poor health.

Three years later on 11 July 1925, Patrick Gaffey – the man who had served six years in India, and every single year in the trenches of the First World War (a war that had also claimed the life of his brother) – died of pulmonary tuberculosis in Colindale Hospital in Middlesex. He was only thirty-seven at the time of his death, and he left behind a wife and three children.

LOST SOULS

Then there were others – the poor unfortunates – who were broken by the war. For these men, there were no counselling services. Shellshock – or post traumatic stress disorder as it is now known – was barely even recognised as a genuine condition. Prior to this, men who had gone out of their minds from the incessant shellfire, or from the horrors of war, were said to have had 'battlefield jitters' or, worse of all, they were branded cowards.

JOHN COLLINS

One day, a woman named Silvia Matthews walked into her hayshed in Portarlington, County Laois. She picked up a pitchfork and started lifting the hay, when suddenly there was a groan from beneath the straw. Silvia screamed in panic, but her fear turned to anger when she discovered a drunken man hidden in her hayshed. She yelled at him to get out of her barn, and the man mumbled something about being a war veteran.

Silvia Matthews had just encountered John Collins from Edenderry, County

Offaly, a former private and officer's batman in the Royal Irish Fusiliers. When Collins had returned to Ireland after the war, he found it very hard to deal with what he had experienced. The war in the trenches weighed heavily on his soul and when he turned to drink to escape, his family disowned him. And so, Collins had ended up in Silvia Matthews' hayshed.

After Collins said he was a war veteran, Silvia calmed down and a conversation ensued. Coincidentally, she was in charge of paying out veterans' pensions in Portarlington, and when she realised that John Collins had never collected his pension, she asked him to show her his war medals to prove that he was ex-army. He did so, and Silvia told him that he was entitled to money. Collins went down to Silvia's office the following day and collected his backdated pension.

John Collins then managed to clean himself up and became a lodger with some relations of the late Sergeant Henry McBryde – the man mentioned earlier in this book who had died of pneumonia in a German POW camp after the armistice had been declared. Collins started work on their farm, but soon drank all of his pension money. Things got worse; the landlord and his family desperately tried to help Collins, but he was lost. Years later, the drink finally took its toll and John Collins fell ill, ending up in Tullamore hospital on his death bed. When his family learned that he was still an alcoholic, they refused to turn up at his bedside, and so he died and was buried with only the family of his landlord present – another Irish victim of the First World War, whose suffering went on long after the guns had fallen silent.

PATRICK AND WILLIAM ROACH

Other men suffered their mental breakdowns due to what happened when they returned home and the Roach brothers from Newport, County Mayo, are also a good example of how some returning Irish soldiers were made to feel by their fellow countrymen. The brothers managed to make it home to Mayo but were shunned by the local people. Mayo was a strongly republican area, with men like Captain Paddy Horkan waging war on the British forces, and this response from friends and family only made the two brothers feel guilty and ashamed. They grew to resent that they had ever been to war.

One of them – Patrick, a former Connaught Ranger – could not deal with what he had been through. He suffered terribly from shellshock and was soon getting into fights in Newport. After one punch-up, he was jailed. He disappeared soon after that and the last the family heard of him, he was in a mental asylum in Berkshire.

The other brother, William Roach – who had previously served with the Royal Irish Rifles in Gallipoli – was so ashamed of himself that he took his army uniform, which he had so proudly worn over the last few years, and buried it in the bog. He wanted to forget the war, to erase it from his memory, and after putting the uniform in the ground, he spoke of it no more. By complete accident, it was dug up by the family decades later. William Roach's uniform was perfectly preserved by the peat.

WILLIAM HAND

Bill Hand could be said to be representative of Ireland's attitude to its First World War veterans as a whole. A Dublin-man, Bill served with the Royal Army Medical Corps in Gallipoli as a stretcher-bearer before being transferred to the Ypres front. One day, while he and a comrade were lugging a wounded man on a stretcher across war-torn land, a blast of heat and noise erupted right in front of him. Bill was left holding two burnt handles – all that was left of his fellow stretcher-bearer and the wounded soldier in their care. A German shell had killed the two of them right in front of him. Bill, miraculously, was completely unhurt.

He returned home after the war, but that incident never left him. When the Second World War began, his shellshock worsened and suddenly Bill Hand was convinced that he was back in the trenches. His condition became so bad that his children placed him in a mental institution, and instead of telling Bill's grandchildren the truth, they told them that their grandfather had passed away.

Years passed and Bill Hand was left forgotten behind closed doors, away from the view of a disapproving public. He died alone in 1963 – his grandchildren believing that he was already long gone. He had left the war forty-five years previously, but the war had never left him.

JOHN OLIVER

Finally, while some were broken and some locked up, there were others like John Oliver. Born in 1887 in Loughrea, County Galway, Oliver was from a particularly poor background – his family lived in a tiny lean-to shack out the Galway road on the edge of town – but he was good friends with the Wall family, who were far better off than his own family. John Oliver was particularly friendly with one of the Walls – Thomas, who was much younger than he was – and both men ended up joining the army at different points. John Oliver enlisted in the local infantry regiment, the Connaught Rangers, in 1905, aged eighteen, while Thomas Wall enlisted in an artillery unit in 1915 – Wall did this because he loved music (he had previously played with a band called The Saharas in Loughrea), and although he would primarily work as a driver, the artillery would also allow him to serve as a bandsman.

When the First World War broke out, Private Oliver was serving with the 1ˢᵗ Connaught Rangers in India, then stationed in Ferozepore. They sailed from Karachi on 28 August 1914 and landed in Marseilles just under a month later on 26 September. By this time, the 2ⁿᵈ Battalion had already been involved in the Battle of Mons and the subsequent retreat. Oliver fought in the First Battle of Ypres and served on through 1915, but then, on 5 August 1915, he was tried by Field General Court Martial in Le Havre, France. The charges were drunkenness, insubordination and 'threatening', and resulted in Oliver being sentenced to thirty-five days of Field Punishment No. 1 – where he would be forced to do hard manual labour while shackled to a heavy object.

On 11 December 1915, the 1ˢᵗ Connaught Rangers left France and sailed to Mesopotamia. Landing at Basra on 10 January 1916, they joined the rescue force detailed to save the garrison that was cut off and surrounded by the Turks in Kut-al-Amara. Here, Private John Oliver would have fought several battles in the harsh conditions of a Middle Eastern winter. The British attempt to break through to Kut-al-Amara failed, but Oliver did not leave Mesopotamia. The 1ˢᵗ Connaught Rangers remained there until 3 April 1918 when they sailed from Kuwait to Egypt before moving on to their final destination – Palestine.

Oliver survived the war and was in Dover in May 1919. What was perhaps strange about his service at this point, for a man who had been court-martialled

Private John Oliver of the Connaught Rangers (left), and his friend, Gunner Thomas Wall (right). Both men were from Loughrea, County Galway, and the photo was taken when they were both on leave at the same time.

for an apparent problem with authority, was that he was still in the army at all. His original period of service – twelve years – expired in 1917, and he would have been free to leave the army by 1919 after the end of the war. However, in that year, John Oliver chose to extend his period of service.

On 24 October 1919, Private John Oliver and the 1st Connaught Rangers sailed for India. When they arrived, Oliver was posted with a detachment to the Solon hill station. During this time, the War of Independence was being fought in Ireland, and when, on 27 June 1920, news of reprisals committed against the Irish people by the Black and Tans and the Auxiliaries reached the main body of the 1st Connaught Rangers – stationed at Wellington Barracks in Jalandhar – they mutinied. However, this was not a violent uprising; it was a protest where the men refused to perform duties while there were still British forces in Ireland. Messengers were dispatched to the detachments at Jutogh and Solon hill stations, and while Jutogh remained loyal to military command, the garrison at Solon joined the mutiny. A leader soon emerged there – Private James Daly from Tyrrellspass, County Westmeath.

The mutiny in Jalandhar ended quickly. Arrests were made and the mutineers were imprisoned in Dagshai. But up in the Solon hill station, the soldiers there did not know what was happening. Rumours began to spread – including one false report that the imprisoned mutineers were being executed – and so Private Daly and about seventy Connaught Rangers mounted a raid on the local armoury to retrieve their weapons (they had stored them there earlier at the insistence of their Catholic chaplain, Father Benjamin Baker). However, the hill station's officers – all Irish – defended the armoury and refused to let Daly and his followers gain access to their weapons. Two mutineers were shot and killed during the fight – Private Peter Sears from The Neale, County Mayo, and fellow Irishman Private John Smyth – while a third was badly wounded before the revolt was finally suppressed (this third man, Private John Miranda, died from his wounds on 22 December 1920, aged twenty-two. From Liverpool, he was the son of a Spanish father and an Irish mother.).

Roughly 400 men took part in the mutiny, which resulted in eighty-eight soldiers being court-martialled. Private John Oliver from Loughrea was one of them. Identified as one of the ringleaders of the Solon hill station mutiny and one of the men who participated in the assault on the armoury, he was sentenced to death along with thirteen others in August 1920 (the rest of the soldiers court-martialled were given up to fifteen years in prison, with some acquitted). However, John Oliver escaped execution. Along with twelve of the other mutineers who had been sentenced to death, Oliver's sentence was commuted to life imprisonment. Only one man would be shot by firing squad – Private James Daly – and on 2 November 1920, the sentence was carried out in the Dagshai prison yard. Aged twenty-one, Daly would remain buried here until 1970 when his body was repatriated to Ireland. Today, his remains lie in Tyrrellspass cemetery. The remains of Private Peter Sears and Private John Smyth were also brought home – they are now buried in Glasnevin cemetery, Dublin. Private John Miranda still lies in Indian soil.

John Oliver was one of only a very few pre-First World War regular soldiers to have taken part in the mutiny. However, as Connaught Rangers Association researcher Oliver Fallon has noted:

> Anything to do with the Connaught Rangers' so-called mutiny in India in 1920 is a minefield. From my research and in my own opinion far too much has been made of what was more or less a very drunken affair, involving a number of hotheads who had a variety of grievances, many of them valid. It was not until they

were chasing IRA pensions in the 1930s that the mutiny took on a more patriotic hue. Little mention is made of the small number of non-Irish who participated.

It is possible that events back in Ireland at the time merely gave the Connaught Rangers the excuse they needed to rebel against grievances that were far more immediate than the distant struggle for Irish independence, and that in the years that followed, their failed mutiny was revised for propaganda purposes to make it palatable to a new Ireland. However, what truly matters most is that three men died, another was executed, and many more were imprisoned. John Oliver was one of the latter.

After his sentence was commuted, Oliver was shipped back to England and arrived in Maidstone Prison in July 1921. While here, he managed to get in touch with Mary 'Cissie' Fallon back in Loughrea. She was the sister of John Oliver's old friend, Thomas Wall, and she was still living in the Wall family home on Patrick Street, Loughrea with her aged parents – only by now she was married to a Connaught Rangers' colour-sergeant, named Jack Fallon, hence the new surname. However, John Oliver was unable to write

Above: *Photograph of Gunner Thomas Wall and his sister Mary 'Cissie' Wall from Loughrea, County Galway. The photo was taken in Loughrea in 1916, and given that Thomas only enlisted in October 1915 and that he is not wearing any service stripes on his sleeve, it was mostly likely taken during a period of post-training leave before he departed for the war. Cissie Wall (later Fallon) would later nurse John Oliver when he returned to Ireland from Maidstone Prison.*

much in his letters and telegrams, due to censorship and restrictions, but he was able to inform Cis and the Wall family that, at the very least, he was still alive.

On 3 January 1923, after eighteen months in prison, it finally looked as if John Oliver's luck was about to change, as on that day, he was granted an amnesty and freed from prison. Provided with the fare for the boat back to Ireland, Oliver set off to return to Loughrea. However, his situation began to deteriorate rapidly. Oliver did not stay out of uniform for long and he joined the National (Free State) Army, only to be discharged after a short period of service on medical grounds. Although he had survived the First World War and escaped death following his part in the Connaught Rangers' mutiny, John Oliver was no longer a healthy man. Worse still, he was now also suffering from shellshock.

The seeds for this had certainly been sown during the years of the First World War since, as Raymond Wall – brother of Cis Fallon and Thomas Wall – recalled, 'I knew him [John Oliver] when I was a small boy. Heard from my family that he used [to] spend his entire war time leaves sitting by our fireside, almost in disbelief that he was still living and that the gentle human comforts of home still existed.' By July 1924, John Oliver was listed as being 'destitute', and it was not long before Cis Fallon took him in. She fed John Oliver, let him sit by the fire, and now had to deal with caring for a broken soldier as well as her elderly parents. He was soon known as 'Poor John Oliver', a reference that the Wall family still use to this day when referring to him.

Then one day, John Oliver attempted to take his own life. He got dressed up in his Sunday best, even though it was during the week, and simply walked out

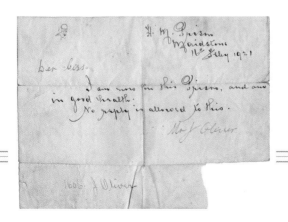

Letter written by Private John Oliver in Maidstone Prison to Mary 'Cissie' Fallon (née Wall) in Loughrea, County Galway. Oliver had just arrived in Maidstone for his part in the Connaught Rangers Mutiny and was not allowed to say much.

Telegram sent from Dublin by John Oliver, after his release from Maidstone Prison in 1923, telling Mary 'Cissie' Fallon (née Wall) to expect him soon in Loughrea. On the back of the letter, Raymond Wall – Cissie's brother – noted that 'on his [John Oliver's] return to Loughrea … he rejected overtures from the nastier element of the IRA to join them in robbery.'

into the lake behind the Loughrea court house. But someone witnessed what he was doing and managed to drag him back to shore. But John Oliver remained determined to end his life. Not long after his attempt to drown himself, Cis found John Oliver choking on several unbroken eggs that he had forced down his throat. She saved his life by crushing the eggs in his throat, and forcing Oliver to swallow them (in fact, Oliver tried to kill himself twice by this method, only to be saved by Cis each time). Then, within a few days of his latest failed attempt, he slit his throat, but the Wall family rushed him to Central Hospital, Galway, and he survived. His wound was stitched and Oliver was kept in hospital until he had recovered. However, according to Cyril Wall – son of Raymond Wall – as soon as he was discharged:

> John walked into a toilet, I believe it was in a pub back in Loughrea, and ripped out his stitches before gouging his throat out of his neck. The poor man must have been absolutely demented.

John Oliver died on 31 January 1932, aged forty-four (his friend and fellow war veteran, Thomas Wall, had died three years earlier on 29 January 1929, aged thirty-four). Oliver's death certificate lists 'sceptic pneumonia' as the cause of death rather than suicide, since the Wall family record that even this final successful attempt did not end his life immediately. He was brought back

The Wall house on Patrick Street, Loughrea, where John Oliver was taken care of by Mary 'Cissie' Fallon (née Wall).

to hospital and lingered on for a time before finally succumbing – the onset of sceptic pneumonia evidently ending his life.

Further evidence that Oliver's death was caused by suicide is to be found in the final chapter of his story. Some years ago, a cousin of Cyril Wall's was attending a meeting in Loughrea Church of Ireland church, concerning plans by the local authority to turn the now-disused building into a new library. During the meeting, additional plans to demolish an old shed in the adjoining graveyard were brought up. An old caretaker mentioned that beneath the shed were unmarked paupers' graves. The caretaker then recalled that, 'There's one of them mutiny Connaught Rangers buried there.' And so John Oliver's last resting place was rediscovered by the Wall family. Oliver was not a Protestant, he was a Catholic, and so the only way he would have been buried outside of a consecrated Catholic burial ground was if he had committed a perceived sin against the church – a sin such as suicide. His grave is still unmarked, and he is the only Connaught Ranger who participated in the mutiny, who is believed to have taken his own life.

THE LAST IRISH WAR VETERAN

THOMAS SHAW

Today, Ireland's First World War veterans are gone, along with the regiments that they served in. The last Irish war veteran disappeared with the death of Thomas 'Tommy' Shaw in 2002, aged 102. Born in 1899, he enlisted in the Royal Irish Rifles in January 1916 – only sixteen years old – and was on his way to the front when he encountered his older brother who was an MP. The brother had Tommy arrested for lying about his age to sign up and sent him back to Ireland. But Shaw refused to quit, and as soon as he was old enough, he re-enlisted and joined the 16th Royal Irish Rifles, fighting at Messines Ridge and during the Third Battle of Ypres. During the Second World War, he was in charge of meat rationing for Northern Ireland, and also worked as a civil servant in Stormont, where he met his wife Eleanor. At the time of his death, Shaw had been married for sixty years. He was buried in Bangor, County Down, with full military honours, and a bugler from the modern Royal Irish Regiment played the 'Last Post'.

THE IRISH REGIMENTS

As for the regiments in which the Irish First World War veterans had served, after the War of Independence and the signing of the Treaty, Ireland had its own government in the form of the Free State and suddenly, the recruiting grounds of the old Irish regiments of the British Army were closed to them. Their supply of men was gone. And so, on 12 June 1922, the Connaught Rangers, Royal Dublin Fusiliers, Royal Munster Fusiliers, Leinster Regiment, Royal Irish Regiment and South Irish Horse were formally disbanded at a ceremony held in Windsor Castle and presided over by King George. The oldest – the Royal Irish Regiment – had been in existence since 1684, the Connaught Rangers had been formed in 1793 and had fought with distinction against Napoleon's armies during the Peninsular War, while the Royal Dublin Fusiliers and Royal Munster Fusiliers had started out as regiments of the East India Company. But now, there was no more need for them, and so the regiments were disbanded and their regimental colours were laid up in Windsor Castle (except for the standard of the South Irish Horse, which is in St Patrick's Cathedral, Dublin).

As for the northern Irish regiments, they went on to fight during the Second

British troops leaving Richmond Barracks, Dublin, as soldiers of the National (Free State) Army march in, to take their place, 1922.

World War, until, on 1 July 1968 – the fifty-second anniversary of the Battle of the Somme – the Royal Inniskilling Fusiliers, the Royal Ulster Rifles (the descendent regiment of the Royal Irish Rifles) and the Royal Irish Fusiliers were amalgamated to form the Royal Irish Rangers. This regiment was, in turn, amalgamated with the Ulster Defence Regiment on 1 July 1992 to create the modern Royal Irish Regiment, which today forms part of the British Army's 16th Air Assault Brigade. Along with the Irish Guards, the modern Royal Irish Regiment is one of only two remaining Irish infantry regiments in the British Army of today.

What all this amounts to is that the Irishmen who fought in the trenches and the soldiering traditions that they were a part off are, for the most part, a thing of the past. All that is left now are memories of men – ordinary men – who had 'fought in the war'. The reasons why these men went to war vary with each individual. It would be foolish to tar them all with the same brush. The truth is that the subject of the First World War and the Irishmen who fought in it is a complex issue. It includes factors such as Home Rule, independence, economic necessity, loyalty, adventure, hope, the coming of age, and the desire for betterment. To claim that these men were all traitors, unless they put their skills to

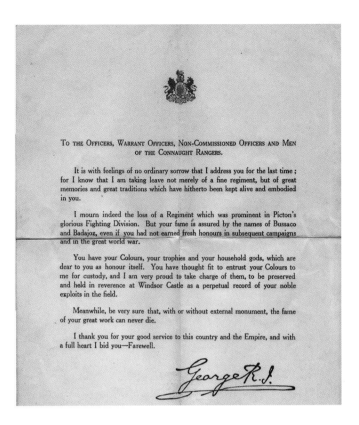

To the Officers, Warrant Officers, Non-Commissioned Officers and Men
of the Connaught Rangers.

It is with feelings of no ordinary sorrow that I address you for the last time ;
for I know that I am taking leave not merely of a fine regiment, but of great
memories and great traditions which have hitherto been kept alive and embodied
in you.

I mourn indeed the loss of a Regiment which was prominent in Picton's
glorious Fighting Division. But your fame is assured by the names of Bussaco
and Badajoz, even if you had not earned fresh honours in subsequent campaigns
and in the great world war.

You have your Colours, your trophies and your household gods, which are
dear to you as honour itself. You have thought fit to entrust your Colours to
me for custody, and I am very proud to take charge of them, to be preserved
and held in reverence at Windsor Castle as a perpetual record of your noble
exploits in the field.

Meanwhile, be very sure that, with or without external monument, the fame
of your great work can never die.

I thank you for your good service to this country and the Empire, and with
a full heart I bid you—Farewell.

George R.I.

A copy of a letter from King George V that was distributed to all men of the Connaught Rangers due to be disbanded upon the formation of the Irish Free State. This one was given to Colour-Sergeant John 'Jack' Fallon from Loughrea, County Galway. He subsequently transferred into the King's Liverpool Regiment, in order to stay in the army and serve out the remainder of his contract.

good use by joining the IRA, is simply wrong. It would similarly be wrong to claim that they were all just misunderstood naïve innocents (as men were still voluntarily enlisting long after the enormous casualty lists had starting appearing in newspapers) or that they were *all* penniless paupers forced into uniform by economic necessity (as this was certainly not the case). The majority were just normal men, trying to get by in a difficult world. Ultimately, their involvement in the First World War must be viewed from primarily emotional and *human* terms, not from a political standpoint. Their experiences of the trenches – what it did to them and how it shaped their futures – are far more important than why they enlisted.

Above: *A Connaught Rangers' colour party during a parade. The colours were the soul of a regiment – they were emblazoned with the unit's battle honours, and it was a disgrace to lose them in battle. This photograph is stamped 'Halksworth Wheeler, Folkestone'.*

Below: *Group of Connaught Rangers, c1920, showing the soldiers in tropical uniform.*

AUTHOR'S FINAL WORDS

It is only now that Ireland is starting to open its arms to its First World War veterans, although sadly this has come about so late. On 17 April 2001, the Irish government officially acknowledged the role of the Royal Dublin Fusiliers in the First World War by hosting a state reception at Dublin Castle for the Royal Dublin Fusiliers Association, and at Messines, the battlefield upon which the 16th (Irish) Division and the 36th (Ulster) Division – nationalist and unionist, Catholic and Protestant – had fought and died side by side, there now stands a replica monastic round tower, funded and constructed by both the Irish and British governments. Named the Messines Peace Tower, it was officially opened by President Mary McAleese and Queen Elizabeth II on 11 November 1998 – the eightieth anniversary of the end of the war – and stands in memory of the Irishmen from both north and south who lie buried in this place.

But while such commemorative gestures take place, and while it is now acceptable to begin writing on the subject of Ireland's involvement in the First World War, people other than scholars or interested students might still ask 'Why should we care?' Looking back from a place in today's Ireland, 1914–1918 is perhaps too long ago, back when people were deathly poor and the population was still reeling from the famine, back when we lived off the land – scraping out an existence in tiny patches of dirt. In the Ireland of the twenty-first century, who cares about 35,000–50,000 dead Irishmen and 150,000 others who were haunted for the rest of their lives?

We should care, because the best way to redeem ourselves – the best way to understand the Irishmen who fought in the First World War – is to remember them, to finally *acknowledge* what they went through and allow their stories to be told. This book is an attempt to do just that – to tell the stories of the forgotten. I would advise anyone who is interested to go and research their forgotten First World War ancestors. A great deal of their service records still exist in Britain, and I would recommend an excellent researcher named Richard Moles (www.richardmoles.com) who assisted me with this book.

Other sources of information are the regimental museums and associations.

The Royal Inniskilling Fusiliers, the Royal Irish/Ulster Rifles and the Royal Irish Fusiliers all have fine museums based in Enniskillen, Belfast and Armagh town respectively. Meanwhile, in the Republic, the Connaught Rangers Association is based in King House, Boyle, County Roscommon, where they also house artefacts relating to the regiment's history. Other associations who do not have permanent museums can be contacted online. A simple internet search can provide you with their contact details.

Find out who your ancestors were, what they went through in the war. You will never be able to understand it or fully grasp the meaning of it all, but if you acknowledge it, and are moved by it, then perhaps that will in some way honour the Irishmen who served in the trenches. They deserve to be accepted and honoured. But not just in the pages of an academic's book. They deserve to be welcomed home to their families.

As for the reputation that Irishmen earned during the war, this short rhyme – although written about one specific Irish regiment – sums it all up. Attributed to Anonymous, it is a fitting tribute to their legacy as soldiers:

> *The Kaiser knows the Munsters,*
> *By the Shamrock on their caps,*
> *And the famous Bengal Tiger, ever ready for a scrap,*
> *And all his big battalions, Prussian Guards and Grenadiers,*
> *Fear to face the flashing bayonets of the Munster Fusiliers.*

BIBLIOGRAPHY
AND FURTHER READING

Arthur, Max, *Symbol of Courage – A Complete History of the Victoria Cross*, UK: Sidgwick and Jackson, 2004.

Arthur, Max, *Symbol of Courage – The Men Behind The Medal*, London: Pan Books, 2005.

Broadbent, Harvey, *Gallipoli – The Fatal Shore*, London: Viking, 2005.

Burgoyne, Gerald Achilles, *The Burgoyne Diaries*, UK: Naval and Military Press.

Burrows, Brig.-Gen. AR, *The 1ˢᵗ Battalion, the Faugh-A-Ballaghs, Irish Fusiliers in the Great War*, Aldershot: Gale & Polden, 1926.

Carlyon, LA, *Gallipoli*, London: Bantam Books, 2003.

Cooper, Maj. Brian, *The 10ᵗʰ (Irish) Division in Gallipoli*, Dublin: Irish Academic Press, 1993.

Cooper-Walker, CA, *The Book of the Seventh Service Battalion The Royal Inniskilling Fusiliers from Tipperary to Ypres*, 1920.

Creighton, Rev. O, *With the Twenty-Ninth Division in Gallipoli,* UK: Naval and Military Press, 2004.

Denman, Terrence, *Ireland's Unknown Soldiers: The 16ᵗʰ (Irish) Division in the Great War 1914–1918*, Dublin: Irish Academic Press, 1992, 2008.

Doherty, Richard and Truesdale, David, *Irish Winners of the Victoria Cross*, Dublin: Four Courts Press, 1999.

Falls, Cyril, *The History of the First Seven Battalions, The Royal Irish Rifles in the Great War,* Aldershot: Gale & Polden, 1925.

Fox, Sir Frank, *The Royal Inniskilling Fusiliers in the Great War*, London: Constable, 1928.

Geoghegan, Brig.-Gen. Stannus, *The Campaigns and History of the Royal Irish Regiment 1900–1922*, Edinburgh: Blackwood, 1927.

Gilbert, Martin, *Somme – The Heroism and Horror of War*, UK: John Murray, 2006.

Gliddon, Gerald, ed., *VC's Handbook – The Western Front 1914–1918*, UK: The History Press, 2005.

Graham, JJ, trans. (revised by FN Maude), *Carl von Clausewitz: On War*, London: Wordsworth Editions, 1997.

Hanna, Henry, *The Pals at Suvla Bay – Being the record of "D" Company of the 7ᵗʰ Royal Dublin Fusiliers on Gallipoli*, 1917.

Hitchcock, Capt. FC, *Stand To – A Diary of the Trenches 1915–1918*, UK: Naval and Military Press, 2001.

Hofmann, Michael, trans., *Ernst Jünger: Storm of Steel*, UK: Allen Lane, 2003.

Holmes, Richard, *Tommy – The British Soldier on the Western Front 1914-1918*, London: Harper Perennial, 2005.

Horrocks, Lt-Gen. Sir Brian, ed., Henry Harris, *The Royal Irish Fusiliers*, London: Lee Cooper, 1972.

Hughes-Wilson, John and Corn, Cathryn M, *Blindfold and Alone – British Military Executions in the Great War,* UK: Weidenfeld and Nicolson, 2001.

Johnson, Lt.-Col. FWE, *5th Battalion Royal Irish Fusiliers in the Great War*, UK: Naval and Military Press, 2004.

Jourdain, Lt.-Col. HFN, and Fraser, Edward, *The Connaught Rangers (Vol. 1, Vol. 2, & Vol. 3),* London: Royal United Service Institution, 1924–28.

King, Edward J, *Haphazard*, Abingdon, Berkshire: The Abbey Press (privately printed), 1962.

Kipling, Rudyard, *The Irish Guards in the Great War – Volume 1 – The First Battalion,* London: Macmillan, 1923.

Kipling, Rudyard, *The Irish Guards in the Great War – Volume 2 – The Second Battalion,* London: Macmillan, 1923.

Lucy, John F, *There's a Devil in the Drum*, UK: Naval and Military Press, 2001.

MacDonagh, Michael,. *The Irish at the Front*, London: Hodder and Stoughton, 1916.

MacDonagh, Michael, *The Irish on the Somme*, London: Hodder and Stoughton, 1917.

McCance, Capt. S, *History of the Royal Munster Fusiliers 1861 to 1922*, (Privately printed 1937) Cork: Schull Books, 1995.

Minford, John, ed. & trans., *Sun Tzu: The Art of War*, London: Penguin, 2003.

Murphy, David (writer) and Embleton, Gerry (illustrator), *Irish Regiments in the World Wars*, Oxford: Osprey Publishing, 2007.

Orr, Philip, *Field of Bones – An Irish Division at Gallipoli*, Dublin: Lilliput Press, 2006.

Orr, Philip, *The Road to the Somme – Men of the Ulster Division Tell Their Story*, Belfast: Blackstaff Press, 1987, 2008.

Ousby, Ian, *The Road to Verdun*, London: Pimlico, 2003.

Rickard, Mrs Victor, *The Story of the Munsters at Etreux, Festubert and Rue du Bois*, London: Hodder and Stoughton, 1918.

Samuels, API, and Belfast, DGS, *With the Ulster Division in France – a story of the 11th Battalion Royal Irish Rifles (South Antrim Volunteers) from Bordon to Thiepval –*UK: Naval and Military Press, 2003.

Taylor, James W, *The 1st Royal Irish Rifles in the Great War*, UK: Four Courts Press, 2002.

Taylor, James W, *The 2nd Royal Irish Rifles in the Great War*, UK: Four Courts Press, 2005.

Walker, Stephen, *Forgotten Soldiers – The Irishmen Shot at Dawn*, Gill and Macmillan, 2007.

Whitton, Lt.-Col. FE, *The History of the Prince of Wales's Leinster Regiment (Royal Canadians) Vol. 1 & Vol. 2,* Aldershot: Gale & Polden, 1924.

Wylly, Col. HC, *Crown and Company: The Historical Records of the 2nd Battalion Royal Dublin Fusiliers, formerly the 1st Bombay Regiment*, London: Arthur L Humphreys, 1925.

Wylly, Col. HC, *Neill's "Blue Caps" – The History of the 1st Battalion, The Royal Dublin Fusiliers,* Dublin: Maunsell, 1924.

Record of the 5th (Service) Battalion The Connaught Rangers from 19th August, 1914, to 17th January, 1916, UK: Naval and Military Press, 2002.

'Athlone started the Volunteer Movement,' by Sean O'Mullany in *The Athlone Annual* (Athlone, 1963).

'British Admiralty Statement on the Zeebrugge and Ostend Raids 22-23 April 1918' in *Source Records of the Great War Vol. VI*, edited by Charles F Horne (National Alumni, 1923).

'Mayo Man was among last to die in World War One' by Michael Commins in *Western People* (Wed. 11 Nov. 1998).

'Tales of Mud, Blood, Shot and Shell' by Michael O'Reilly in *The Leinster Express* (issue unknown, 1991).

SERVICE RECORDS

Service Record of Ahern, Michael; UK National Archives; WO363/A222

Court Martial Record of Clonan, Joseph PS, Series Number: A471, Barcode: 6973596; National Archives of Australia

Service Record of Clonan, Joseph PS, Series Number: B2455, Barcode: 3260214; National Archives of Australia

Service Record of Culhane, Timothy (10532); Irish Guards Archives

Service Record of Curley, Michael; UK National Archives; WO363/C1682

Service Record of Dease, Maurice James; UK National Archives; WO339/7579

Service Record of Finn, Michael; Agency: AABK, Series: 18805, Accession: W5537, Box/Item: 96, Record: 0040050; Archives of New Zealand

Service Record of Finn, Patrick; Agency: AABK, Series: 18805, Accession: W5537, Box/Item: 96, Record: 0040051; Archives of New Zealand

Service Record of Fitzgerald, Michael; UK National Archives; WO339/73104

Service Record of Fowler, Francis Reginald; UK National Archives; WO339/46707

Service Record of Fowler, John Gerald; RG 150, Accession 1992-93/166, Box 3247 – 49; Library and Archives of Canada

Service Record of Fowler, Richard Tarrant; RG 150, Accession 1992-93/166, Box 3248 – 39; Library and Archives of Canada

Service Record of Fowler, William Henry; RG 150, Accession 1992-93/166, Box 3249 – 27; Library and Archives of Canada

Service Record of Gaffey, Martin (9956); Irish Guards Archives

Service Record of Gaffey, Patrick, UK National Archives; WO363/G6

Service Record of Grey, Edward (4283); Irish Guards Archives

Service Record of Grey, William (11288); Irish Guards Archives

Court Martial Record of Hope, Thomas; UK National Archives; WO93/49

Service Record of Kennelly, Patrick; UK National Archives; WO364/1988

Service Record of McArevey, Joseph Betrand; UK National Archives; WO339/45908

Service Record of McElroy, George EH; UK National Archives; WO339/110067 and AIR 76/13

Service Record of McGrath, Michael; UK National Archives; WO363/M164

Service Record of Monks, Edward; UK National Archives; WO364/2529

Service Record of O'Keefe, William Henry; UK National Archives; WO339/25387

Service Record of O'Sullivan, David; UK National Archives; ADM159/135

Service Record of Rooney, Thomas; UK National Archives; WO363/R1329

Service Record of Saker, Frank Harrison; UK National Archives; WO339/19054

Service Record of Stewart, George Alexander; RG 150, Accession 1992-93/166, Box 9309 – 56; Library and Archives of Canada

Service Record of Stewart, Hugh Ferguson; RG 150, Accession 1992-93/166, Box 9312 – 41; Library and Archives of Canada

Service Record of Stewart, Isaac Irwin; UK National Archives; WO363/S2455

Service Record of Stewart, William Morrison; Series Number: B2455, Barcode: 3014434; National Archives of Australia

Service Record of Sullivan, Eugene (7504); Irish Guards Archives

Service Record of Whelan, Michael; UK National Archives; ADM188/860, ADM188/914, and ADM 188/1103

Service Record of Whelan, Thomas; UK National Archives; WO363/W1547

WAR DIARIES

1st Connaught Rangers; Jan. – Apr. 1916; UK National Archives; WO95/5106

2nd Connaught Rangers; Oct. – Nov. 1914; UK National Archives; WO95/1347

6th Connaught Rangers; Dec. 1916; UK National Archives; WO95/1970

6th Connaught Rangers; Jun. – Jul. 1917; UK National Archives; WO95/1970

6th Connaught Rangers; Nov. 1917; UK National Archives; WO95/1970

1st Irish Guards; Aug. – Sept. 1914; UK National Archives; WO95/1342

1st Irish Guards; Jul. 1917; UK National Archives; WO95/1216

2nd Irish Guards; Jul. – Aug. 1917; UK National Archives; WO95/1220

2nd Leinster Regiment; Aug. – Sept. 1916; UK National Archives; WO95/2218

2nd Leinster Regiment; Mar. 1918; UK National Archives; WO95/2308

2nd Leinster Regiment; Oct. 1918; UK National Archives; WO95/2308

2nd Royal Dublin Fusiliers; Aug. 1917; UK National Archives; WO95/1974

7th Royal Dublin Fusiliers; Sept. 1916; UK National Archives; WO95/4830

8th Royal Dublin Fusiliers; Aug. 1917; UK National Archives; WO95/1974

9th Royal Dublin Fusiliers; Aug. 1917; UK National Archives; WO95/1974

6th Royal Inniskilling Fusiliers; Dec. 1917; UK National Archives; WO95/4585

6th Royal Inniskilling Fusiliers; Nov. 1918; UK National Archives; WO95/2843

1st Royal Irish Fusiliers; Mar. – Apr. 1915; UK National Archives; WO95/1482

1st Royal Irish Regiment; Dec. 1917 – Sept. 1918; UK National Archives; WO95/4583

6th Royal Irish Regiment; May – Jun. 1917; UK National Archives; WO95/1970

2nd Royal Irish Rifles; Jul. – Oct. 1916; UK National Archives; WO95/2247

2nd Royal Irish Rifles; Sept. 1917; UK National Archives; WO95/2247

2nd Royal Irish Rifles; Nov. 1917; UK National Archives; WO95/2502

14th Royal Irish Rifles; 22 Jun. – 2 Jul. 1916; UK National Archives; WO95/2511

14th Royal Irish Rifles; Nov. 1917; UK National Archives; WO95/2511

14th Bde. Royal Field Artillery; Oct. 1918; UK National Archives; WO95/1203

40th Bde. Royal Field Artillery; May 1917; UK National Archives; WO95/1400

4th Royal Fusiliers; Aug. 1914; UK National Archives; WO95/1431

1st Royal Munster Fusiliers; Jun. 1917; UK National Archives; WO95/1971

2nd Royal Munster Fusiliers; Mar. 1918; UK National Archives; WO95/1975

8th Royal Munster Fusiliers; Jul. – Sept. 1916; UK National Archives; WO95/1971

1/8th Worcestershire Regiment; Jun. 1918; UK National Archives; WO95/4249

14th Worcestershire Regiment; Apr. – May 1917; UK National Archives; WO95/3105

Various "Combats in the Air" reports to 24th Sq. (RFC) and 40th Sq. (RAF); Feb. – Jul. 1918; UK National Archives; AIR 1/857/204/5/414

INTERVIEWS

Ahern, Michael – interview with Tim Aherne

Blackwood, James – interview with Michael Blackwood

Callinan, Patrick – interview with daughter

Cascani, John – interview with Gordon Hudson

Clifford, James – interview with Bart Clifford

Clonan, Joseph – interview with Tom Clonan

Collins, Michael – interview with Michael Barry

Collins, John – interview with Anne Sands

Coote, Luke – interview with Thomas Coote

Corkery, Daniel – interview with Kevin O'Byrne

Crowe, Matthew – interview with Matt Crowe

Culhane, Timothy – interview with Charlie Cavanagh

Curley, Michael – interview with Mike Johnson and Sean Malone

Dowling, Edward – interview with Joe Dowling

Doyle, Anthony – interview with Peter Doyle

Finn, Michael – interview with John Finn

Finn, Patrick – interview with John Finn

Fitzgerald, Jeremiah – interview with Noreen Doolan

Fitzgerald, Martin – interview with Jimmy Dunne

Fitzgerald, Michael – interview with Brian, Marian and Fionnuala Fallon

Flood, Bernard – interview with Derek Molyneux

Flynn, Michael – interview with Eilish Blacoe

Flynn, Richard – interview with Eilish Blacoe

Fowler, Francis Reginald – interview with Peter Langley

Fowler, John Gerald – interview with Peter Langley

Fowler, Richard Tarrant – interview with Peter Langley

Fowler, William Henry – interview with Peter Langley

Gaffey, Martin – interview with Eileen Kavanagh and Tony Gaffey

Grey, Edward – interview with Assumpta Murphy

Grey, William – interview with Assumpta Murphy

Hickson, Patrick – interview with Deborah and Marie-Louise Fitzpatrick

Holian, John Thomas – interview with Tom Holian

Holligan, Thomas – interview with Ger Holligan

Horkan, Paddy – interview with Mairead Horkan (based on information from an interview with Paddy Horkan, conducted by Peter and Sean Horkan)

Kelly, Fred – interview with Pat Conlon

Kelly, John – interview with Padraig Broderick

Kennelly, Patrick – interview with Michael Barry

Kerr, Thomas – interview with Arthur Kerr

King, Edward – interview with Alison Schwalm

Lalor, Thomas – interview with Anne Sands

Lawrence, Matthew – interview with Brendan Lawrence

Lawrence, William – interview with Brendan Lawrence

Mangan, John – interview with Pat McCale

Manley, James – interview with Mary Kennedy

McBryde, Henry – interview with Anne Sands

McGrath, Michael – interview with Mary O'Neill

McLoughlin, James – interview with Mark McLoughlin

McLoughlin, Michael – interview with Steve McLoughlin

Molloy, Lawrence – interview with Eddie Molloy

Monks, Edward – interview with Peggy Whelan

Moran, Michael – interview with Terry Moran

Morrow, Robert – interview with Geraldine Conway

Mullen, Joseph – interview with Geraldine Murphy

Nevin, James – interview with Stephen Nevin

Newman, Thomas – interview with Cllr Michael Newman

O'Donnell, Patrick – interview with May Neary

Oliver, John – interview with Cyril Wall

O'Rourke, John – interview with Michael O'Rourke

O'Sullivan, David – interview with David O'Sullivan

O'Sullivan, Fr Donal – interview with Donal O'Sullivan

Rivers, John – interview with Peggy Lovell

Roach, Patrick – interview with Michael Roach

Roach, William – interview with Michael Roach

Rooney, Peter – interview with Eugene and Peter Rooney

Rooney, Thomas – interview with Eugene and Peter Rooney

Sinnott, John – interview with Patricia Dolan

Spain, Joseph – interview with Brian Spain

Stewart, George Alexander – interview with Morrison Stewart

Stewart, Hugh Ferguson – interview with Morrison Stewart

Stewart, Isaac Irwin – interview with Morrison Stewart

Stewart, William Morrison – interview with Morrison Stewart

Toal, Peter – interview with Anne Shanks and Peter Toal

Whelehan, Thomas – interview with Sean Hefarty

White, Kieran – interview with Kieran White

INDEX

ALPHABETICAL INDEX